T0162448

READY TO COME ABOUT

READY TO COME ABOUT

a memoir

SUE WILLIAMS

DUNDURN
TORONTO

Some names and identifying details of characters in this book have been changed.

Cover image credit: Sue Williams
Printer: Webcom, a division of Marquis Book Printing Inc.

Library and Archives Canada Cataloguing in Publication

Title: Ready to come about / Sue Williams.
Names: Williams, Sue, 1956 October 26- author.
Identifiers: Canadiana (print) 20190047402 | Canadiana (ebook) 20190047453 | ISBN 9781459743908 (softcover) | ISBN 9781459743915 (PDF) | ISBN 9781459743922 (EPUB)
Subjects: LCSH: Williams, Sue, 1956 October 26-—Travel—North Atlantic Ocean. | LCSH: North Atlantic Ocean—Description and travel. | LCSH: Sailors—Canada—Biography. | LCSH: Adventure and adventurers—Canada—Biography. | LCSH: Transatlantic voyages. | LCSH: Boats and boating—North Atlantic Ocean. | LCGFT: Autobiographies.
Classification: LCC G530.W55 W55 2019 | DDC 910.9163/1—dc23

1   2   3   4   5   23   22   21   20   19

 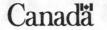 

We acknowledge the support of the **Canada Council for the Arts,** which last year invested $153 million to bring the arts to Canadians throughout the country, and the **Ontario Arts Council** for our publishing program. We also acknowledge the financial support of the Government of Ontario, through the **Ontario Book Publishing Tax Credit** and **Ontario Creates**, and the **Government of Canada**.

Nous remercions le **Conseil des arts du Canada** de son soutien. L'an dernier, le Conseil a investi 153 millions de dollars pour mettre de l'art dans la vie des Canadiennes et des Canadiens de tout le pays.

Printed and bound in Canada.

VISIT US AT

 dundurn.com | @dundurnpress | dundurnpress | dundurnpress

Dundurn
3 Church Street, Suite 500
Toronto, Ontario, Canada
M5E 1M2

In memory of my father, (John) Lawrence Walsh
And to my husband, David,
with gratitude and love

I'm not afraid of storms, for I'm learning how to sail my ship.
— Louisa May Alcott, *Little Women*

Inia, anchored off Ilha da Culatra, near Olhão, in the Algarve region of Portugal.

PROLOGUE

IT'S DARK LIKE MIDNIGHT. We're a mere speck tossing about in twenty-foot seas on the vast North Atlantic Ocean. Two hundred nautical miles north is Newfoundland, the closest point of civilization. Winds are screaming through the rigging. There's a fierce clanging against the hull. David pokes his head up from the companionway to investigate as streaks of salt foam fly horizontally across the deck — drenching him, yet again. I stay huddled below decks on the makeshift bed of cushions arranged on the cabin sole, blankets tucked under my chin. My body braces for the next breaking wave, which I know will soon pound against the fibreglass walls of our small sailboat, *Inia*. I smell the brininess. I scan the edges of the floorboards for signs of water seeping in as the bilge-pump light turns on, then off, then on again. I vomit in the bucket beside me. Three days after leaving the shores of the Gaspé Peninsula, *Inia* is hove to and we are riding out a full-blown gale, just my husband and me.

This was David's dream, not mine. Far from it. I loved family and friends, our dog, our home, my job as an occupational therapist. Appliqué was my idea of a thrill. I didn't have an adventure-seeking bone in my body.

Christmas Eve 2005 changed everything.

While doing last-minute shopping, David had a grand mal seizure of such violence his spine fractured in two places and cuts on his head took fourteen stitches to close.

The doctor said stress and sleep deprivation were likely the cause. And it made sense. Over the preceding years, he had worried non-stop about our three sons. So had I. As they headed toward adulthood, we questioned their lifestyles, fretted about their plans, wondered if they would ever be able to make their own way, feared they might never find their spots in this world — all this while David was being buried alive at work. In retrospect, something had to give.

It could have been worse; he could have been disabled by a stroke or even died from a heart attack. He made a full recovery. The seizure was a warning for which we were grateful.

When David returned to the office, the scars still raw, he attended a pre-arranged meeting that he thought was to finally address his impossible workload. Instead, he was fired. "Restructuring," the CEO called it.

I was immobilized by the news at first, the feelings of betrayal, the hurt. In time, though, I realized this, too, was a blessing in disguise.

"If you want to cross an ocean, this is your opportunity," I said. David's eyebrows spiked. "And freedom's what the boys need now, time and space to figure things out for themselves. So I'll go, too," I said, surprising even myself.

May 21, 2007, David and I, both in our fifties and with no real blue-water or night-sailing experience, cast off the dock lines in Hamilton Harbour, the westernmost point of Lake Ontario, and headed east. Destination: the Atlantic Ocean.

That was six weeks ago. Now, with barely a thousand miles under our belts and potentially another ten thousand to go, David is worried about storm damage and I'm cold and sick and afraid. I pray for reprieve. I long for solid ground. And I can't help but ask myself, *What the hell was I thinking?*

ONE

WINTER 1981, in our second-floor apartment of an old brick house in downtown Ottawa, I sat at the drop-leaf table David had set with a faded chintz tablecloth, a pair of candlesticks, and the sparkling cutlery we had been given as wedding presents, while he prepared dinner. There were blizzard-like conditions beyond the frosty panes of glass, but the kitchen's baby-blue radiator kept us warm.

"What's cookin'?" I asked, watching him turn stove dials up and down, lift and lower pot lids, and open and close the oven door like a one-man band.

"My own recipe." He stirred a dollop of butter into a steaming pot. "Pork Shake 'n Bake, except on chicken," he divulged with pride.

Gotta love 'im. I giggled to myself.

After serving up two plates of his concoction with Minute Rice, mixed vegetables, and sprigs of parsley placed just so, he sat down, uncorked a bottle of Mateus, and poured us each a glass.

"Happy anniversary, my dear," he said.

"Happy anniversary," I said, smiling.

We had been married seven weeks. He thought that was cause enough for celebration. My heart swelled as our glasses clinked.

We ate at a leisurely pace, but chatted with passion about our new life together.

Ottawa, with its green spaces and vibrant arts scene, had a lot to offer. Perhaps we'd even make it home. Kids? *Absolutely.* When? *Soon*, was my thinking.

"Well then …" David said with a glint, and we laughed.

And workwise, we were off to an auspicious start. He had been promoted to permanent status as an entry-level accounting clerk in a high-tech firm. The pay was good, his colleagues were collegial, and he could bike to work — perfect for the time being.

I had just completed a week of orientation as staff occupational therapist in the rehabilitation wing of a nearby hospital. The department was a beehive of optimism: an amputee being trained to feed himself using prosthetic arms in one area, a quadriplegic learning to drive a power wheelchair in another. "The OT mission is function with dignity. The vision is possibility," I explained to David.

"You'll be so great at it," he said, his soft blue eyes moist.

I scooped up a forkful of veggies and considered that he was absolutely right.

"It feels like what I was meant to do. And to grow old and ugly with you," I joked. "Seriously, everything's just so perfect right now." My eyes welled as I took a bite.

That's when he said, "The only thing I regret about being married is I won't ever sail an ocean."

I stopped chewing — and, momentarily, breathing — and studied his face.

He was serious.

"Didn't even know you sail," I said as evenly as possible.

"Oh yeah. I did. My Aunt Caroline gave me a small sailboat my grandfather had built. I used to sail it on Lake Yosemite, an irrigation lake about seven miles from our house. My mom would drop me off there on her way to work. I'd sail back and forth all day long and imagine I was crossing an ocean, even though it was only a mile wide. Silly."

Why was I just hearing about this for the first time now?

Why did he presume I'd be unsupportive?

And just how regretful was he and would he be with the passage of time? Would he become one of those bitter old men who look back on their lives with despair? Worse, would he blame me?

"More chicken?" he asked.

"God! I can hear it already; you introducing me as 'my wife, Sue, the dream wrecker' to our tablemates in the nursing home!"

"Whoaaaa! What the —"

"Don't you whoa me!" I said, determined to nip any notion I might be overreacting in the bud.

David backtracked as best he could: it was a poor choice of words; he even surprised himself with the comment; he couldn't be happier. "It was a childhood fantasy, nothing more," he insisted.

But as he told the story, his face lit up in such a way I wasn't entirely convinced he had left this fantasy behind. So, determined to seem open to the preposterous idea, I remarked with as much conviction as I could muster, "You know, anything's possible."

And we finished our meal listening to the radiator gurgle and ping.

TWO

AFTER A COUPLE OF YEARS of marriage, we started our family. In less than four years we had three healthy boys — Ben first, then Brian, followed by John — and they became the centre of our universe. There were the practical activities: diapers, night feeds, the Tooth Fairy, cuddles. There were the edifying activities: bedtime stories, Cub Scouts, homework, paper routes, music lessons, film and drama camps, and attempts at just about every sport known to man. And then there was the just plain fun: afternoons at the beach, summer music festivals, backyard barbecues, and road trips. Yes, our family actually did like road trips! We didn't have the time or inclination for much else. House and home were all that mattered. And life was good.

The topic of sailing came up rarely and only superficially in the boys' early years. Now and then David would dig out his childhood sailing log book. When he'd read the part that said "I got to thinking that if it doesn't rain, we might not have enough water to fill the lake. At least there's wind," they laughed, every time. There were the school science fair projects about lift that David would find himself doing. And, of course, there was the frequent retelling of the story about their famous distant uncle,

Oliver Hazard Perry, Commodore of the U.S. Fleet — two ships, two brigs, one schooner, one sloop — in the Battle of Lake Erie during the War of 1812, to which the boys invariably responded, "But, so, why'd they name him Hazard?"

A decade or so later, that changed. After moving to the southwestern Ontario city of Guelph, we booked a cottage, sight unseen, on the Bruce Peninsula for David's two weeks of summer holidays. We expected a rustic abode, nestled in trees, on a pristine lake. What we got was a plywood shack in scrub brush on a stagnant body of water, not a single fish to be caught.

On the third day, having played dominoes until we saw spots in our sleep, we piled into the minivan and headed to Tobermory, a town on the tip of the peninsula known for its candy store.

As the five of us strolled along the harbour, devouring jawbreakers and jujubes, I noticed sailing dinghies flitting every which way, like mammoth winged bugs on the water, and David staring at a man sorting a web of ropes on a yacht at a dock. "Maybe we should give sailing a shot as a family," I said.

Desperate to salvage the holiday, the very next day we headed back home and joined a local boating co-op. By week's end, the five of us were huddled on the shore of a little man-made lake on the outskirts of Guelph. Each wearing a mildewy faded orange life jacket, we stared at the fourteen-foot club boat David had rigged, our standard poodle Leiah curled at our feet.

"C'mon, let's go," John said. All the boys fidgeted, raring to jump in.

"Not so fast," David said with unexpected gravity. "We need to get a few things straight first."

The boys and I went quiet and exchanged puzzled glances.

"I'm captain," he announced.

I looked at the tiny boat, paint chipping, lying askew in the weeds, and grinned, certain he was pulling our legs.

"I'm serious," he continued. "And, as captain, I'm responsible for the safety of this vessel and the welfare of its crew."

Glancing across the little splash of water, the boys began to snicker. I tried to think of sad things like death and famine so as not to join them.

"So you must abide by everything I say, no —"

"All righty then," I said, biting my inner cheek.

"No questions asked."

"Or should I say 'Ahoy matey.'" My eyes began to water.

"Dear, I mean it."

"No, it's 'Aye aye, cap'n!'" Brian said, explaining he had watched his share of Popeye reruns.

The four of us erupted into gales of laughter. David stood stone-faced and waited us out. Only after each one of us swore a solemn oath of loyalty did he move a muscle. I didn't know what had gotten into him. Whatever it was, I hoped it would soon pass.

It was a warm, humid August afternoon. We set sail in a light breeze, the lake all to ourselves, only the sounds of ripples against the boat and birds chirping in the distance. Moving by the power of wind felt like magic.

As the boat sliced gracefully through the water, David talked about how to adjust the sails depending on where the wind was from, known as the points of sail. He told us about the technique called tacking, or coming about, used to change direction, and the command-response system between captain and crew to coordinate it. He had us try it a few times to get a feel for how it worked.

It was easy — that is, until we were at the far end of the lake and the wind freshened. As the boat began to tilt, I slid down to the floorboards, leaned toward its high side and held on to the edge, or gunwale, with a vice-like grip, convinced we'd all soon be swimming.

With calm authority, David ordered me back up, then bellowed, "Prepare to come about."

"Ready to come about," the kids and I stuttered.

"Coming about!" he confirmed, pushing the tiller hard over, as we ducked under the boom, stepped over Leiah, and scurried to redistribute our weight.

After we had barely settled, a huge blast of air caused the boat to lurch, momentarily submerging the lower gunwale. I screeched and we tilted en masse in the opposite direction until the wind abated. Just as we began to relax again, a bigger, more sustained gust hit, upon which David ordered Ben and me to "hike out" by securing our feet under a toe strap on the floor of the cockpit and extending our bodies beyond the gunwale, to create enough counterbalance so we wouldn't capsize.

In no time, Ben was precariously stretched out over the whitecaps.

"Dear, this is craziness," I protested.

"Now!" he said.

Soon I was doing this previously unthinkable manoeuvre, too, and just as quickly, the boat's stability was restored. By the time we reached our shore, we were executing these procedures like a well-oiled machine.

Once back on land, the boys all said how awesome sailing was. Then they ran off with Leiah while I helped David put things away.

"That was pretty scary," I said as we folded the sail together. "I mean, at first, when it got windy I thought for sure ... but ... we would've been in trouble if not for ... you were great out there." I watched him lock up the storage shed. "What I'm trying to say is, sorry for earlier."

"It's okay," he said as we walked to the car.

"It's such a small lake. I never expected —"

"It's okay."

That outing rekindled David's interest in sailing. We began discussing boats. He said larger ones with heavy keels were almost untippable. I said a cabin for the occasional family sleepover might be fun.

In the fall of 1996, we bought a single-masted, fin-keeled Tanzer 26 and christened it after David's grandfather's boat. The *Killarney II* marked the end of cottage rentals and the start of marina-to-marina sailing on Lake Ontario and the Bay of Quinte, which carried on through the boys' teenage years.

In 2000, before Ben left for university, we chartered a sailboat in the British Virgin Islands, where we spent two glorious weeks tootling among the islands and basking in the company of our three growing sons. Once back home, realizing they'd all soon be flying the coop, we found ourselves wondering what we were going to do with our free time — and the rest of our lives, for that matter. That's when my library of craft books expanded and David's childhood dream of crossing an ocean resurfaced. It'd be a retirement goal.

The boys left home, one right after the other, and the home winds began to shift.

By fall 2003 Ben, having had a few shots at different university programs, was becoming disillusioned with the whole post-secondary experience. The poli-sci prof peppered every single lecture with his own political views. In film studies the class was told what movies they were supposed to like and why. According to Ben, liberal arts was anything but liberating.

"Try to keep an open mind, Ben," I said.

"I *am*," he said. "But it's like they go out of their way to *stop* us from thinking for ourselves. I'm not sure it's for me." He wanted to take a year off and to stay in Toronto, where there'd be more job options.

Subsequently, Ben unknowingly worked for free for several weeks at a café. When he attempted to collect the back pay he was owed, he found a bankruptcy notice on the locked front door. Short stints as a private gardener, a tree pruner, and a day labourer followed. I expressed disappointment that there was no job security, concern that the jobsites were unsafe, fear that the work cultures were demoralizing. "So what?" "Says who?" "Settle down!" he'd respond.

Then he was swindled out of two months' rent by a slumlord who cleverly skirted the Landlord and Tenant Act by referring to her rat-infested house as an inn, after which he moved to a small room that had a large single-pane window, no insulation, and no heat. I encouraged him to move back home to regroup, to take a time out, to maybe reconsider school — a different program, a brand-new place. He wouldn't think of it. Instead, he borrowed a rusty department-store bike and became a courier, and, with the space heater and old blankets we had given him, he moved into a windowless basement room of a rental duplex that was packed to the rafters with young, single newcomers to the city in search of something, but not yet sure just what.

Brian, in his second year of college, switched programs and moved off-campus with three friends. Before long, he reported he didn't like this second program any better than the first.

John, in his first year of classical music studies, was starting to wish he played jazz instead.

That Christmas David stumbled on a small ad: "Alberg 37 for sale." We made arrangements to check it out over the holidays for something to do.

The broker, Mike, met us at the marina gate. He was a compact man, wearing a puffy winter coat, down mittens, a toque, big boots, and a grimace that said he'd much rather be home drinking eggnog than amusing us in the swirling lake-effect snow. We followed his car tracks to the boat's location. It was on a cradle at the far end of the yard, alone, all wrapped up for the winter. After climbing the ten-foot ladder, we crawled along the boat's deck under the sooty canvas tarp and descended the companionway into the main cabin.

The living space was like a garden shed, twelve feet at its longest and my arm span wide, but cozy, with lots of teak, homespun cushions, unbleached cotton curtains with leather tie-backs, and paraffin lamps dangling from the handholds. And there were pull-out berths to sleep on; an ice chest in which to store food; a gimballed kerosene stove for cooking; lights to read by; a two-piece head, or bathroom; and a navigation (nav) station equipped with a very high frequency (VHF) radio, radar, and a drop-down table for charting.

"It's ten tons, with ratios of a serious blue-water vessel," Mike said. Sensing interest, he added, "It's never tasted salt water. Sad, really."

Back in the car David turned on the ignition, then looked at me and switched it back off. We ogled the lovely sleek hull.

"It's got pretty much everything," I finally said.

David agreed.

"And it's beautiful," I added.

"It is that."

"Dear, if you're serious, I'm thinking this is the boat."

His eyes met mine. "Really? Are you saying you'd —"

"Me? Uh-uh. No way. It takes six bloody hours, *if* we're lucky, to sail from Hamilton to Toronto!"

I had privately contemplated the concept of an ocean crossing, but just couldn't fathom the attraction. Abandoning our boys, my mom, our trusty dog, friends, my career — vocation, more like it — our house, our garden, all our stuff. This in exchange for weeks and weeks out of sight of land in a tiny floating capsule, just him and me. The prospect of storms, pirates, maybe even icebergs like the one that sank the *Titanic*. The probability of growing soft and lumpy. The promise of going crazy. After all, how long can a person look at water? No, I simply didn't get it.

"I'm sorry. I just can't. You'll have to find crew for the crossing," I said. "But I'll happily fly over and meet you on the other side."

At that, we hightailed it home and made an offer, conditional on a spring survey. The name of the boat was *Inia*.

A week after making the offer on the boat, David almost aborted the deal.

We had given Brian a lift back to his new apartment before the start of the winter semester and discovered it was a notorious high-rise in the roughest part of Toronto. My heart pounded as the three of us walked through the lobby filled with snarling faces and vacant eyes. It nearly stopped as we rode an elevator to the fourteenth floor with two guys who were as high as kites.

Brian's unit offered precious little solace. It was sparsely furnished: a settee, a TV on a stack of milk crates, a giant glass cage housing his friend's pet python, and an adjacent smaller cage filled with live mice that, Brian explained, would eventually become the snake's dinner.

"What, Ma? It's natural. Just life. The food chain," he said.

"But still, Brian." I sipped my instant coffee and helped myself to an Oreo cookie from the chipped plate.

When David and I left the building, the parking lot was surrounded by yellow tape and filled with police cruisers. A bystander told us a young man had plunged to his death from an upper balcony. Was likely pushed. A suspected drug deal gone wrong.

I called Brian the instant we got home. "When out, don't engage. Keep your head down. Use a buddy system at all times," I advised. I also informed him that pythons, despite their apparently docile dispositions, could actually kill. "They swallow porcupines whole," I remarked to drive the point home.

"He giggled and called me insane," I said to David after the call. "He seems oblivious to danger!"

David picked up the picture of *Inia* from the counter. "We need to back out of the deal," he said. He went on to say it was impulsive, stupid, pure selfishness on his part. The boys needed our stabilizing influence now more than ever. They had always come first.

I was aghast. His retirement was at least ten years off. Surely to God by then …! And they all knew about the boat offer and the dream. What kind of message would we be sending them? I insisted the deal had to go through. Right then the purchase was not about a trip, but about hope, for all of us.

The following May *Inia* became ours. It felt right.

THREE

DECEMBER 23, 2005, after my last three house calls, I trudged through the grocery store parking lot to join the throng of pale-faced shoppers jostling for frozen turkeys, hunting for cranberry sauce, and standing in meandering lines of brimming carts as the checkout clerks in Santa hats robotically wished everyone season's greetings.

As much as I loved my job as a community occupational therapist, I was exhausted from the pre-Christmas stress and the usual flood of clients being discharged home from hospitals needing wheelchairs, portable ramps — and needing it all yesterday. And I had my own household to worry about.

Back home, with the groceries unpacked and the fridge and cupboards stocked for the holidays, I pulled out the yellowed recipe card and began to bake. Danish pastry was a twenty-plus-year tradition. Soon the kitchen was like a sauna, with the dense aroma of sweet yeast dough filling the steamy air. It was an aroma I had come to associate with all things Christmas, the anticipation, the joy, and the chaos of the season I lovingly endured. And family harmony, especially family harmony.

The phone rang. It was Ben, again, this time announcing he wouldn't be coming home. Christmas Eve was one of the busiest days for bike couriers, delivering all those bottles to Bay Street.

"We aren't asking you to move back for good. Two bloody days, that's all," I said. Maybe I should have avoided sarcasm.

When I played the "John'll be here and expects you to be, too" card, he said he wished he was in Whistler like Brian.

I asked why he'd say such a thing and he growled that he hated Christmas, all the commercial bullshit, that's why.

Then I made the colossal mistake of reminding him about when he was over-the-moon to receive that action figure with wings and a jet pack, and how he used to spend hours making superhero ornaments for the tree with the hot-glue gun.

"That was when I was friggin' six," he screamed. I practically felt his spit through the receiver.

I hung up, reeling.

We had been such a tight little family by everyone's standards. My mom used to insist I'd never have to worry about the boys. "You're lucky in that regard," she'd say over and over. And I had thought she was right. I truly believed if we just loved enough, listened enough, tried hard enough, nothing could go wrong. What the hell had happened? I had no idea. All I knew was I missed the family we once were, the closeness we once had. The loss of it made me ache. And I feared nothing could bring it back.

By six o'clock it was dark. I wiped the patches of crusty flour and sticky jam off the counter and stacked the filled pastry tins to one side as the glow of headlights appeared on the living room curtain and slowly turned into the driveway. Like clockwork, the front door opened and David came in through the blowing snow.

"Hey, honey, I'm ho-ome!" he said in his usual goofy way. And I giggled on cue.

He was unshaven and wearing a wrinkled white shirt and the same baggy-kneed flannel pants he'd worn the day before.

I told him the grocery store had been an absolute zoo, the baking marathon was done, frozen lasagna was in the oven.

"Care for a glass of wine?"

"Would love one. Maybe two," he replied.

We slouched on the couch, sipping wine and watching TV with our feet up on the coffee table.

"God, I can't believe how pathetic we are," I said, watching a mother and her kids elaborately ice a gingerbread house on TV. "Just two days to go and we don't have a tree yet, or even gifts for each other."

"Doesn't matter," David said.

"Yes, it does matter!" I said. "The boys'll think we don't care anymore. Or I should say 'boy.' Singular. Ben called. He's not coming."

"He can't spend Christmas hovering over that space heater."

"I know. But you utter the slightest little thing and you're a control freak."

David reached for the phone and dialed.

"Ben, it's Dad. We understand. We respect that you want to — that's not true, Ben. It was John's choice, not ours. Again, not true. We think the break'll do Brian good. It's just that he can't mountain bike forev— yes, we've always said you can accomplish anything if you — enough already, Ben! Would you just come home? If you feel the need to work tomorrow, I'll pick you up after. Mom's spent the whole damn afternoon baking Danishes. Please, Ben! Fantastic. I'll be outside your place at four."

David hung up, closed his eyes, and let his head flop back on the couch cushion.

"He's changed his mind?" I asked with guarded optimism.

"We'll see," he replied.

Smelling a waft of burnt cheese, I hurried to the kitchen.

"Dinnertime, my dear!" I returned with a plate of dry lasagna in each hand and containers of no-name Parmesan cheese and chili peppers under my armpits. "So then, about tomorrow. I know you're busy, but —"

"Roy plopped a stack of files on my desk this morning, just to make sure I won't be bored over the holidays," David said, mindlessly covering his food with a mountain of grated cheese.

Years before, David had been asked to take on the role of chief financial officer. He hadn't aspired to that position. I had pointed out that he'd be great at it nonetheless. Besides, with the kids' post-secondary years looming, the added cash would come in handy. So he had felt he couldn't say no.

"If you ask me, that man's bordering on abusive. Even his all-caps emails feel mean," I said.

"He also happens to be the CEO. But about tomorrow, we'll hit the mall first thing, then do a decorating blitz that'd put Martha Stewart to shame."

"Before you get Ben? Will there be time?"

"As long as you can jump into a moving vehicle."

"You're so silly."

He picked up the TV remote and speed-clicked through basketball and football games, news programs, and quiz shows, settling on the Weather Network. We sat hunched over our plates, gulping wine and crunching crispy noodles as the meteorologist droned on.

Eight o'clock, we hit the sack.

Midafternoon Christmas Eve, I drew back the curtain. David was sitting semi-reclined in a hospital bed, wearing a greyish-green gown, his arms outstretched on the over-the-bed table in front of him, his head thickly wrapped in white gauze.

"You look like you're going to tell my fortune," I said.

His bloodshot eyes twinkled.

"I predict you'll be having Christmas without me," he slurred. His tongue was thick and purple and his lips were swollen.

"Jeez, you're good!" I leaned over and kissed his cheek. He flinched. "God, what? Sorry!"

"Uggh! My back." He grabbed both bedrails and gingerly adjusted his upper body, flinching some more. Then his eyes darkened. "What happened? All I remember is splitting up to shop for each other, then feeling hot, really hot. And the mall lights swirling. And trying to find a bench."

I sat down on the vinyl chair beside the bed, breathed in deeply, blinked back tears, and then began to explain. "I was walking down the mall corridor, heading to Starbucks to meet you, when I saw someone lying in a pool of blood. There was a crowd gathering around him. *Poor soul,* I thought. *Christmas can be such a sad time.* I hurried over to help, thinking *I know CPR,* fearing that I knew CPR. Then I spotted the bootlace with green masking tape on the end, and I realized that poor soul was you!" I stroked his arm and began to cry. "Blood was literally gushing out of your forehead. And you were thrashing about. And you looked scared, so, so scared. Dear, it was just awful."

Our conversation was interrupted by a young, rosy-cheeked nurse in a pink two-piece uniform and powder-blue runners. "Hi, Mr. Williams. I'm Kelly. Just going to take your vitals."

I glanced down at my cellphone, tears falling onto the screen while she listened through David's yeows, efficiently moving the stethoscope up and down his shoulder blades.

"Am I still breathing?" he asked, settling back down.

"You are indeed." She smiled and recorded the information on a pad from her pocket. Then off she went.

"I called Ben first thing to let him know you won't be picking him up," I said, drying my eyes with the hem of my shirt.

"What'd he say?"

"Dead silence at first. I thought the phone had cut out. He seemed pretty upset. Wanted to know what it was. I told him we're still waiting to find out."

"Hopefully he'll come home anyway," David said. "I hate the thought of him spending Christmas in that basement dump and —"

"Remember yesterday? He made it abundantly clear he has no desire to be here."

"— and being all alone."

"Frankly, I'm not sure I even want to see him right now, but it's entirely up to him. I phoned the other boys too. Brian cried and said he was sorry."

"Sorry for what?"

"That you're in here and that he's too far away to come home."

"Poor guy. Tell him not to worry. When I can talk like a normal person again I'll give him a call myself. And John?"

"I waited 'til noon, but still woke him up. Good thing, 'cause he slept through his alarm and would've missed the bus. The band played at a house party last night, then partied *with* the party 'til four this morning. He sounded pretty rough but is on his way. Of course, he's upset, too."

A lanky, kind-faced man entered with a stethoscope around his neck and a clipboard in hand. "Good evening, Mr. Williams. I'm Doctor Pereira. To cut to the chase, you had a seizure, a violent grand mal. You sustained two compression fractures of your thoracic spine and multiple lacerations as collateral damage. Took fourteen stitches to close you up. Your family doctor will arrange a battery of tests to determine the cause."

"Oh my God, the cause!" I blurted, as terrifying thoughts of brain disorders and inoperable tumours flooded my mind.

"Mrs. Williams, seizures can be brought on simply by stress."

"Well, I had to shop in the mall on Christmas Eve, so ..." David said with a contorted smile.

"Yet he still didn't buy me anything!"

"Aggghh! Don't make me laugh." David grimaced, lifting and shifting, careful not to twist.

The doctor smiled gently. "As I'm sure you can appreciate, Mr. Williams, this was a major assault on your body. Assuming it was a stress-induced seizure, they tend to be singular events — if the precipitating factors are mitigated." He turned to leave, then looked back. "But I concur, Christmas Eve at the mall is definitely bad for one's health."

The chuckling ended abruptly as there was a commotion outside the curtain. "He's my dad," we heard. Then Ben flew in, past the doctor and me, and headed straight for the bedside.

He was wearing an army-green canvas coat with a black hoodie underneath, faded jeans, and worn runners lined with grocery bags secured with elastic bands around each ankle to keep his feet dry. He had long blond dreadlocks and he smelled like damp earth.

"Hey," he said, sizing up the various tubes and electrodes attached to David.

"Hey, Ben," David replied. "Not exactly the Christmas we had in mind. But glad you're here."

"No worries."

Christmas morning, I got up extra early and slipped into the kitchen. Under the dim glow of the stove light I made a pot of coffee and set the breakfast table for three. Then I peeled and chopped potatoes into one pot of cold water and turnips into another and began breaking up sausage in a frying pan with onions, celery, and sage for the turkey dressing.

Stress. That was likely it. It was as if a bomb had exploded at the core of our family, blasting it apart, sending our sons hurtling unprepared into the adult world and rendering our once-stable home life almost unrecognizable. There were car accidents. Bike accidents. Post-secondary woes. Sketchy jobs, unsafe jobs, and no jobs at all. Apartments with rats in the walls and gangsters in the stairwells. Partying, pot, and heartbreaks we wished we could mend. When the boys were little it had seemed so easy to protect them from harm and make their hurts all better. Now, no longer.

David and I fretted in circles about their safety, their health, their happiness, and their futures. This while he was being buried alive at work. Stress, the seizure — it made sense.

Hearing footsteps upstairs, I put bacon on the back burner on low.

John soon appeared at the kitchen door wearing black jeans and a striped shirt partly tucked in, his unwashed hair sticking up every which way.

"This must be the middle of the night for you," I said. "Did I wake you?"

"Couldn't sleep."

"Coffee?"

"Sure."

"Merry Christmas," I said, handing him a steaming mug.

"Same to you," he replied reflexively.

We winced at just how far that was from the truth.

"Ben says Dad's worn out," John remarked, stirring milk into his coffee. "He's gotta take better care of himself."

"That's easier said than done."

"Is it?"

I wanted to say, *Obviously, you don't get it. Don't get him. Don't get that his paycheque has covered vehicles and tuition and first and last months' rent more times than I can count. That he loves you three more than anything in the world. That he'd walk through fire if he thought it would help any of you out.* But I bit my tongue.

"We'll have breakfast, then head up to the hospital."

"Sounds good."

Just then, Ben walked in. "Hey, hoser."

"Hey," John replied.

"Why did you answer to that?" I asked John, pouring Ben a coffee.

"'Cause that's his name," Ben said. They both laughed, a sound as warm and lovely as a favourite sweater.

I got out a loaf of bread and a carton of eggs and began to prepare breakfast.

"How's school?" Ben asked.

"It's good. And me and a few guys started a band, Max Galactic and the Cloud of Evil."

"Are you Max?" Ben asked.

"No, I'm part of the cloud, a quarter of it to be precise," John said with a smile. "We played a slew of gigs leading up to the holidays."

"Cool," Ben said.

"Sometimes 'til four in the morning," I jumped in.

"Oh, the other night. That was hilarious," John said. "Ever hear of Dance Dance Revolution?"

We both shook our heads no.

"Well, just as things were dying down, a guy shows up at the house party with this video game. DDR he calls it for short. He presses a button, music plays, lights light up, and he starts moving his feet on this floor mat. As the music goes faster and faster, so does he. He's supposed to be dancing. But his arms and legs are stiff as a board. And he's deadly serious. Like this." John got up and did a Frankenstein-on-crack manoeuvre about the kitchen as we stepped out of his way and chuckled. "It was the most ridiculous thing I've ever seen," he said, sitting back down. "But that didn't stop the rest of us from trying. I can't remember anything funnier. Still a bit sore, though."

I placed a bowl of scrambled eggs; plates of crispy bacon, sliced tomatoes, and toast; and jars of strawberry jam and hot sauce at the centre of the table, then topped up all the coffees and poured us each a glass of orange juice.

"Go ahead. Dig in," I said, joining them at the table.

"How's the courier thing going?" John asked Ben while spooning eggs onto his toast.

"It's awesome," Ben said. He loaded up his plate like he hadn't eaten in weeks.

"Even in snow?"

"Especially in snow! I went all the way to North York and back in that storm."

"That's crazy," John said.

"Good grief!" I said. "Do you wear an orange vest or something so cars can see you?"

"Nope."

"Tell me you wear a helmet at least."

"No helmet, either."

"Dear Lord, Ben. I work with people with brain injuries and I've seen the devastation —"

"I said no. No helmet and no fuckin' orange vest," he said, shaking hot sauce over everything in sight.

"I wish you wouldn't use language like that."

"Or what? I'll go straight to hell?"

"You sound like a trucker, that's all."

"What's wrong with being a trucker?"

"It's a figure of speech, Ben. You know full well I have no problem with people who drive trucks for a living."

"As long as it's not one of us."

"That's not —"

"Not everyone's destined to be an accountant like Dad. And besides, how's that working out for him?"

I got up and scraped my full plate into the bin under the sink, then busied myself loading the dishwasher, periodically swiping at the tears running down my cheeks. Ben and John finished their breakfast in silence.

"Is there time for a shower?" John asked, cleaning off his plate.

"Yes, certainly," I said, avoiding eye contact. "There are clean towels in the hall closet."

I heard the water start to run in the bathroom. Ben walked over to me with his plate.

"Look, I know you care but —"

"You have no idea how much." By now I was bawling.

"But I'd rather stick needles in my eyes than sit through another PowerPoint presentation of nine essential things I need to know. I'm not going back to school."

"You're a smart guy, Ben. We're worried you might regret it."

"If so, that's my problem. Not yours."

"We want you to have a good life. To feel fulfilled. To be happy."

"That's what I have, what I am, right now — as a bike courier. I feel free out there, more alive than I've felt in years. Maybe ever. And I'm good at it. When the weather's shitty and others wimp out, the dispatcher can always count on me. Maybe it won't be forever. And what follows, who knows? But one thing I'm certain about is I need to figure things out for myself. You guys are smothering me. I gotta goddamn breathe."

In that instant I knew Ben was right. As an occupational therapist, I understood the importance of autonomy and self-determination. If Ben were my client, I'd be a fierce defender of his unique lifestyle choices, and I'd champion his unique personal goals. So surely, as my son, he deserved no less.

"Will you please just wear a helmet?"

"Jesus friggin' Christ."

FOUR

ON DECEMBER 27, before heading back up to the hospital, I opened the kitchen window a smidgen to let cool air in
and the lingering smells of days-old bacon fat and turkey grease
escape while I mopped the kitchen floor. I've always liked this
post-Christmas ritual, the ridding the house of festive clutter and
excess, the restoring of order. It brings a sense of renewal, a spiritual cleansing of sorts.

I gathered up the latest Christmas cards and arranged
them in a neat pile in the centre of David's desk, knowing he
wouldn't want to miss any — except perhaps the annual news-
letter from our ex-neighbour Judith, whose family undoubt-
edly had had another "simply maaavelous" year and once again
felt truly humbled by their good fortune. But that, too, was a
twenty-plus-year tradition.

I glanced at the bulletin board above the desk and scanned
its haphazard collage of family pictures, school photos, brittle
newspaper clippings of birth and death announcements, and
crayon artwork from the boys' early years. I stopped at the curled
three-by-five snapshot of *Inia*.

Soon after the deal had been finalized, David quietly tacked
her picture in the middle of the board and began to methodically

prepare for his retirement adventure: studying celestial navigation, going to seminars, watching documentaries, and reading
every account of ocean sailing he could get his hands on.

But now, depending on the outcome of the neurological
assessment, his plans might come to a crushing halt. *Please, God,
tell us stress caused the seizure and not anything more ominous. I know
he can get over fractures and bruises and cuts, and pretty much anything
else that's thrown his way, so long as he has a positive vision of the
future. However, if this cockamamie dream of his is shattered … well,
that could be unbearable.*

The desk phone rang. Its shrillness at this early hour made
me jump. It was David calling from the nursing station, impatient to tell me the doctor had just made rounds and declared
him well enough to be discharged and that he had declared
himself well enough to take me out for Indian food. It was our
twenty-fifth anniversary.

FIVE

EARLY JANUARY, David walked out of the bedroom wearing a white hairnet through which I could see the raw scars and shaved patches on his skull. A pouch, slung across his chest, sat on his hip. Electrodes were stuck in the centre of the shaved patches, a wire from each running to a monitor in the pouch. He was undergoing an ambulatory electroencephalogram, or EEG. And he was dressed for work.

"You can't be serious," I said. "Honestly, dear. It's way too soon. You need more time to —"

"I'm fine."

"And ... well ... you look —"

"I'll just say I'm communicating with Martians." He made theremin sounds and pretended to adjust dials to tune in to foreign lifeforms.

I didn't know whether to laugh or cry and ended up doing a hysterical combination of both.

"You know how wild year-end is. If I'm not there, it'll mean more work for others, and the whole department's run ragged. Sue, I've got to go. But I'll talk to Roy after it's over. See if I can offload a few things."

"Promise?" I said.

"I do," he said, removing every unessential paper out of his briefcase so he could carry it.

He bit his bottom lip while reaching down to pull on his boots and tie the laces, and when he straightened up, his face was beet red. He wrestled on his heavy winter coat, carefully stretched his toque over the electrode assembly, put on gloves, snapped his briefcase shut, and headed out the door.

He was a godawful mess, clearly in no shape to return to the office. I fully expected he'd be ordered back home the minute upper management laid eyes on him. But he wasn't. Instead, he convalesced at his desk over the winter. Not a single deadline was missed.

During this time, he underwent an exhaustive series of tests: an MRI, an ECG, an EEG, a bone scan, and a CAT scan, along with the ambulatory EEG. All were negative, leading the neurologist to conclude the seizure was a stress-related event. Stress could have just as easily caused a stroke and permanent disability or a heart attack and death, rather than the seizure. We were lucky and we knew it. However, the seizure was a warning. We needed to make some serious changes in our lives, or next time we might not be so fortunate.

As promised, David scheduled a meeting with Roy after the year-end crunch to hand off the non-accounting responsibilities that had crept up on him over the years. So, it was just a matter of time before his workload would become more manageable.

On the home front, we started to appreciate that our perceptions of our sons' situations and needs, however clear they seemed to us, were not necessarily shared by them. And our efforts to solve their life puzzles, however well intentioned, could have even, inadvertently, been a deterrent to their abilities to find their spots in this world.

My eighty-six-year-old friend Charna, a great-grandmother several times over, told me to think of this stage like springtime. It's unsettled, often stormy, but full of promise. The best thing parents can do for their children at this stage is to give them time and space, freedom to grow into themselves, secure in the knowledge that summer will inevitably follow.

I had to agree. Thinking back to that in-between stage in my own life, the confusing transition to adulthood, I asked myself whether my parents would have wanted to protect me from life's troubles and pain. Probably. Could they have? Not likely. In retrospect, would I have wanted them to? No. I needed space to figure me out for myself. How can you know who you are if you've never been given the opportunity to find out? It was only when I struck out on my own that I determined what I really cared about and began to develop my own world view.

Our sons needed independence. For all our sakes, it was time for us to let go.

David met with the CEO toward the end of February to discuss his workload. Late that afternoon, I showered and put on comfy jeans and my old Aran sweater. This was a leaf-turning occasion, worthy of a celebratory burger and beer at the Wooly, our favourite neighbourhood pub. I felt rested, healthier, happier, just anticipating the restoration of a normal work-life balance.

I'll never forget the pain on David's face when he walked through the front door at the end of the day. "I'm being let go," he said, barely above a whisper.

I was stunned. We hugged as tears rolled down his cheeks.

"Sid was there, too," he eventually continued. He hung up his coat on the hall hook and wiped his eyes. "So I knew it was going to be bad. They don't call him the Angel of Death for nothing."

I followed David to the bedroom and sat on the side of the bed while he changed.

"Roy said they're restructuring," he said, tossing his dress pants and shirt into the hamper.

"The liar."

"Sid explained they don't see me in their view of the organization from thirty thousand feet." He zipped up his jeans and put on a flannel shirt. Then he sat beside me.

"If they felt you were damaged goods, they should've at least had the decency to tell you so in January. But no. They let you put in ten-hour days with a broken back, even a head full of electrodes."

"They've asked me to stay on through another accounting cycle to update department manuals and arrange backup of the systems."

"Eleven years. Loyal to a fault."

"And to give them an opportunity to find my replacement."

"The department loves you. How could none of that matter? How could *you* not matter?"

He flopped back on the bed. "There'll be a package in the end, so I can take time to figure out *what next?*"

"Cold-blooded snakes."

"Maybe this'll turn out to be a good thing in the long run," he said, closing his eyes and rubbing the flaming scar on his forehead.

I lay back beside him and stared at a cobweb on the ceiling, tears matting my hair and dampening the comforter below. The two of us were in an out-of-control downward spiral. Why was it happening? What had we done to deserve it? How would it all end?

"Tell Sid he isn't funny and he can't sing," I said.

SIX

"JUMP!" DAVID YELLED.

"I'm gonna die!" I yelled back.

"Now!" he said, pushing himself off the swaying seat, then gliding to a graceful stop in the powder-like snow.

I scissored my skis, landed, and fell. The chairlift jerked forward, depositing successive pairs of skiers close by while I struggled to get back on my feet.

David's thinking was *When in Rome*. But we weren't in Rome. We were in Whistler, British Columbia.

Early March, I suggested we visit Brian. He had to see for himself that his dad had recovered. John and Ben both needed a break. David and I couldn't walk around like zombies forever. The winter had been a particularly brutal one for the entire family. It would do us the world of good.

At the last minute, Ben said he couldn't make it.

"Okay, fine," I said. But it was neither okay nor fine. His absence would be conspicuous, unnatural. It could possibly ruin the trip for us all. My heart sank.

Now I stood on the summit of Blackcomb and took in the view: the mountain blanketed in white and miles of winding spruce-lined trails, the rays of sunshine piercing the cotton clouds, the sparkling snowflakes floating from the sky. "I had no idea," I said. "It's just so beautiful." I looked at the ant-sized people criss-crossing below. "And so ... big! It's shockingly very big. Are you sure —"

"There are green markers everywhere, dear. This *is* the bunny hill." David skied twenty feet down, then stopped and waited for me. "C'mon. Just take your time. You'll be fine."

Knees bent, pigeon-toed, I inhaled the steely air, gritted my teeth, and poled off.

Veer left, wi-ide turn, veer right. Big turn left. Big turn right. Left then right. Left, right.

"Good, Sue. You're doing great," he said as I got closer.

I straightened up and beamed, losing my concentration and that all-important V. As I passed him, I picked up speed. So I did the only thing I could think to do: I sat down on my skis. And I went faster yet, crossing the path of parents teaching their toddlers to ski, narrowly missing a pair of boys on snowboards who gave me the finger as they whooshed by. It would have ended badly if not for the snow fence and the ski patrollers who untangled me from it.

"Well, that was embarrassing," I said to the young men, adjusting my rental goggles. "But I'm okay. Go ... now ... really, I'm fine."

"'Fraid we can't, ma'am," said the guy with the ponytail and ear stud, pointing out that my left ski was across the tips of theirs.

"Geez Louise," I said, shuffling ahead to set them free.

"Take it easy out here, will ya?" he said.

"Wouldn't want you to break a hip," his chisel-faced partner added with a wink, and they skied off.

David had seen it all; worse, he had heard it all. His valiant attempt to keep a straight face failed. It was the most he had laughed in a long time.

After giving me a brief refresher on the mechanics of the snowplough, he led me gradually down the mountainside, with stops to stretch and to hydrate and to eat a high-protein lunch midmountain. Four hours later, I came to an entirely respectable stop near the chairlift line-up at the base.

Shielding his eyes from the afternoon glare, David scanned the various runs to spot the boys while I leaned on a post, sipping coffee and acting like being there was the most natural thing on earth.

"We'll see them when we see them," I said, refusing to flinch as racing yahoos came to hockey-style stops mere feet from me. Then, watching the steady stream of Gore-Tex glide by, I joked, "It's like they're coming off a conveyer belt with —"

"Christ," David said, pointing to a guy running, sliding, jumping down near-vertical drops in hot pursuit of an errant snowboard on the double black diamond run.

"Oh my God. It's —"

"Definitely Brian."

"Then where on earth's John?"

"See that plume of snow halfway up?"

John was doing moguls. On his back.

When Brian met up with his snowboard at the foot of the run, he tucked it under his arm and darted to where John was headed. David and I followed.

"It was a mistake, a wrong turn. I tried to warn him," he explained.

The three of us watched John's luge-like descent in silence.

When he swirled to a stop at the bottom, we hurried to his aid.

"Yo, John," Brian called out.

John dizzily rose to his feet. "I'm okay," he eventually said, as we all dusted him off. "But, what the hell —"

"You even caught air, dude," Brian said.

They looked at each other and cracked up.

Just as I had insisted, flying down snowy mountains on slippery boards was a risky endeavour, fraught with danger, even for people with a modicum of skill. In my case, it was utter recklessness.

I did it anyway. Despite my better judgment, I skied Whistler. And I experienced sheer terror, but also exhilaration and beauty and joy unlike anything I'd known before.

As the four of us left the mountain, sunburnt, sore, and laughing ourselves silly, I felt tired, blissfully so. We were able to have fun. Our family was evolving as it should, as it must. Calamity had released its stranglehold on David and me. And I, of all people, had skied Whistler.

It was a day of triumphs. I would have swaggered if I could have, but as it was I could barely walk.

I tossed and turned, unable to sleep.

Whistler had been fantastic. I still felt the afterglow. No, it was more than that. Much more. But I didn't quite know what.

I fluffed up my pillow, stared into the darkness, watched the clock radio blink.

God, we had such a great time! It was different without Ben, but more natural than unnatural, when I really thought about it. And it was different in general, the way Brian and John related to each other, them to us, us to them. All of it was subtly different. Adult to adult. Nice.

David was the happiest I'd seen him in a long time. He talked more. He laughed a lot, mostly at me, but that's okay. I might find the snow fence encounter funny too ... in time.

He wasn't worrying about Roy and Sid out there. That's the main thing. They might have destroyed other people's lives, but not his. Not ours. I now know we'll be okay.

I looked over. David's breathing was even, peaceful. His face, worry-free.

I can't remember when he last slept this soundly either. Maybe he was right when he said his getting fired might someday turn out to be a good thing. Maybe it already is.

It was past midnight. I needed to sleep, too. I flipped my pillow over and kicked off the covers. That felt cooler, better, sort of. But the thoughts kept coming.

His days of having to answer to that heartless duo are numbered. The end's in sight. Next spring he'll be free.

But then what? Back to the same old grind? God! Perish the thought!

David never wanted to be an accountant. Can't even add! But he took that first office job for me. Didn't want my parents to think I was marrying a deadbeat. Hilarious. Truth is, they adored him. Might have even considered slipping him "a little something" to propose to me, if he hadn't taken the initiative. And then, it was for the boys, for lessons, for sports, for travel, for school, for … for … and it hasn't stopped.

They aren't asking us for money. Not at all. But it's what we parents do. We're hardwired to provide support if we're able, if it'll make their lives easier.

With no covers at all, I felt chilly, exposed. I dug out the top sheet and pulled it up … there … perfect.

Here's Ben, with an eviction notice. New owners plan to convert the house back to a single-family dwelling. He'll likely need help to secure a new place, through no fault of his own. Brian's working not one, but two jobs in Whistler, yet he can't even afford a season pass. Ironic or what! And, as talented as John is, everyone knows being a musician is a tough row to hoe.

So we naturally continue to help them out, with no end in sight. But is it necessary? Is it still truly helpful? When they're no longer in school, is it even right?

In my heart of hearts, I believe the answers to all of the above are no. Autonomy, true autonomy, is what they really need. But if that's so then —

I threw the sheet back and sat bolt upright, my body jittery, my thinking crystal clear.

"David?"

"Hmmm."

"You awake?"

He looked at the clock, "It's two thirty."

"I figured it out," I said. "The *what next*. I know what it is."

"Can't it wait 'til morning?"

"You need to go sailing."

He rolled over, lifted his head off his pillow, and studied my face in the clock radio's faint light.

"If you want to go, this is the perfect opportunity," I said. "Think about it: you've got the boat, the health, and you'll soon have the time. You can look for another job after."

David turned on the bedside lamp and we propped ourselves up against the headboard.

"And the boys aren't asking for our help anymore. Nor do they need it. As Charna says, freedom's what they need now, time and space to figure things out for themselves. So I'll go, too."

"You? But you've always —"

"I've changed my mind. If we have a proper ocean-going vessel — and we do — we'll likely be fine. You've said so your-self."

"Well, there's a little more to it than —"

"And plus, I'm now an adrenalin junkie. Remember last week? Whistler?"

David laughed. He said sailing off was certainly an intriguing concept. Perhaps we could do the popular Ontario jaunt, down the Intracoastal Waterway to the Caribbean and back. Then, if successful, we could venture farther afield in retirement.

"No," I said. "An ocean crossing's what you've dreamt of doing, so that's what we'll do."

If there was one thing the seizure had illustrated, it was that one's health could change in a heartbeat. There was no assurance we'd even be alive in ten to fifteen years' time.

"I have to say I didn't see this coming," he said, leaning over and reaching for the lamp. "We'll have to think this through, give it some serious thought." He turned out the light.

"But I'm still not sleepy," I said.

"Me neither," he said, pulling me closer, curving his body around mine.

SEVEN

OVER THE NEXT COUPLE OF WEEKS, we studied Pilot Charts to learn about historic wind and weather patterns on the world's oceans, and we read Jimmy Cornell's book, *World Cruising Routes*, from which we made our plan: we would circumnavigate the North Atlantic Ocean starting from New York City, leaving in spring 2007. And since I had a job to return to and David had a job to find, the trip would be done in a year.

The complexity of temporarily shutting down our land-based life was mind-numbing. What about my mom? I talked to her every day. Who would fill the inevitable void created by my absence? Then there was Leiah. Who would take care of her? And would they take the right kind of care of her? Let her watch TV on the couch? Sleep on their bed? Generally rule the roost? After all, that's all she had ever known. What about our friends, our house, the car, the business of our daily lives? Most importantly, what about the boys? How would they fare without the security of a home base? Without Danishes at Christmas? Without us? Really, truly, how would they fare?

Then, just what did we need to do to get ourselves ready to go and to prepare *Inia* for the biggest job of her life?

So much to sort out in so little time.

We visited my mom to tell her in person. With the three of us sitting around her maple kitchen table, my mom midcrossword, David broke the news. She knew he intended to do an ocean voyage in retirement, so although the timing was unexpected, the trip itself came as no surprise to her. But she was taken aback to hear I intended to go, too.

When I was growing up, doing crafts was my concept of excitement. Outside was the place I walked through to get to fabric stores and yarn shops.

Family togetherness was everything to me. When my brothers left home they were pumped, my parents were proud, and I cried enough for all of them.

And no one was more of a homebody. I could see my mother thinking *Australia*. In my last year of university, hearing my classmates go on about their grand plans to work abroad after graduation, I applied for a job down under. But that Christmas, when my parents gave me luggage and a world map to support my newfound spirit of adventure, I burst into tears and continued to sob inconsolably throughout the rest of the festive season. I didn't want to go to Australia. The mere thought of Australia made me hopelessly homesick. There was no way I'd go to Australia, let alone roam the world.

"When's this supposed to happen?" my mom asked.

"Next spring," David replied.

"Oh, next spring," she said, getting back to her crossword puzzle, apparently certain I would change my mind.

The following week we went to Toronto to have lunch with Ben. The agenda was to sort out his latest shelter crisis, and now additionally to tell him about the trip. While the three of us walked along a commercial strip looking for a restaurant, David told Ben about the sailing plan.

"Mom, too?" He looked at me. "Really? You?"

I imagined he was recalling when I got seasick aboard the *Killarney II* while it was tied to the dock in Prinyers Cove, or perhaps when the boys went into Welland to watch *X-Men* because I steadfastly refused to depart the marina in three-foot waves. And he was very likely considering that I didn't actually know how to sail.

That there were doubts about me was entirely justified. Based on all the evidence, I was the last person on earth to embark on an adventure of this magnitude. But it was like a switch had been flipped. Once I made the decision to go, I was convinced it was meant to be. I could no more stop this plan from proceeding than I could the earth from spinning.

"Yup," I said. "How about Mexican? I've got burritos on the brain."

Over lunch Ben said that he was thinking of moving to Vancouver when his lease was up.

"What's there?" I asked.

"Don't know yet," he said, with a smile.

David asked how he was going to get there. He hoped by train, *if* he could save the money.

"Looks like a great city for biking," I said, pinching David's knee under the table. "From what I saw of it anyway. We got a glimpse of it on the way to Whistler."

"Oh, about Whistler," David said, proceeding to recount our mountain mishaps, following which he and I took turns commenting on the bean burritos, the weather, the latest movies, the guacamole, the salsa, the bean burritos again — everything we could think of other than money.

When Ben left for the washroom we agreed now was the time.

"Mom and I talked. We'll cover the train fare and a month's rent," David said as Ben sat back down.

"I'll pay you back."

"It's a gift, not a loan. But this is it, Ben. No more."

"Cool."

"After this, you're on your own."

"Cool. That's cool," Ben repeated. "Awesome. I'm good with that."

EIGHT

FROM READING AND TALKING to experienced sailors, it soon became evident that, aside from being a blue-water vessel, what constitutes an ocean-ready boat depends. Some sailors go offshore with minimal electronics, lights, and perhaps a global positioning system, or GPS, believing the less you have, the less that can go wrong. At the other extreme are boats outfitted with electric winches, water-makers, hot showers, washers, dryers, flat-screen TVs, and gigantic generators to run them all.

We tended toward the minimalist side. Living simply had appeal, and financially we had little choice. On our own boat-readiness checklist, safety was the top priority; comfort and all else a distant second.

On the electronics front, the ability to communicate was paramount. We would install a marine single-sideband ham radio for long-distance communication and the ability to download GRIB files (compressed files of weather data) and to email over radio waves. We would also take a new VHF radio with distress-signalling capability. For navigation, in addition to our handheld GPS, we'd install a wall-mounted Garmin.

After much deliberation, we decided we'd insert a keel-cooled refrigeration system in our ice locker. Although refrigeration would be a significant draw on power, we agreed that meal options beyond beef jerky would be essential to our mental and physical well-being.

"We need a CD player, too, perhaps with a built-in AM/FM radio," I said. "Music's food for the soul. Our salvation depends on it," I added, feeling clever.

David added a CD/radio to our list of needs.

Rather than only relying on the engine to recharge the battery bank, we'd install solar panels and a wind generator to harness natural sources of energy to meet our demands for power.

We'd also mount a CapeHorn self-steering unit on the transom. Self-steering systems enable a boat to steer itself and are essential for single-handed sailors and short-handed ones travelling long distances, like we'd soon be. Our existing autohelm was battery-operated. This new pendulum wind-vane unit would enable us to control *Inia*'s direction mechanically by the wind.

One Saturday afternoon, David slapped a pamphlet on the kitchen table. Without asking me first, he had enrolled the two of us in a one-day course, Fundamentals of Marine Diesel Engines.

"Tell me you're joking."

"Dear, it'll be just you and me out there."

Although I had committed to going on this voyage, having to actually *do* stuff on it — particularly diesel-engine stuff — hadn't, until then, crossed my mind.

As the big day drew nearer, I started to consider that maybe David saw something in me I hadn't yet seen in myself. Maybe I could become one of those modern women who sews and tinkers with diesels on the side. Perhaps this wasn't an entirely ludicrous plan.

On the course day, we got up early, put on our faux-grubbies, and headed out. Down an alley in the east end of Toronto, past rusting cars and pieces of twisted metal, was the classroom — also known as a garage. Parked in the gravel lot between other vehicles, waiting for the instructor to arrive, we sipped take-out coffees and stared at the greasy plate-glass window plastered in decals advertising oil and engine additives.

"It'll be great. Probably really helpful," David said, breaking the silence.

A BMW pulled up, out of which emerged a tanned, heavy-set man in his sixties dressed in a loud Hawaiian shirt, cargo shorts, and Crocs, and a scrawny twenty-something-year-old with Levi's dangling precariously from his skeletal hips. The older man unlocked the garage door, went inside, and turned on the fluorescent lights while the other waved us in.

A blast of hot air and fuel fumes hit us at the entrance. Inside was a large square space with folding chairs arranged in a semicircle around two glimmering hunks of steel mounted on pedestals like objects of worship. I claimed the seat at the far end. David was to my immediate right followed by five other men. Everyone talked in reverential whispers before the class began.

I tried to settle in and relax; no reason not to. I had just as much a right to be there as anyone, I reminded myself.

"Mornin' and welcome," the Hawaiian-shirted man began. "I'm Fred, the proprietor, and this is Micky, my ace mechanic. Today we're gonna talk about the marine diesel engine, an invention of pure genius."

"Just bought a boat, so gotta learn this shit," said a gnarly man with a baseball hat on backward.

"Then let's get right at 'er." Fred held up a tiny round rubber object. "Does anyone know what an impeller's for?"

"Skewering people," I said into David's ear. "Impale, skewer — get it?"

David kept looking straight ahead, but by the jab in my ribs I knew he had heard me.

"When we exercise, we heat up and our bodies need water. Your diesel's no different. When she's working, this here helps run water through to keep her cool. But being rubber, it needs replacing from time to time. Take a good look. It's a job you'll have to do, guaranteed."

So began an exercise in which engine parts, haphazardly stacked on a side table, were passed around slowly while their functions were described. Everyone watched the objects move from person to person. Feeling like I was glowing with no place to hide, I received a fuel filter, fuel injectors, an engine belt, and so on, and unnecessarily commented on each.

"Last but not least," Fred said, "we have the pistons and the —"

"Go, Lakers!" I said, looking around with a giant grin, bubbles coming out the sides of my mouth.

My classmates squirmed and David hissed to give it a rest in response.

"The pistons and the crank shaft," Fred continued, undeterred. "When the crank shaft turns, the pistons compress air, and compressed air gets hot. Naturally, you inject a little diesel and *kaboom*, your engine starts." Locking eyes with me, he added, "For your model diesel, with a flywheel, it's akin to starting a fire without a match. Understand?"

"I, I think so," I said, slinking down in my seat.

"No spark plug. No nothing. Pure genius." He glanced at his handwritten notes. "'Kay. Next, we're gonna list what spare parts you should have onboard."

As Fred and Micky ploughed on, I settled down. And to their credit, by five o'clock, in spite of myself, I had learned a thing or two.

"I'm glad we have one," I said, watching a lone trawler chugging along the shoreline of Lake Ontario on our drive home.

David looked over, confused. "One what?"

"A flywheel. Seems someone wasn't listening!"

Over the next several months we became regulars at our local sail lofts, rigging shops, and chandleries, during which we acquired a storm sail for use in near gales, new halyards to withstand the pummelling of the sea, heavy-gauge lifelines to prevent us from falling overboard, a life raft in case we sank, an emergency position-indicating radio beacon (EPIRB, 406 megahertz) to signal we were in peril and where, and an abandon-ship bag, or ditch bag, which David filled with what he deemed minimally essential to take into the life raft. It included a handheld GPS, a handheld VHF radio, a compass, flares, first-aid supplies, identification in a Ziploc bag, packets of sterilized water and energy biscuits, a blanket, a mirror, a horn, and a bell. *Plan for the best; prepare for the worst* was his motto. *If I find myself in the life raft ringing that little orange bell ... that'd be the very worst,* I thought.

NINE

AFTER A YEAR OF LIVING in Whistler, Brian decided to move to Victoria, on Vancouver Island, for more job opportunities, a milder climate, and its proximity to the ocean. One day in the late fall, I flew out west, rented a hatchback at the Vancouver airport, and drove up the Sea-to-Sky Highway to help him move. The next day, the two of us rose at the crack of dawn and, by noon, the sum total of his earthly belongings was packed in and on the vehicle, and we were on our way.

When we arrived in Victoria, we booked into a downtown hotel and immediately began browsing the internet and reading the classified ads to check out work and apartment prospects. It soon became clear the job market was grim and the apartment vacancy rate was grimmer. Nevertheless, every day, all day long, I drove him around and, armed with his accordion file full of resumés and lists of personal references, he filled out applications, went for interviews and, along with the legions of other people desperate for a place to call home, met with building superintendents. Although I got discouraged as the week progressed, he didn't.

By week's end, he had landed a job in an upscale wine store on Victoria's trendy waterfront.

"I didn't realize you knew that much about wine," I said when he got back in the car with the news.

"I don't." He loosened his tie. "It's amazing what you can pull outta your butt under pressure," he added with his signature giggle.

But as for an apartment, still nothing. And I was leaving the next morning. In the absence of an affordable alternative, we moved into a two-bed efficiency unit in a rundown motel on the edge of town. I paid for a month's stay, after which Brian, like Ben, would be on his own. We carried his garbage bags of clothes, boxes of keepsakes, and bikes up the rusty iron stairs, past cloudy plate-glass windows, and into a stale, dark-panelled room. Then we hit the sack.

In the morning, I saw that there were women's panties in the wastebasket by the toilet. Black, lacy, see-through panties.

I bolted out of the washroom and informed Brian. "And they're not mine," I said. "I wouldn't want you to think —"

"*Awk-ward!*" he replied.

"Don't touch them."

"I won't."

"And call the manager and ask for housekeeping to clean this place, will you?" I zipped up my duffel bag, fighting to suppress the lump growing in my throat.

"Mom, don't worry," he said. He unpacked a coffee mug, his Walkman, and a stack of CDs, and organized the space to make it homey. I was struck by the irony: I had gone there to support him, but I was the one who needed it.

"You gotta go," he eventually said.

"I know. Yes, I do realize that," I said, picking up my purse and bag.

He gave me a bear hug, then waved from the second-floor walkway as I got in the car and pulled out of the parking lot.

I drove to the ferry terminal under threatening skies.

Back on the mainland, I made my way to downtown Vancouver and met up with Ben at the corner of Robson and Granville Streets. We went to a Chinese restaurant for dinner. Between his trips to the buffet table, he told me he had landed a courier job — with potential benefits, no less. He had tried surfing in Tofino a couple of times. That was quite the rush. And he was living in a garage for $160 a month. He couldn't believe his luck. Great. Just great, I said.

After dinner, I dropped him off in front of his roll-up door and drove off in tears through blackness and torrential rain to find a hotel.

Early the next morning, I flew back to Ontario with an ocean voyage to prepare for.

On a late November afternoon, I changed from work clothes to jeans, put on an extra layer to shield myself from the bitter north wind, and headed out with Leiah for our daily walk. She knew the route, down the Edinburgh Road hill and onto the tree-lined path along the Speed River.

My mind was spinning with terms like *wave propagation, ionosphere*, and *transducers*. To use our ham radio, we needed an amateur radio licence. The self-study course consisted of physics and math and the essential components of a radio system. I protested to David that we make toast without having to know how the toaster works. David advised me not to waste my energy. Had I met a "ham," I would realize the course curriculum was non-negotiable.

"But conspicuous by its absence is any instruction on how to operate the radio," I said.

"Well, that's for us to figure out," he said, as though that was at all logical.

I spotted Ken partway down the hill. His son, Marcus, had gone through school with our kids. If parental bragging were an Olympic event, Ken would be on the podium. Over the years, I had put up with his stories about Marcus. Marcus the genius. Marcus the artist. Marcus the athlete. Marcus the perfect son, the perfect person, with the perfect life. But with Ben now living in a garage, Brian in a sleazy motel, and John having just announced he had abandoned aspirations for an orchestral career to "do his own thing" — and with us not only leaving our sons be, but actually *leaving* them — today was not one of those days. I yanked Leiah's leash with such ferocity her eyes bulged. Before Ken had a chance to see me, we were headed east on Waterloo at a serious clip.

North on Dublin, we passed by Saint Stanislaus, the eight-room elementary school tucked in the corner of the Church of Our Lady parking lot, dwarfed by the cathedral spires, where the boys had gone so long ago. I could recall the smell of Elmer's glue and Lysol and hear Miss Butler threaten to banish her seven-year-old pupils, or "flowers" as she liked to think of them, from God's garden for things like forgetting to put their runners on their desks at the end of the day, printing outside the lines, and having an independent thought, notably none of which Marcus ever did. The day she made good on her threat to Lewis, one of the boys in John's class, and removed his construction-paper daisy from the three-by-six-foot construction-paper garden, John came home utterly traumatized, devastated for poor Lewis and fearing his own spiritual ruin. The next day, when I saw the daisy lying alone on the blackboard ledge and questioned the practice, Miss Butler explained she was preparing the children for the real world.

I said, "You've got to be kidding! It's not the world I know, nor the world I want my kids to know." Then I flew into the principal's office, demanding Lewis be put back in the damned garden, now.

Leiah and I cut through Sunny Acres Park. A dozen or so guys were playing ball hockey in the rink area, where their tennis balls and boots would be exchanged for pucks and skates the minute there was ice. Ben had balked at skating lessons so much we let him stop partway through. But on this neighbourhood rink, given the freedom to figure it out for himself, he became an overnight pro. Many a winter evening he'd come home rosy-cheeked with smelly wet socks and frozen toes after a game of shinny.

I paused to listen to the familiar sounds of sticks clacking. This was a new generation out there now, not a single familiar face among them.

Leiah and I went in through our gate, up the porch stairs Brian used to fly down on his bike, and into our kitchen through the back door. The house was quiet, cold, museum-like. Leiah curled up on the corner of the couch. I sat at the kitchen table, sipping Earl Grey tea.

Our sons weren't Marcus. They weren't each other. And they weren't us. They were unique individuals, taking risks, choosing paths less travelled, learning to skate their own way. It took courage. I should have told Ken so.

David called from work to say he had an email to send, after which he'd be on his way.

"Let's sell," I said.

"But we'll need a place to come back to."

"And we'll find one," I said. "What's the ionosphere again?"

"The layer of atmosphere that radio waves bounce off," he said. "You sure?"

"Yes, I'm sure. Right, of course, the bouncing waves."

New Year's Eve 2006, our neighbours Colleen and Roger came over to celebrate. After a dinner of David's killer beef curry, we got comfy in the living room. David put a B.B. King CD on and refilled the wine glasses. Then he brought out our globe of the earth.

He placed it in the centre of the coffee table and everyone leaned in. David slowly rotated it while tracing our route with his finger. "We'll cross to the Azores, then to Portugal; from there, head down to the Madeira Islands —"

"That reminds me of my uncle Jouni. 'Have some Madeira, m'dear. It's much more delightful than beer,'" I interjected.

"Then the Canaries," David continued, "where we'll catch the trade winds and fly back across."

"Wow!" Colleen said. "That's a whole lotta ocean." She sat back, staring at the expansive patches on the globe.

Just then the kitchen phone rang. When David left the room to answer it, she and Roger studied me as though I had suddenly sprouted a second head.

"Aren't you at all scared?" Colleen finally asked.

"There's nothing to fear but fear itself," I said, giggling. "No, seriously. We worry *waaaaay* too much. Remember when we did fireworks for the big Y2K? Spent the whole damn evening fretting we'd burn down Guelph?"

"That's 'cause all the neighbours' roofs had Roman candles smouldering on them," Roger said.

"Sue, you're talking about crossing a bloody ocean," Colleen said.

"Stop right there. Really. I mean, seriously, you have more chance of being run over by a bus when you're crossing the street than drowning in an ocean."

"Oh, for Christ sakes! Says who?" said Roger.

"You know what the biggest risk is?" I said. "You'll never guess."

Colleen began to answer.

"Boredom!" I blurted before she had a chance. "Honest to God. Not storms, not sharks — it's boredom!" I repeated louder, with more conviction. "Our friend Cameron said his dad told him a friend of a friend —"

"Good grief, Sue," Colleen said, looking over at Roger.

"Surprising, I know. Ironically, having a knitting project will be more important than a life raft!"

David returned carrying four tiny flutes of Grand Marnier. "It was the real estate agent. They signed the offer. Didn't even counter."

"Yippee! We just sold the house!" I said. "And I didn't even have to clean the closets!"

David explained to Colleen and Roger that we had planned to list it mid-January. But the agent had asked to bring a couple through that afternoon, and they had liked it.

"Cheers to homelessness!" I said.

We all raised our glasses and Roger started to laugh. "You're becoming unhinged before our very eyes."

"I can see why it might appear that way," I said. "But to tell you the truth, Roger, the exact opposite is true."

The clock struck midnight. We hugged and kissed and wished happy new year all around, then flopped back down and drained the glasses.

Colleen and I continued to talk into the wee hours of the morning, while the men's heads began to bob.

"Maybe Rog and I will meet you on the other side."

"That'd be great!"

"We'll collect your mail."

"Thanks."

"And check in with your mom from time to time."

"She'd love that."

"And about your boys —"

"It'll be a fantastic year for them, too. Colleen, seriously, it feels like destiny."

"Destiny. Fuckin' looney tunes!" Roger said, giggling to himself before his final nod.

TEN

DAVID'S LAST DAY of work was April 5. My leave of absence was to start April 14. We had to be out of the house by April 30.

In the cold winter evenings and on weekends, we cancelled phones, cable TV, hydro, newspaper and magazine subscriptions, and house and car insurance; suspended our professional memberships and provincial health insurance; arranged a box at the post office so we could have our mail redirected; and rented a storage unit, into which we began to deliver carloads from our home.

I started taking detours to drive by a little yellow cottage I had gone through during a real estate open house the year before. It had long since been taken off the market, but the way it looked made me suspect it hadn't sold.

"There's a rug draped over the fence," I kept saying to David.

"So what?" he'd respond.

"So, new owners don't leave rugs on fences," I'd explain. Finally, he looked into it. My hunch had been right.

Late February 2007, we privately bought the thousand-square-foot fixer-upper built in 1866. The closing date was May 1, 2008. One more uncanny sign it was all meant to be.

In March, it was discovered David had a hernia. Instead of going to work on his last scheduled day, he went for a hernia repair. There probably wasn't a good time to have this procedure, but with boxes, bags, and crates overflowing onto our front porch and mere weeks to clear out of the house, this was about the worst.

In the days immediately following David's surgery we focused on non-physical tasks — finding a home for Leiah the most pressing among them. Recognizing we were in a pinch, my no-nonsense cousin Jaana agreed to board Leiah for the year. We drove five hours to deliver her to the family farm. As David carried in her toys and I her thirty-pound bag of food, Leiah sniffed out her new digs and Jaana laid down the ground rules. Leiah would be treated no differently than their two dogs. Of course, I said. And she'd sleep on the floor on a *dog* bed where *dogs*, even poodle *dogs*, belong. Okey-dokey. And she'd eat what the other dogs ate, forget that organic designer shit.

"Really? But the breeder specifically said —"

"Yes, really," Jaana said.

Back in the car, I began to cry. I hated leaving Leiah behind, but bringing her with us was out of the question. David reminded me she would have friends for the first time in her life and more room to roam than ever before. I glanced in the rear-view mirror. She and her new canine pals were deking each other out in the open field. He was right; potential weight gain notwithstanding, this year would likely be good for her, too. Perhaps she wouldn't miss us at all. I cried some more.

Less than a week after the surgery, David was lifting boxes with abandon. He said he had healed. I was grateful for the medical miracle.

April 30, in a state of numbness, we left the home in which we had raised our family, took a last load to storage, booked into a hotel in town, and crashed for the night.

The next morning, we drove to the Whitby marina — no house, no jobs, and most of what we needed for the year in the trunk of the car. I felt light. Unencumbered. Free.

ELEVEN

MAY 1 WAS GREY, drizzly, cold. *Inia* was still on the hard. The launch was scheduled for May 7, our departure for the 21st.

David put on his worn winter coat, a toque, and goggles and began sanding the boat's bottom while I made trips up the ladder with the duffel bags of clothes; plastic bins of equipment manuals, spare parts, and first-aid supplies; and shopping bags of books, CDs, and knitting materials until the car was empty and below decks chock full.

A place for everything; everything in its place. Whoever said that must have lived on a boat, I thought as I began to organize our miniature floating home.

Friday, May 4, our friend Cameron arrived. We'd met him and his wife, Leslie, through John. Both were professional musicians and, it turned out, serious boaters, too. Not only were they excited about our voyage, but they were eager to crew for a leg of it. Cameron came to help get *Inia* ready for Monday's launch.

A high-pressure system moved in, bringing daytime temperatures in the low teens, fine for painting. I put on a disposable full-body suit made of white paper, zipped up the front, and tightened the hood around my face. Looking prepared for chemical warfare, I painstakingly taped the boot stripe while

Cameron and David took off in our car on what they referred to as fact-finding assignments.

As they came and went, I painted. When I eventually questioned the division of labour, Cameron pointed out that my contribution was physical, theirs cerebral in nature. In boat preparation, both were necessary and of equal importance, they stressed while they dropped off more little bags of hardware and I continued to paint. By the time their "assignments" were completed, I had finished the boot stripe and applied a layer of antifouling paint over the entire keel, my arms were about to fall off, my eyelids glued open with toxic red splatters.

After cleaning up, we went to a pub for dinner, throughout which their nonsensical banter continued. I feigned irritation but was delighted to be part of the team.

Saturday and Sunday David and Cameron worked topside, resealing chain plates for the main backstay, epoxying the radar mount, and fixing the mizzen-mast–step base, while I applied second coats of paint everywhere.

"The boot stripe looks great. Red was definitely the right choice. It's striking against the cream hull," Cameron said as he was leaving. I thought so, too.

Launch day, David and I waxed and polished the sides, brought fenders onboard, and tested the engine. While tying on the last of the dock lines, we heard a low rumble. It was the travel lift heading our way.

Before *Inia* was picked up and carried off, I stood back and did a final once-over. Sparkling from stem to stern, she looked the best she ever had, pleased with her spiffy new self, ready to face the challenges ahead, like a young woman at her graduation. And I beamed with a parental sort of pride.

The following weekend, Cameron returned, this time with Leslie, to firm up our plans. Sunday morning, with *Inia* now in the water tied to a marina dock, we sat outside around the cockpit table, eating warmed croissants, drinking coffee, and poring over literature on the Azores.

"We're all booked. We'll fly to São Miguel. Then July twelfth we'll hop on a smaller plane for Faial," Leslie said, pointing to the two islands on a map of the Portuguese archipelago. Faial was where we'd depart to do the passage to Portugal together.

"July twelfth's perfect," David said. "That gives us oodles of buffer." According to his conservative calculations, if we averaged 100 nautical miles a day, we'd likely arrive weeks ahead of them.

"We'll be happy to just kick back, maybe do a little sightseeing while we wait," David said.

"We'll scope out a good restaurant for when you get there," I said.

David added, "Hard to believe that's in just two months!"

"Wow!" we said, in three different keys.

After Cameron and Leslie left, I occupied myself rooting through the fridge to figure out supper. Thoughts of the boys seeped in. Last I knew, Brian had been looking for a new job. I hoped he remembered that a bird in the hand was worth two in the bush. John had been worried he had missed a deadline for a music competition and would let his teacher down. I had resisted the temptation to reinforce the importance of good organizational skills and of writing things down on a big calendar. We hadn't heard from Ben in months. What was with that? And it was Mother's Day. This Mother's Day in particular, I needed to hear from them.

I had thought our sons would benefit by our taking off. But what if *they* didn't see it that way? What if letting go was one thing, leaving another? What if they felt abandoned? I found myself on shaky emotional ground as the afternoon wore on.

Just as we sat down to eat, the phone rang. It was Brian. He wished me happy Mother's Day and was excited to report that his job search had been successful. He'd gotten a job at a small manufacturing plant that made fibreglass dinghies. He got to thinking that, since boats and boat-building were in the family, perhaps this line of work was a natural fit. And this was a good place to start.

"Could be. I think you'd be great at it," I said, pleased with his news.

As soon as I hung up, John called with best wishes and also to let me know he hadn't missed the competition deadline after all. It was a typo. I thanked him, expressed relief about the typo, and asked how things were going otherwise.

"I'm a little listless," he replied, explaining that the school year had just ended, his roommates had gone to their homes for Mother's Day, and he was on his own.

"Oh God!" I said, painfully aware he had no home to go to. "They must think —"

"I said I'm listless, not dying. It's weirdly quiet with everyone gone, but things should be back to normal around here tomorrow." He added, "And just so you know, my friends think that what you and Dad are doing is awesome. Mike said you're their heroes."

The two of us, in our fifties, greying, a little lined, *heroes* to twenty-year-old guys. After the initial shock, I was thrilled about the remark. The notion that our trip might be a source of inspiration to our sons and their friends as they moved into their adult lives with goals and dreams of their own was almost motivation enough for me to cast off. Almost.

"Why don't you get a pizza and rent a movie or something?" I said.

"A call's coming in from Nick. Gotta go."

Well into the night, David and I were awakened by a different ring tone. It was a voicemail message from Ben. With traffic sounds in the background, his voice cutting in and out, he said, "I'm in Montreal … got no time on the phone so … anyways … happy Mother's Day … I guess that's it … bye."

I lay in the berth, looking at the stars through the overhead hatch, happy they had each called, pleased they were each taking steps, once again trusting they'd each find their place in this universe. It turned out to be a good Mother's Day, under the circumstances.

On May 15 our equipment upgrades were completed. Over a seven-hour session, the men who installed our electronics taught us how to collect the GRIB files and send and receive email over radio waves, how the refrigeration unit and the echo-charger worked, and how to read the control panel of gauges to monitor everything. And they recommended that, rather than leaving from New York, we go down the St. Lawrence River for a shakedown cruise to test out these new systems before heading offshore. We suspected they were more worried about us than our systems, but we agreed it was a good idea, on both fronts. We altered our route, with plans to hit New York City on the way back.

By then, David and I were anxious to leave Whitby. Marinas are like little towns. The work being done on *Inia* was attracting more attention than we liked. Neighbours were eager to help. And unsolicited advice was flowing freely. "Why get refrigeration? Just stock up on rye crackers and Cheez Whiz." "Don't leave before you get every last job done. You won't be able to do work underway, and you'll regret it." Then, "Don't wait until you have every last job done or, mark my words, you'll never leave."

I started to hide below when I saw legs through the portholes and to do mad dashes down the dock when the coast was clear.

May 17, while David was on deck waiting for Fred to show up to recheck our new stuffing box, a round couple with matching windbreakers sauntered up to him and suggested we might want to consider flying to Portugal. "It's much cheaper," they said.

That was it! The minute the inspection was complete, David and I bundled up for the cold and cast off.

From Whitby we backtracked to the Hamilton Harbour to say goodbye to my mom and to do our official departure from our home port. We arrived in Hamilton on the Victoria Day long weekend.

My mom invited us to stay over in her condo. David didn't want to leave *Inia*. I insisted we go. "For heaven's sake, a night won't hurt, and it'll mean a lot to her," I said. "You've gotta understand, my leaving's huge."

He pointed out that my mom was in regular contact with my brothers and she had a giant network of friends with whom she played bridge, hiked, golfed, gambled, and partied. "She'll be fine," he said, locking up the companionway. "And I don't get how sleeping over makes a difference," he added as we walked down the dock.

"One lousy night. That's all," I said. "It's important to me, too. If not for her, then do it for me." I looked back at *Inia*, the life raft mounted on the bow, the wind generator spinning on the mizzen, solar panels sparkling above the dodger. "She's ready for the ocean," I said. "I'm sure she can survive a night alone at the dock."

My mom was leaning against her car at the far end of the parking lot, waving to us.

"Too bad we can't see the boot stripe anymore," I said, both of us waving back to her. "Stupid that I didn't anticipate the added weight. All that fussing about colour, all that work, for nothing."

David glanced over his shoulder while I nattered on.

"Sounds silly, but I'm disappointed," I said. "The red added a certain *je ne sais quoi*!"

We gave my mom a hug, hopped in her car, and headed to her condo for the night.

David and I sat at her kitchen table. While she made meatballs and sour cream gravy at the stove and I peeled potatoes, we talked about the year ahead. I explained how "sailmail" worked and said we'd provide regular updates. I also said she could trace our progress using Google Earth. She expressed amazement at the new technology. She said my brother, Brian, had offered to keep our car in his lot for the year, and she'd drive it there.

"We appreciate the help," I said. I gave her the contact information of ham volunteers at the radio museum in Guelph who planned to try to connect with us mid-ocean, and told her she was welcome to join them for the scheduled calls. She said she might just do that.

Throughout the evening, David checked his phone, looked at his watch, and stared off into space.

"You were rude," I said, slamming around the kitchen after my mom had gone to bed. "Here she went to all this effort. Couldn't you have at least tried —"

"I need to go back to the boat."

"Don't be ridiculous. We're leaving in the morning!"

"Sue, I need to."

Hearing urgency in his voice, I grabbed the keys from the kitchen hook and we snuck out.

In the glow of the marina lamps, David leapt aboard *Inia*, went below, and flipped on the bilge-pump switch. And to my shock and horror, water gushed out at the stern. A locking nut had come loose on the just-inspected stuffing box. *Inia*, the vessel that we had just invested tens of thousands of dollars in and our home for the year ahead, was sinking at the dock!

When David tightened the nut, the inflow immediately stopped. As the heavy stream continued to pour out of her, the boot stripe rose back up into view. He confessed its disappearance had bothered him, too, but differently.

Luck was on our side. Had we waited, had we slept first *as I had wanted* . . . God, I still shudder at the thought!

Driving back to my mom's, David said that maybe someday we'd tell the story, but given the imminence and magnitude of our plans, now was not the time. I agreed, adding that maybe someday we'd even laugh about it, although I highly doubted it.

We tiptoed into the condo and slipped into the warm, clean bed.

Departure morning.

After hot showers, my mom drove us back to the marina. We had breakfast at a waterfront coffee shop, after which we joined a small gathering of friends at *Inia* to make a toast with champagne.

On May 21 at 1043, under a clear blue sky, in a light south-southeast wind and a lovely 15 degrees Celsius, David and I cast off the dock lines in Hamilton Harbour, pointed *Inia* east, and embarked on the most enormous adventure of our lives.

TWELVE

OUR FIRST STOP was Toronto. We tied up to a wall at Queens Quay in the heart of the city, walking distance from the Nautical Mind bookstore and marine suppliers. Because of our route change, we needed charts for the St. Lawrence River.

David also wanted to fix the toilet while we were here. The toilet, or head, on a boat usually has two hoses. One leads to a holding tank under the floorboards. By law, to protect the environment, when boats are cruising on lakes or near shore, waste must be discharged into this tank, which gets pumped out by machines at marinas. The second hose goes through the hull, taking waste directly out to sea. A lever opens one valve and closes the other. The sea hose was cracked.

While David left in search of a replacement hose, I went by cab to the waterfront Sobeys, where I spent a half day strolling the aisles, stocking up on the basics: eggs, non-refrigeration milk, butter, coffee, flour, sugar, rice, pasta, cereal, Thai sauces, packaged marinades, Indian spices, vacuum-packed chicken, salmon, beef, fresh fruits, salad ingredients, an assortment of cold meats and cheeses, bagels, whole-wheat bread, chocolate bars, and cookies. Eating cold beans would be required in an emergency situation only.

David returned empty-handed and frustrated. Our sea hose, a non-standard size, was available only in — where else? — Whitby! We'd have to stop there again on our way through.

Late afternoon we went to Nautical Mind. While the wiry clerk, in his Mountain Equipment Co-op outfit, gathered up the thirty-four additional charts and navigational publications for the St. Lawrence, I told him about our plans.

"Wow!" he said. "When're you thinking of going?"

"Tomorrow," I said.

"Tomorrow!" His brow furrowed. "Spontaneous or what!" he said, rolling the giant stack of papers into a massive bundle.

"Oh, not at all. We made the decision a week ago," I said.

His face twitched.

"Wait. Hold on!" David said. "She meant to change our route. The decision to change our route." He looked my way. "He thinks we decided —"

"Oh God, that's hilarious," I said. "Yup! We're crossin' the Atlantic tomorrow. Spent a week plannin'," I joked.

David clarified that we'd spent essentially a year getting ready.

A year was still on the quick end of the spectrum, but better, the clerk responded. He tallied the charts up on his cash register. "So that'll be nine hundred and seventy-five dollars, for the St. Lawrence, all told," he said. "What else can I get for you?"

"Holy … nine hundred and seventy-five dollars, eh! Uh, that's all, I guess," David said. "No, nothing else. We've essentially got our route covered. So I guess that'll be it."

We paid up and walked out.

"Except the Bay of Quinte," David said, standing outside the store. "We have every chart except the Prinyers Cove area of the Bay of Quinte."

"Dear, you *do* know that area," I said, making eye contact with the clerk through the window.

"True. We *have* sailed there a fair bit," he acknowledged. He readjusted his grip on the heavy roll. "Yeah ... we should be okay."

I waved goodbye to the clerk.

"Spent the whole damn week plannin'," I repeated, as we chuckled our way back to the marina.

Since we were to sail around the clock to the Bay of Quinte the next day, we made it an early night. Around 2300, when nature called, I shuffled to the head. Half-asleep and trying to stay that way, I depressed the foot pedal and pumped the three-foot handle to flush, creating a geyser of ice water.

Hearing me shriek, David jumped out of the berth in his underwear. "Sorry!" he said. "I can't believe I forgot to switch the valves." He pushed the lever over, handed me a towel, then wiped down the walls and mirror with another.

"Could've been worse," I said like a sport while changing into dry flannelettes.

May 26, we left Toronto and, after a brief stop in Whitby to pick up the sea hose, we headed for Prince Edward County, with plans to meet up with Cameron and his father, Bob, in Prinyers Cove. This was my second night sail ever, and the first time I was more than just a body onboard. Anticipating being alone in the darkness while David slept, I wondered how I'd do. Would I be afraid? Would I be cold? And how would I fare from a fatigue point of view? I was simply useless without proper rest.

We agreed to a schedule for night watches: three hours on, three hours off. And we set two cardinal rules: one, wear a harness at all times, and two, never leave the cockpit unless the other was on deck.

After sunset the air was cool and crisp. From our "telltale" wind indicator — a strand of wool tied to a shroud — the little wind there was, was pointing right at us. So we motored. Before my watch, David turned on the autohelm to keep *Inia* on course.

I surfaced wearing my new red insulated overalls and matching foul-weather jacket, the hood snug over a baseball cap. I was armed with a novel, a book of crossword puzzles, a Walkman, CDs, a flashlight, an insulated travel mug of tea, a baggy of cookies, and a banana.

"We're talking three hours," David said with a grin.

"Your point being?"

He laughed and went below.

The night sky was clear, the water still. Between the hourly plotting of our position on the chart, I did five puzzles, read a chapter, drank all the tea, ate all the food, and listened to a Rick Fines CD twice. Before I knew it, David was up and ready to take over.

His watch flew by, too.

Buoyed by this experience, I was confident the two of us could manage twenty-four-hour sailing on the ocean. It would be the same, just more of it.

Approaching Prince Edward Bay, we made a spur-of-the-moment decision to spend the night at an anchorage off Waupoos Island that Cameron had raved about. After setting anchor, we sat out the rest of the afternoon, soaking in the island's bucolic setting. Sheep roamed freely; willows swayed in the gentle breeze; ducks bobbed lazily along the shoreline. It was every bit as lovely as Cameron had described it.

In the morning, after a relaxed breakfast of coffee and bagels with ginger marmalade, we got underway.

Prinyers Cove was around a point of land, a half-day sail, tops. The only hazard to worry about was a notorious shoal called Green Island.

"There it is!" I said, pointing to a rock barely below the surface.

"Good eye," David said. He gave it an extra-wide berth and we sailed on. The air was fresh, winds moderate, sky a royal blue. It was an exhilarating ride.

"Looks like the dinghy's lost some air," I commented, glancing at the puckered Zodiac bouncing in our wake.

"Sonofabitch!" David shrieked, springing to his feet. "Rock to port!" he yelled, while making a sharp right turn.

Thud!

Rock was to starboard, too.

A wave rolled in from behind, causing *Inia* to lift, shift, and thud again. Then another wave. Then yet another. When she came to a final stop, jagged rock was below the surface to the left, right, front and back of her. *Inia* was hard aground, a mile from shore, smack dab in the centre of Green Island.

We put out more sail, hoping to tilt enough to float off. The hull got another severe beating. Then David tried to back us off the way we had come. Hearing more crunching and grinding, he quickly abandoned that idea. Try as we might, we couldn't free ourselves.

"I have to call a pan-pan," he said.

"Isn't that the 'Hey, everyone, I'm an idiot!' call?"

"That's the one."

"Alternatively, we could just wait," I suggested. "Another boat's bound to show up. Or a rogue wave might eventually blast us off."

"Sue, if the rudder gets damaged, we're in far worse trouble." He swallowed hard, went below, and radioed the Canadian Coast Guard.

Within minutes, a fishing boat stopped about two hundred feet away. It was a homemade steel affair with rods sticking out every which way like a giant pincushion. There were three people onboard, two men and one woman, all built like refrigerators, wearing rubber overalls and standing side by side along the stern rail.

Looking at us through binoculars, the captain made radio contact. "Yo, *Eye-nigh-ay*, is it? It's the *Molly Mae* here. Over."

"Hi, *Molly Mae*. It's *Inia, in-ya*," David replied. "It's an Amazon dolphin. Over."

"I'll be damned. A dolphin named *Inny*. Well, *Inny*, looks like you've been summarily introduced to our Green Island. Over."

"Unfortunately, yes. And we'd really appreciate a tow off. Over."

"Be more than happy to, *Inny*. Just bring me a line, and we'll have you off lickety-split. Over."

"*Me* bring it to *you*? Over."

"Roger that. Over."

"Can you come any closer?"

"No can do, *Inny*. Gotta take care o' my ship and my men. We're talkin' friggin' Green Island here. Over."

David retrieved spare anchor rode from the locker. Since rode is rope (or chain) meant to weigh down an anchor, it is characteristically heavy and non-floating. So it was far from ideal for towing, but it was the only rope we had that was long enough. After tossing it into the inflatable Zodiac, he lowered himself down. Noticing the dinghy had lost more air, he stomped on the foot pump to refill it.

The crew of the *Molly Mae* and I watched from our respective vessels as David motored over. After handing them the bitter end, he headed back to *Inia*, meting the rode out along the way.

As it grew wetter it became heavier. The dinghy moved slower and began to deflate at an observable rate. Then its 3.5 horsepower outboard stopped and the shrivelling dinghy started to drift backwards and sink, at which point David began to row like hell.

The crew members of the *Molly Mae* were now riveted. We were clearly not the first vessel they had pulled off this shoal over the years, but we were likely the most entertaining.

Was it sheer will or divine intervention? Who knows? But David made it back and, chest heaving, heart-attackish, he clambered aboard, attached the other end of the rode at our bow, then signalled we were good to go. And in a matter of minutes, *Inia* was turned around, pulled over a few more lumps and bumps, and set free.

Just as the fishing boat motored off, a red and white Zodiac zoomed up with two uniformed men onboard. It was the Coast Guard. David immediately informed them we had already been helped, there was no damage, we were fine now and anxious to be on our way, you know, to make up for lost time and all. And he thanked them profusely for coming.

But perceiving yet more pleasure from our pain, from the Coast Guard no less, I saw red.

"This wouldn't have happened if the government wasn't so cheap," I said, choosing to ignore David's semaphore-like gestures beyond their line of sight. "There's only one spar buoy to indicate this hazard to the east. But from our approach, nothing, nada."

When I was done, the more senior official turned to David. "Captain, just need to ask if you have the current marine chart for these waters onboard," he said.

With that, even I knew the buck stopped with David. Damn. If only I had picked up on his cues. He so regretted not buying that chart from the outset. And the punishment was already severe. He didn't need a public flogging.

"No" was David's shame-filled response.

When the officials circled and headed back to Kingston, we continued on to Prinyers Cove. As we entered the bay and headed toward the marina, a light flashed on an exterior panel, indicating the engine was overheating. It was a troubling discovery, but right then our concern was bringing *Inia* to a safe landing. She was a challenge to dock. It required our undivided attention.

The marina was busy. Vessels of all types were coming and going, and the docks were packed with boaters engaged in storytelling competitions. Standing to one side, waiting for us, were Cameron and Bob — engineer and mariner extraordinaire Bob.

Just as David was about to head *Inia* into the wind, a couple of Jet Skis buzzed across our bow, causing him to lose his precious turning opportunity, and his focus and footing. Soon all ten tons of *Inia* were barrelling toward the dock.

I hugged the mast stay and heard "Slow down, jackass!" from the wide-eyed men; then we hit.

"Hurry. Toss me a line," Bob yelled as we ricocheted off.

David and I each pelted him. Cameron snatched the spring line and together they scurried to tie us down. Fortunately, no one was hurt, the pier remained intact, and we already knew how to repair gouges in our fibreglass hull.

When the commotion subsided, Cameron and Bob boarded *Inia* and I excused myself and went below "to tidy up." The reality was, I just couldn't handle what was to come. But I could still hear them, or more accurately, Bob, who positioned himself right next to the companionway. As soon as they sat down, he began, "What the hell took you guys so long? Cam and I joked that you must've hit Green Island. Really? Say it ain't so. Jesus, everyone and his sister knows about Green Island! Seems your engine's overheating, eh? Forcing it when aground'll do it, but I'm sure you knew that. What on earth happened to your dinghy? Christ, it looks like you're towing a giant pancake."

After every last detail of our sorry day had been exposed and analyzed to death by Bob, Cameron asked if there was anything we needed in town. David said we could use a few extra jerry cans and more milk and bread. Bob wondered aloud why we hadn't just said so. And off they went.

When they had disappeared, David went onto the dock to have another look at the hull and to adjust all the lines and I reorganized the fridge, none of which needed doing.

A couple of hours later they returned with spare fuel cans and water cans, a stowage board they had fabricated for them, a bag of groceries, and a couple of bottles of wine. Then, following an awkward silence, Cameron said, "So … you still heading off tomorrow?"

His question was simple, but loaded. He suddenly wondered if we were ready. His concern for our safety was palpable.

"Well, there are a few new wrinkles to iron out. But yeah, that's the plan," David replied.

"Well then, we'll see you in about six weeks, I guess!" Cameron said.

They both shook our hands, more firmly than normal, then mercifully left us alone to lick our wounds in private.

But before we could indulge in self-pity, we had a diesel engine to repair — more precisely, an impeller to replace. Unlike in the diesel course, where the engines were on pedestals in the centre of the room, our engine was housed deep in a small compartment in the stern, under the cockpit and behind the companionway stairs.

Discovering that the schematics in the engine manual were like ancient hieroglyphics, our first challenge was finding the impeller. David removed the stairs panel, praying it was on the accessible bow-facing aspect. No such luck. The only other way to the engine was a one-by-two-foot cut-out through the side wall of the quarter berth. He shimmied into the coffin-like space and, with a telescoping mirror, eventually located it at the very back, directly above the bilge.

The bilge is a deep cavity that runs along the centre of a boat. It's where water drains, and where dropped objects are lost forever. David's daunting mission involved unscrewing four tiny flathead screws, removing a cover plate, removing the damaged part, inserting a new one, and finally reattaching the plate and the screws, all while lying twisted on his side with no ability to see the task at hand.

I sat on the settee handing him screws and listening to him mutter, "Don't drop it…. Don't drop it…. Do-o-o-on't drop it…. Shit. Don't dro— shit. C'mo-o-n, don't … shit. Shit. Shit!" Finally, three excruciating hours later with the last of our spare screws, the new impeller was in place.

In an effort to salvage the evening, I made a steak dinner, but neither of us ate a thing. However, we did drink. And we took stock. Up to that point, *Inia* had been in the water for a little more than a week and had travelled only about 150 nautical miles from home, during which she had almost sunk, the head had exploded, the Zodiac had sprung a leak, we had run aground, and both the outboard and diesel motors had broken down. Yet we were heading for the Atlantic Ocean where there would be no stores, no help, and no turning back. I wondered if Cameron was right to be worried. Were we crazy? Right off our rockers? I hit the sack, seriously, seriously shaken.

However, in the fresh new morning light, the week didn't look so bad. As David pointed out, yes, we had had a few mishaps, but they either had been resolved or were resolvable. He was right; obviously we could and would manage. There was simply no logical reason to stop.

I waved a hardy goodbye as we motored past Cameron and Bob, who stood at the end of their dock and watched us head off for the mighty St. Lawrence. And I marvelled at the power of a good night's sleep.

THIRTEEN

MAY 29, OUR INAUGURAL night at the mouth of the St. Lawrence River, *Inia* lay at anchor in a misty cove off Wallace Island, in sight of the Thousand Islands Bridge. We sat out in the cockpit, breathing in the pungency of spring, a jumble of ropes at our feet, anticipation coursing through our veins. The St. Lawrence would take us to Sydney, Nova Scotia, from where we would head offshore.

David had set his sights on leaving Nova Scotia on June 21 at the very latest. His reasons were practical. From a sailing perspective, May is too cold on the ocean. Although June to November is officially hurricane season, the risk is low in June. And, according to the Pilot Charts, June is favourable in terms of mean oceanic winds and waves at the latitude we'd be travelling. Also, he wanted to be in the Azores before Cameron and Leslie to get a head start preparing for our departure to Portugal with them. Since their return flight to Canada was July 27 out of Lisbon, they had a finite window in which to do the passage. Leaving on the 21st, the worst-case scenario, we'd beat them by a week, which was as fine as he wanted to cut it.

It meant we had to cover roughly 700 nautical miles in a little over three weeks, or 210 a week, or 30 a day, to get to the Atlantic Ocean.

"It's all unfamiliar territory from here on," David said, whipping the end of the new floating polypropylene tow line.

"At least we've got all the charts now." I untangled the spring line from the spare anchor rode. "And really, when you think about it, how complicated can the St. Lawrence be?" I said, looking down the glasslike river.

We rewound all the lines into tight bundles and stowed them neatly in the starboard lazarette.

Inia headed out alone. In the damp, cool spring weather, we motored past small-town Upper Canada, trees budding pink and yellow along its shores.

Somewhere past Brockville, while I was at the helm, another pleasure boat appeared for the first time. It was behind us, in the distance. As they say, the definition of a race is two sailboats on the water.

"Eat my dust!" I smiled as I pushed down the throttle a tad and began to cut all the river corners.

"Christ, Sue! Pay attention!" David shrieked, climbing up the companionway.

When I looked back over my shoulder I couldn't see my sailboat opponent any more, or anything else — other than a freighter. "I swear it wasn't there a minute ago," I said, darting to the right of the channel.

As the four-hundred-foot-long wall of rusting red and green steel plowed past and *Inia* tossed about in the rolling hills of displaced water, two crew members called down from the bridge.

"Sounds Spanish," I said, waving to them. "What d'you suppose they're saying?"

"We're better off not knowing," David said, grabbing the wheel to get us back under control.

"Who knew those massive suckers could be quiet enough to —"

"Would you please, please pay attention?" David said.

From then on, *Inia* and ships the size of apartment complexes shared this buoyed, surprisingly narrow, often shallow waterway.

Before entering the Quebec portion of the St. Lawrence, I emailed Ben to tell him we'd be stopping in Montreal, to ask him if he was still there, to request a response from him of some sort. I didn't hear back.

June 3, after a quiet, cold thirteen hours on the water, we put into the Longueuil marina. The next day we took the metro into the heart of Montreal. Walking around the gentrified Old Port district, David and I checked and rechecked our phones. But there was no message. I found myself expecting Ben to bike up to us on the waterfront boardwalk, run down the basilica stairs waving in our direction, or step into our subway car. Of course, he didn't.

The following morning, with heavy hearts, we left for Trois-Rivières as soon as we had refuelled.

Midafternoon, the Canadian Coast Guard broadcast that remnants of Tropical Storm Barry were headed our way. As the extreme-weather advisory was issued over our VHF radio, angry clouds gathered over our heads. Our choices were to anchor in nearby marshland or to carry on for another 24 nautical miles. Hearing rumbling from every direction, David veered off the main channel. I knelt at the bow pulpit, hollering directions as we wove our way through clumps of bulrushes and wispy weeds until the horizon flashed white and a freak gust nudged us into a ridge of soft brown muck. No sooner did we run aground than the sky went black, a violent crack of lightning shot across the water's surface, and a torrential downpour began.

I took the helm. David lowered himself with our spare fisherman-style anchor into the repaired dinghy. Amid bolts of lightning and horizontal sheets of rain, he rowed out and set the anchor thirty yards to beam. Back aboard, with the anchor rode attached to our main halyard, he winched it in, causing *Inia* to heel and the keel to eventually break free. Watching the depth sounder, I steered *Inia* to a clearing where we dropped our main anchor. Then David jumped back into the dinghy and rowed out to reset the spare, after which the two of us scrambled below, sliding the companionway panels down behind us.

"Holy moly!" I said as we peeled off our dripping outer layers. "Thank goodness we're here and not, you know, out there." I hung the sopping gear out of the way on wall hooks in the head.

David marked our waypoint on the GPS and engaged the anchor alarm. "Actually, theoretically, we'd be better off in the middle of the ocean," he said, studying *Inia*'s movements on the radar screen.

"Theoretically." I shouldn't have bristled when Aunt Caroline had called him an *academic* ocean sailor. That's what he was.

I wiped the foggy porthole with my sleeve. The tempest swirled around us. Trees swayed wildly. The outer channel churned. "I hope we won't be testing out your theory any time soon," I said, as the wind roared and erratic flashes of white lit the cabin.

Bedtime, the cabin walls were clammy. So were the sheets, the pillows, the comforter. The hatch above began to drip. I watched David duct tape paper towel on the corner of it. I wondered where on earth Ben was, how Jack Bauer made out on the season finale of *24*, if moss can grow on human skin, as I dozed off in this godforsaken swamp somewhere along the St. Lawrence.

The morning of June 6 was calmer, but still gloomy, rainy, and only 6 degrees Celsius. In the flickering cabin light, David lit the stove to boil water, then busied himself studying charts and setting more waypoints. Lamp oil and kerosene hung thick in the dank air.

I needed another layer.

"Everything's wet!" I said, discovering another leak, this time in the closet. "And I'm cold."

"Here, wear my sweater," David said, undoing his coat.

"I don't want your sweater. I want my own sweater."

"We'll do more caulking in Trois-Rivières."

"My own dry sweater. To be warm and dry. And to have connected with Ben. Is that too much to ask?"

He wrapped a musty wool blanket over my shoulders and handed me a mug of coffee. "The thing is, we didn't," he said.

"And why not?"

"Believe me, I'm disappointed too. But the fact is —"

"He'd want to see us before we head offshore, wouldn't he? Why didn't he even respond?"

David leaned against the counter, his hands wrapped around his coffee mug for warmth. "Look, Sue, who knows what's up with Ben? Your guess is as good as mine. He called on Mother's Day. He's likely fine. In any case, you were the one who said the boys are adults now and they need to be free to make their own choices, even bad ones."

"Yes, but —"

"But what? Do you believe it or not?"

"I do. I really do. But …" I started to tear up. "But … yet … it's hard. Just so damned hard."

He sat down and put his arm around me. "It *is* hard. But it's also the right thing to do. We raised three decent, capable human beings. We need to trust in that." He paused, then added, "Fortunately we'll soon have a perilous ocean adventure to focus on instead."

I snorted when I laughed.

The rain stopped. We opened the cabin up and went out under a dappled sky.

The short trip to Trois-Rivières was choppy. David helmed and I sat, curled under the dodger, still wrapped in the blanket.

"Did I ever tell you I wanted to live in a tree house?" he said. "My mom was beside herself when I told her."

"But there isn't a boy who doesn't dream of doing that."

"I was seventeen at the time."

"Good God! What other precious nuggets have you kept from me?"

"It was California in the early seventies. The environmental stuff was big there, even back then. I took the whole anti-materialism movement seriously. That freaked her out. See, when she talked about upward mobility, she wasn't thinking tree-tops." He looked out over the water with a wistful smile. "She would've been ecstatic to know I made CFO."

"What about now?"

We passed a sailboat flailing at anchor. "Looks like they had to ride out the storm there in the open," David said. "Must've been pure hell."

"I mean, what d'you think she'd think of this trip and all?"

As we approached the harbour channel, boats flew out of it like they were shooting rapids.

"That I'd choose travel over building a retirement nest egg? Don't even want to go there."

I surveyed the shoreline, the entrance wall, the shoreline again. "Dear, um, maybe it's just me but … I think we might be going backwards."

David glanced down at the knot meter, then he fixed on a spot on the entrance wall. His eyes went big, his stance wide, his grip vice-like. With the engine full throttle, *Inia* had barely enough power to override the strong ebb flow.

"All that I care about is how *you* feel," David said. We jumped ashore and lashed *Inia* down. "Personally, I've never been happier in my life."

He dug out a spiral-bound booklet from a plastic bin and set it next to the chart for the morning. Tide tables had begun to matter.

✺

The marina staff in Trois-Rivières were friendly but spoke very little English. I told David not to worry. I had taken French in high school. At the risk of bragging, my marks were in the nineties. I proceeded to ask directions to the centre of town.

"That sounded an awful lot like English," he said when I had finished.

"There are definite similarities," I said. No, I had never tried having a conversation in French with an actual person before. And no, I wasn't quite sure what the manager's response was because I had learned *Parisian* French. I'd need a bit of time to train my ear to this local dialect.

A grin spread across his face.

"Stop it!" I punched him in the shoulder. "High school wasn't exactly yesterday."

The manager brought out a map of the city. The downtown area was an hour's walk. Off we went for some much-needed airing out and exercise.

"*Pont* in French," I said as we walked by a painted steel bridge. "And church is *église*," I said, pointing to an ancient limestone structure. "See? It's all coming back."

"Look, Sue!" David said. "La children playing la Frisbee!"

"*Ferme la bouche.* That's French for shut the hell up!" I said, punching him again.

June 7, the sky cleared. With a favourable tide and the ever-present flow out to sea, we flew to Quebec City — 68 nautical miles in nine hours, record speed — and landed in a marina within view of its iconic castle-like skyline.

While walking along the cobblestone streets of Old Quebec, David suddenly stopped. He had to make a call on his cell, something about insurance.

"Not good!" he said when the call ended. "Believe it or not, our coverage ends here."

We were in front of a bistro and decided to go in. David asked the waitress about their specialty.

"Poutine," she said. "Deep-fried potatoes with gravy and melted cheese curds."

Artery clogging, I thought.

"Sounds great!" he said. As she walked away, he continued. "And they're asking for way more information for offshore coverage, like proof of *Inia*'s seaworthiness; the safety, communication, and navigational equipment we have onboard; our route; approximate itinerary …"

"No biggy."

"And our crew list: number onboard, proof of competence."

"Competence! Eeeek!" That wasn't good news at all. "Okay, okay, so, write down we did the BVI," I said.

"The BVI — shit!" Although sailing the British Virgin Islands was technically ocean sailing, it was line-of-sight navigation, in the shelter of islands, in the company of a zillion other boats, in broad daylight. "The biggest challenge is snatching a mooring ball before happy hour!" he said.

"But does Lloyd's of London know that? Oh, and, I know, tell them I crewed on the *Chief Commanda* for three years."

"Sue!"

"What? It's true."

"You were a waitress on a party boat that did day excursions on Lake Nipissing, not on an ocean."

"Just so you know, I happened to love that job."

A platter piled high with bubbling poutine was plunked down on the table between us.

"For three summers, not three years."

"Now's definitely not the time for hairsplitting." I watched him load a shimmering brown clump onto his plate. "Hope there's a defibrillator in here!" I said, pulling a gravy-drenched fry from an edge of the heap. "And I *did* help an elderly passenger once. She was sick and her partial plate fell behind the toilet in one of the stalls and I —"

"I'm not putting the *Chief Commanda* in." He jabbed the air with a dripping forkful like he was making an exclamation mark for emphasis, then began to eat.

"I'd go so far as to say it was the best job ever," I said, taking a tentative bite.

Then we inhaled the rest in silence. It was comfort-food perfection.

June 8, still moored in the Quebec City marina after photocopying, scanning, and emailing, we waited.

David walked around *Inia*'s deck with a screwdriver and wrench, tightening turnbuckles. I sat out and pretended to read. I thought about Doug, from our home port. He planned to retire aboard his sloop in the Florida Keys, investing his life savings in the vessel, his heart and soul in this dream. He had named her *TANGSUN* and delighted in explaining it stood for "there ain't nothing gonna stop us now." We had watched them sail off amid much fanfare, only to come putt-putting back into the marina a month later. Something did stop them, namely a half-century-old criminal record for stealing hubcaps, for which he was turned away at the U.S. border. He never sailed anywhere after that. I couldn't look at the boat's peeling name without wanting to cry.

I peered over the top of my book. David was now lying on his back, staring up as though checking if the mast was true, but he, too, was bracing for the sudden snuffing out of his dream. I could tell.

The silence was painful, but there was nothing to say.

I went below and emailed family and friends: The weather's finally good. Scenery's great. Freighters are big. Quebec City's old. Into tides. Entering salt water. Practising my French. Yikes! And hoping to be in the Gaspé within a week. *Instead, we might be back home, looking for a job, a place to live, a reason to get up in the morning.*

"Woo-hoo!" David yelled from above. "We're good to go!"

I bolted onto the deck and he gave me a rib-crushing hug.

"Never doubted it for a moment," I said, giddy with relief.

Then he told me the cost. The premium for offshore coverage was more than our house, car, medical, life, and Great Lakes boat insurance combined.

"I expected as much," I said, a bigger lie.

My head swam as I mentally tallied the growing list of financial surprises: the electronics, double what we had budgeted; the storm sail, bought last minute at a premium because the contracted sailmaker "forgot" about our order; the charts to St. Lawrence, another grand just like that; now this bombshell invoice. What choice did I have? None. Not that I could see by then, anyway.

"Dear, just pay Lloyd and let's get going — before he changes his mind."

"That's why I love you!" David beamed.

Up to Quebec City, the St. Lawrence had been one main channel. At this point it widened into an estuary, and we had three options: the north shore, the south shore, or down the centre.

"Let's go north. It says here it's the most scenic route," I said, referring to the cruising guide.

"But it's also the longest," David warned.

"And there's a marine park. We might even see whales."

"With far fewer places to stop."

"I've never seen a whale."

North we went.

June 9 at 1000, precisely two hours before high water, we departed Quebec City for Tadoussac. Winds were northeasterly, so pointing right at us and funnelling down the whole fetch of the river. It was slow going and, after sunset, eerie in the bone-chilling cold.

Entering harbours in the dark, especially unknown ones, is discouraged. On the only night sail we had done as a family, with the boys and I asleep below, David arrived at our destination before dawn and, dead tired, chose to bring the *Killarney II* into port. In the morning we found ourselves sandwiched between two submerged oil drums. It was a miracle that he didn't hit either, or both. He swore never to do this again. But this night on the St. Lawrence, he decided to stop — for me.

According to the chart, the next safe harbour deep enough to accommodate our six-foot draft in low tide was Cap-à-l'Aigle. Near midnight he announced we were almost there. I squinted at a blurry cluster of lights on a black band of land.

"There should be two reds and a yellow," David said, shining a flashlight on the chart to show me the symbols.

I scanned the shoreline with binoculars. "Seems there's only one red light, and no yellow," I said, feeling a mixture of gratitude and guilt.

"They have to be there. Take your time."

"Don't see them," I said, hoping we wouldn't regret this.

He headed toward what looked like the harbour entrance, the stone shore growing ever closer before the second red light appeared. But still no yellow.

"Some port of refuge," I said with growing trepidation as we crept along the dark corridor. But then, just as I was about to suggest we head back out, a twinkling marina, nestled among rock cliffs and tall pines, unfolded.

"*Bonne nuit!*" we heard from two men running up the lamp-lit docks to catch our lines.

"Thank you. *Merci!*" David and I said.

There never was a yellow.

June 10, at the break of dawn, we left for Tadoussac again, in north-easterlies *again*.

The Tadoussac entrance was dicey at the best of times because of sandbars, reefs, and crosscurrents created by the confluence of the St. Lawrence River and Saguenay Fjord. A particularly treacherous phenomenon, dubbed the *boeuf du Saguenay*, occurs with a falling ebb tide and a strong northeast wind blowing contrary to the river current. Daylight entry and precise timing is essential to avoid it.

Within hours these headwinds had built to 25 knots and *Inia* was like a bucking bronco. By 1300, with only 24 nautical miles to go, David pulled into Port-au-Persil, a small cove with minimal shelter and a gravel bottom. There was no way we could make Tadoussac before dark in these conditions. And there was no other protected harbour before it.

He went to the bow, got the anchor ready, then repeated the drill. "Watch my hand signals, head into the wind, slow to a crawl, and when I say, put the engine in neutral and then give it a shot of reverse to set the hook."

I surveyed the unforgiving shoreline, then proceeded. While I waited for the telltale swinging motion indicating we were set, *Inia* headed toward a massive boulder, like metal to a magnet.

"Get outta here! Fast!" David screamed, frantically pumping the manual windlass to lift the anchor.

I re-engaged the motor and steered *Inia* back out into the chaotic river, where we flailed and circled and psyched ourselves up to try again.

"Number three's a charm," David said as we headed back out after failed attempt two.

"Please don't say things like that."

"Why not?"

"Just don't."

For attempts four through eight, David tried dropping the anchor, then tossing the anchor, then said we should drift back farther for Christ's sake, and we should let out more goddamn scope.

On our ninth try, as the sun touched the horizon, *Inia* was finally secured for the night in Port-au-Persil, a measly 13 nautical miles downstream from Cap-à-l'Aigle.

We wolfed down cheese sandwiches and cups of hot chicken broth. Then David set his watch alarm and we went to bed fully dressed, to get yet another early start for Tadoussac.

Well before the alarm went off, David and I were sitting out under a crisp crescent moon, breathing in the salt-like aroma of the river and the fresh peppery scent of the forest nearby. As the sun rose, I took in the scenery for the first time: the mountainous terrain, the modest white clapboard church, the decaying wharf on the pristine bay. The cove was a favourite destination of artists with easels. No wonder. It was breathtaking.

After draining a Thermos of coffee, we raised the anchor, shifted *Inia* and ourselves into gear, and headed out.

While we motored along this ruggedly beautiful stretch, the tide changed. *Inia* was now travelling one knot per hour. So, slower than walking speed. And the last thing I wanted to do was to return to the picturesque cove.

As my patience started to wane, David pointed to three large white humps rising from the water off our port bow. They were whales. Scanning the surface, we saw another two here, three there, then a couple of black torpedo-shaped ones hovering before melding into the gentle seas, and later a long, dark mass with a dorsal fin that dove below followed by its tail. Beluga, minke, and finback whales. *Inia* was surrounded by them.

With all this excitement, next thing I knew, the dangerous mouth of the Saguenay was behind us and David was pulling up to the sparse Tadoussac marina, where the dockhand was waiting. He was a skinny, weathered man in his late fifties, with a receding hairline and a thin grey ponytail, dressed in a worn denim jacket and jeans.

"What d'you think of our welcoming committee?" he said while tying *Inia* to metal cleats.

"Amazing!" I said, hopping onto the floating dock. "I hoped we'd see *one* whale."

While the three of us walked up the wheeled dock ramp to the marina office, he explained that the upwelling of cold water near the mouth of the Saguenay Fjord created conditions for plankton and krill that whales like to eat.

"You can keep your tulips. They're our sign of spring!" he said, bursting with local pride.

David and I walked around the bay to the hillside village to buy a few groceries. Then we stopped at a café for a bite to eat. The wind had died. With the late afternoon sun blazing, we opted to sit out to soak in the soothing rays.

After settling at a table, I noticed the dockhand was on the patio, too. He was sitting alone, partially reclined with his bare feet propped on the chair beside him, sunning, smoking, sucking on a beer, looking at one with his universe. I found myself staring at him, curious about his story. Where had he started out? How did he get here from there? I doubted it was in a straight route, or that this tiny village on the north shore of the St. Lawrence was a lifelong destination. Yet here he was, and it suited him. And I thought about our boys' mysterious journeys with optimism and wonder.

From our table, we had a panoramic view of the bay: the whale-filled entrance, the shoreline that was emerging as tidal water receded, the phantom-like beachcombers appearing from nowhere to ply their trade.

David said, "I wish we could stay longer, but —"

"I know. Cameron and Leslie." They would arrive in the Azores in four weeks. Our buffer, which had seemed ample to start, was disappearing fast. We agreed we had better cross the St. Lawrence in the morning.

$$\int \mathcal{U}\tau$$

Cameron wrote.

> You probably have the following already: North East winds are forecast for the entire gulf of St. Lawrence, mostly 15-20 knots, possibly up to 25.... Cool.... Best wishes for an end to the north easterlies.

June 13, the dockhand undid our lines. While tossing them onboard, he warned us to bundle up and be careful. North-easterlies had, in fact, returned with a vengeance. He said he wouldn't be out in that wind.

"We'll be fine," David said.

As we headed off, I took the helm. Covered from head to toe in his bright yellow foul-weather gear, David rushed forward to attach the inner forestay so we could use our storm sail if need be. While watching him work, I noticed wild burbling beyond the bow. Too late. We were committed.

"The boeuf's dead ahead! Hold on!" I screamed.

David dropped to his knees and grabbed the bow pulpit with both hands. As we entered the blood-curdling patch, *Inia*'s bow shot skyward, then twisted and turned and buried itself in the foaming seas.

"Please, please, hold on!" I repeated, my grip tight on the wheel, my sights set on the calm in the distance.

Then a wave of icy salt water roared over the deck, blasting his feet out from under him.

"Good Lord!" I screeched. David lay horizontal, writhing, with waves washing over him.

Once we reached the other side, he got on his knees and crawled back into the cockpit.

"I'm surprisingly dry," he said, glancing back at the boiling cauldron, then at me, through dripping bangs and spotty glasses. Then he took over the helm.

We carried on in the headwinds. As *Inia* slammed into eight-foot waves, frothy spray shot up and over the deck.

Bam. Spray. Bam. Spray. Bam bam. Spray.

It was so cold it even smelled like snow.

I checked for emails at the nav station. "My mom wrote," I said, climbing back outside. "She said her friend Josie slept over. They had a great time, chatting late into the night."

"Great! Sounds like she's doing fine." David stood at the wheel, his nose dripping onto his moustache and beard.

"But then they had to get up early to tee off at seven fifteen."

"To golf?"

"Mmm-hmm. Ladies' day, best ball foursome." I sat on a lazarette cushion, puffs of my breath drifting off. "It's thirty Celsius there."

"Thirty!" David said.

"It's probably uncomfortable with the humidex."

We exchanged frozen smiles.

Bam bam. Spray. Bam. Spray.

After docking in the Rimouski marina, we paid for a slip, had a simple dinner, crawled under a heap of blankets and hibernated for the night.

First thing the next morning, we took a taxi to downtown Rimouski, where the bemused owner of a sporting goods store led us down to the cavernous basement and left us alone to root through boxes of her winter stock.

While David was at the checkout paying for a stack of lined toques and insulated gloves, I looked at the store mannequins decked out in shorts and T-shirts, and half seriously questioned if I'd ever see my arms and legs again.

June 15, we finally got a weather break, a moderate south-south-west wind, perfect to do an around-the-clock push for the Gaspé. We departed at 0430 and sailed wing on wing for the better part of the day.

Evening, I took the first shift, nine to midnight, my customized watch kit by my side. The temperature was pleasant, the sea state calm, the sky a bright sapphire long after the sun had set. It was near the summer solstice, when evening twilight lingers and the night is its shortest.

I looked behind. There was no traffic. I checked the radar screen. Nothing. Plotting our position on the chart took all of two seconds. I put a homemade CD in the Walkman, put my headphones on, opened a bag of trail mix, and began to hum and munch.

Al-lay-loo-ya ... The mixture was a healthy alternative to cookies, especially if I only ate the dried apricots. *Mmm hmm ... dooo ya* ... The apricots and raisins ... *What's it tooo ya ...* Currents, papayas and bananas. Only the fruit. *La da ... throoo ya ...* And the candied ginger. *Ooo ooo ooo oo yaaa!*

Close to midnight David resurfaced, rested and ready to take over. I went to bed, a cornucopia swelling in my gut.

Around 0300, I got the dreaded call. The wind had died; so had the motor. David needed my help. I grudgingly put on my insulated pants and coat over my PJs and, thinking *fuel air exhaust oil, fuel air exhaust oil,* I clambered up to the cockpit.

David unfurled the genoa. It flapped and snapped and fell limp. So he rolled it back in.

With *Inia* adrift on the St. Lawrence, he went below to troubleshoot while I watched for freighters. What could we do if I saw one? I wasn't quite sure, but I opted not to ask.

He quickly determined there was no problem with the exhaust, there was no air in the fuel line, and the engine oil was full. As *Inia* continued to bob along in the river current and seagulls squawked and swooped under our running lights, he set up an elaborate gravity system, bypassing the electric fuel pump, to top up the diesel. He pressed the start button. Click. It wasn't a fuel issue either.

"We're snookered," I said, resigned to calling another pan-pan as morning twilight emerged.

"Seems someone wasn't listening," David joked, wielding a three-foot iron crank from the bottom of the engine compartment. "It's like starting a —"

"Oh my God, like starting a fire without a match!"

He inserted the heavy shaft in the flywheel on the front of the engine. With veins bulging in his temples, he turned the shaft in circles, slowly at first, then faster and faster, beads of sweat spraying off him. "Hit it!" he yelled.

"Okay. All right," I yelled back, shoving down the compression levers.

The engine burped and sputtered and burped some more, then turned over.

"It *is* genius!" he exclaimed, plopping down on the settee, his T-shirt blotchy with perspiration.

"An Abbott and Costello kinda genius," I said, laughing.

"Genius nonetheless," he said.

We were back under power around 1000. By then, although the wind hadn't changed, the sea state had. We had entered the wide-open Gulf of St. Lawrence.

Inia rolled along in ten-foot swells until late afternoon, when she rounded a substantial breakwater of boulders at the tip of the Gaspé Peninsula, beyond which was shelter, calm, and the friendly fishing village of Rivière-au-Renard.

FOURTEEN

INIA WAS THE ONLY BOAT tied up to the long dock that ran along the inside of the breakwater. I sat on the bow at dusk and took in the simple maritime village on the hill; the commercial fishing vessels of miscellaneous colours and conditions resting for the night at the main pier; the bright-red Canadian Coast Guard cutter in front of the marina, polished and ready; the smells of salt and fish and the sea.

After stowing the tools and containers of engine oil, David came up on deck with two glasses of wine. "Well, I have to say, it was quite the shakedown cruise," he said, settling down beside me.

"Unbelievable," I said, watching teenagers gather wood for a fire at the water's edge on the mainland. "Yet I'm glad we came this way. I doubt any place can top this, right here in our own backyard."

"But this isn't exactly in our —"

"And I have to admit the electronics guys were right to be concerned, about me, at least. I was pretty darned naive. I mean, I actually expected the St. Lawrence to be a piece of cake."

"It was anything but, that's for sure. Two weeks of freezing headwinds didn't help."

"Honestly, dear, I say enough's enough," I said.

"Maybe this should wait 'til morning. Neither of us got much sleep and —"

"I'm ready for the Atlantic."

"You're ready? Ready for the Atlantic?"

"More than ready. Frankly, I'm tired of worrying about tides and land to get stuck on and freighters hogging narrow waterways."

"Wow! I wasn't expecting that. Personally, I'd be happy to skip Sydney altogether."

"I'm so looking forward to just going where the wind blows us."

"It'd shave off some time."

"Even to boredom, bring it on!"

"If we're able to deal with the engine and provision, we could even leave from here."

"Sounds good."

"All right. Okay then."

"Let's do it!"

"You didn't bang your head on the engine compartment, did you?" he joked.

I looked over at the blazing bonfire, smelled the burning wood, listened to the music and laughter. "How perfect is that!" I said as we headed below.

Through dense sleep, I heard people talking. Where was I? Oh yeah, on *Inia*, in Rivière-au-Renard. The clock said 2:00 a.m. It was a dream. No. I heard them again, male voices, drunk male voices, and they seemed nearby. But we had the dock to ourselves. Didn't we?

"Dear —"

"I hear them, too," David said.

We lay on the berth, still, looking, listening. "Sounds like they're getting closer," I said, hearing footsteps.

Shadows moved past the portholes and across the hatch. *Inia* swayed.

"Christ! They've boarded!" David said, putting on his glasses and stepping into his jeans.

"Oh no! Dear, don't go out!" I said, sitting up on the berth, hugging the blanket.

He stood on the bottom stair and peered through the porthole. "This is our home!" he said, sliding the companionway roof open. After lifting off the door panels, he stepped outside, bare from the waist up.

Inia rocked as though from a boat's wake. I heard "*Maudit!*" "*Tabarnak!*" "*Sacrament!*" scuffling, beer cans rolling on deck. Then all went quiet. I remained frozen until David descended the stairs.

"Just guys from the party," he said, looking over his shoulder. "I think they were more surprised by us than we were them!"

"Thank the Lord," I said, watching their silhouettes stagger off into the darkness, aware that from here on, it would be just David and me to deal with whatever came our way.

June 17, early morning, we went for a walk to scope out the village, passing empty docks, the fishermen already gone to work. Although the party had thinned, a few diehards were still huddled around the fading embers, arguing unintelligibly.

"Remember that incident with John?" David said, seeing another reveller passed out beside them on the lawn.

"Do I! And I thought he was up in his bedroom asleep when we got the call from emerg in the morning to come and get him!" I said. "Reminds me of *me* at the Oak Hotel, too."

"The Oak Hotel?"

"That's what they called a high-school hangout in Sturgeon Falls. It was at the foot of a hill under a railway trestle. Being the opposite of cool, I didn't even know how one hangs out. I soon learned that drinking was a large part of it there. I had rye, of all things. Way too much of it, way too fast. I remember trying to climb the hill and falling back down, rolling over rocks and tree stumps. I was numb, but aware it should hurt. I didn't care, but thought I should. In the morning, I came to in a strange bedroom in a strange house, reeking of vomit, cold, aching. Even my hair follicles hurt. At school Monday, everyone high-fived me with 'Wicked party!' and 'Man, were you wasted!'"

"And your parents, how were they?"

"Essentially, terrified, especially my dad. Until then, he was certain only *other* kids did those kinds of things. It would never be me." We heard retching behind us. "I wouldn't want to be that age again!"

"I bet a few parents are pacing in their Gaspé kitchens right now," David said.

"*Plus ça change, plus c'est la même chose* ... more French ... the more things change, the more they stay the same. See, I'm switching naturally now."

We meandered through the streets and found a grocery store, a laundromat, and a marine supply store, essentially everything we needed, all within easy walking distance.

It was decided we'd head offshore from Rivière-au-Renard.

Back aboard *Inia*, I was sitting out with a pad of paper, listing final to-dos, when the fishing vessels roared back in from the Gulf. The wharf was soon alive with mounds of flopping fish and dock workers hustling to sort, weigh, and pack their morning hauls for shipment.

David spent the afternoon testing fuses and circuits to determine why the engine had stopped in the first place and why it wouldn't restart the normal way. It turned out the echo-charger, a new device dedicated to charging the starter battery and electric fuel pump with solar and wind energy, was defective.

A replacement was arranged under warranty. It would be couriered to the marina. That meant staying put until at least the 21st, David's original deadline, likely longer.

While we waited, David dismantled, cleaned, and reinstalled the burner assemblies on the kerosene stove, changed the engine oil and fuel filters, topped up the water tanks, and replaced the shear pin on the dinghy engine. I varnished the companionway and, between coats, sprayed our wrenches and pliers with WD-40 and put them into baggies to prevent the corrosive effects of salt water.

Gaston, a crew member from the Coast Guard cutter, having no emergencies to attend to the entire time we were preparing for departure, was happy to oversee our work. He asked if we thought we had enough fuel, informed us that kerosene causes respiratory and neurological problems, suggested we stow at least double the amount of water we had. "I'd really hate to get 'the call' and find the two of you bobbing at sea, clinging to each other, dying of dehydration."

"Good grief! Just how often do you get that call?" I asked.

"Never. Not once in my twenty years. The point is, it *could* happen. And it'd suck if you were the first."

Late Friday the echo-charger arrived. We emailed Cameron:

> Our plan is to leave Rivière-au-Renard on high
> tide Sunday (the 24th), bound for the Azores.
> We still think we can beat you there!

Saturday a fierce wind howled. While David installed the new part, I took off on a "what else could we possibly need and what do we need more of" trip to the grocery store. I returned with gum, chocolate bars, peanut butter, frozen bread dough, more batteries for our handheld electronic devices, sunscreen, and, of course, more water.

As *Inia* writhed and her dock lines snapped, David and I deflated the dinghy and lashed it to the deck. Then we hung our canvas weather cloths from the lifelines on either side of the cockpit to provide us with shelter from the sea. I stood on the dock, looked at the maelstrom in the bay, then back at the foot-high cloths. *Are they up to the job?* I wondered.

"How 'bout a final poutine?" David said.

"Sounds good," I said, pulling the corners of the canvas as tight as I could.

The restaurant was on the highway, on top of the hill. We trudged along the shoulder through twirling fast-food wrappers and blowing sand.

At a table away from other patrons, we took turns phoning family and friends on our cellphone to let them know we'd be leaving for the Atlantic in the morning, all communication would be by sailmail over the ham radio until landfall, the forecast was perfect, and we were happy, great, very *very* prepared, excited, actually raring to blast off.

John said he'd received David's email about our wills.

"Oooh yeah, that." I apologized and admitted the timing of sharing that information was less than stellar. "You guys should've known this stuff well before now."

"Along with instructions to break into the file cabinet to get at them," he added.

"*If* need be," I stressed, acknowledging the wording wasn't the best either. "Honestly, John, we'll be fine. We're *ultra*prepared."

Brian considered the note about our wills disturbing, too. However, he had just heard a radio documentary about a sailor, Robin Knox-Johnston, who, at sixty-eight years of age, solo-circumnavigated the globe.

"If that old geezer could do it alone, you guys should be fine," Brian said. "Inhaling resin and fibreglass all day long might be riskier." He went on to explain that by the end of his first week on the dinghy job, he had thought his lungs were seizing up. So he had moved on from the boat-building industry to cabinet-making.

"Seems right up your alley. I love the spice rack you made me at school," I said.

"But he hated that program," David said after I hung up.

"I know, but I guess that was then and this is now."

On our return trek along the top of the hill, the bay below looked like whipped meringue. We leaned into the wind and talked about our departure in the morning. "The earlier the better's my thinking," David said.

Oh … my … God!

FIFTEEN

THE MORNING OF JUNE 24 was cloudy. A cold light drizzle fell. Waves lapped against the breakwater. Gulls cried out from
on top of its glistening boulders. With the engine running, David
untied *Inia*'s dock lines.

Gaston hopped off the cutter and ran in our direction. Too late.

"We're off," David yelled to him across the bay while pushing the stays and stepping aboard.

"Be safe, my friends," he yelled back, stopping to watch us go.

By 0730 we were underway.

Beyond the breakwater, David raised every sail, winched
them taut, and doused the motor. The rigging hummed as *Inia*
sailed close-hauled, southeast to cross the Gulf of St. Lawrence,
beyond which was the Atlantic Ocean.

Late afternoon I made dinner: chicken curry, green beans
and rice, yoghurt and fresh strawberries for dessert. Bundled in
layers, we sat in the cockpit and ate, the electronic autohelm
keeping us on track.

"You've totally outdone yourself," David said, surprised by
the spread.

"As they say, a well-fed sailor's a happy sailor," I said. "I boiled
the rice in the same water as the beans," I added.

"Clever."

"Gaston made me nervous."

"We'll be all right, as long as we're careful. But good thinking."

The wind was constant through the night, and a light rain began to fall.

By dawn on June 25, we had travelled 126 nautical miles, so halfway across the Gulf. It was 10 degrees Celsius, but felt colder in the dampness. A thick fog rolled in. The swells built. David resumed helming, now by radar. I went below to make coffee. The smell of it made me gag.

Back on deck, I took in several deep breaths of the chilly mist.

"You okay?" David said.

"I'm fine," I said.

"Take some Gravol and go lie down."

"I'm fine," I repeated. "But maybe you're right, a bit more sleep won't hurt. An hour, tops." I left him with the full Thermos of coffee and snuck a ginger-flavoured Gravol on my way to bed. It, too, made me gag.

When I awoke the fog had lifted, the rain had stopped, and a near-full moon was glowing. We were in the Cabot Strait, within sight of land. It was the middle of the night. I had slept the entire day, throughout which David remained in the cockpit, managing *Inia*.

"God, you must be starving," I said through the companion-way, my stomach spasming as *Inia* rolled and pitched. "I'll whip up something, something nice 'n' hot."

Under the cone of the galley light I made grilled cheese sandwiches, yawning and burping and sweating at the stench of fried butter and melted cheese. I then bolted on deck with the food and insisted on taking over the helm.

Standing at the wheel, I let the fresh wind wash over my face and focused my watery gaze on the moonlit cliffs.

"You look a little pale," David said, dipping his sandwich in ketchup.

"An empty stomach's the problem," I replied, forcing myself to eat, too.

Around 0200, we reached the tip of Cape Breton and could see a village on its shore. The houses, with their smoking chimneys and soft yellow porch lights, looked so warm and cozy, so inviting, so safe. As we passed by them and entered the shimmering blackness of the Atlantic Ocean, my sweat turned cold and I began to shiver. Were we truly prepared? Did we really want to do this? Did *I* really want to do this? Was I — the mom, the health-care worker, the homemaker — even remotely capable of such an undertaking? If not, now would be the time to say so.

I looked at David. He was at peace in the darkness, moved by the night sky, utterly joyful to be on the cusp of his childhood dream at long last. His poise gave me the strength I needed at that moment. I didn't say a word. On we went.

After the moon had set and the village had disappeared behind us, stars shone brighter. I watched *Inia*'s lace-trimmed wake roll away and away until a faint glow emerged to the east. It was morning twilight, the start of a new day, already. There was immense comfort in that.

No longer in sight of land, David and I stood in the cockpit and stared out at the vast Atlantic Ocean in daylight for the first time.

"It's awesome," he eventually said, putting his arm around my shoulder, squeezing me close.

"Yup," I peeped.

How could I be so sick in all this awesomeness? After having lived aboard for almost two months, having had weeks of increasingly big seas, without a problem? After wearing motion sickness bracelets, sucking on Gravol, fixing on the damned horizon?

I broke free from his grip, threw my upper body over the lifelines, and let cheesy gingery slime fly.

"Sorry," I said, wiping saliva off my chin, my body still draped over the gunwale.

David rubbed my back with one hand, steered *Inia* with the other. "It's not your fault," he said.

Seeing the orange splat on the side of the hull and the patch of floating goo, I vomited some more, this time just strings of sour spit. "I can't help it," I said, drenched in sweat, aching all over.

"I know. It's not your fault," he said again, his eyes welling. "I just wish there was something I could do."

"Oh God," I said, feeling guiltier, heaving again.

"If it's any consolation, from books I've read —"

And again.

"— it supposedly goes away in time."

"What about you? You've —"

"Don't worry about me," he said, insisting he could manage single-handedly until I got better. "I can't sleep now anyway. Honestly."

I went below, yanked open the berth in the main salon, and flopped, face down, spread-eagled across it.

It was dusk again when I reawakened and wobbled to the head to pee. Perched on the toilet, I saw moisture pooling around its base. When I went on deck to tell David, he was looking out over the water, letting the genoa out, steering.

"The autohelm broke late morning," he explained.

"God! You should've woken me up," I said, taking over the wheel so he could investigate the suspicious water.

He discovered the toilet's through-hull fitting was leaking, so he closed the seacock. Waste would be discharged into the holding tank instead of out to sea until the fitting could be replaced. He assured me it was nothing to worry about.

Afterward, he took the opportunity to set up the wind-vane self-steering system, which would be almost like having another crew member, we both said, hopeful. We then sat in the cockpit together, I weak and sore, David nearing exhaustion, both of us making monumental efforts to pretend otherwise.

"Look," he said, breaking the disquieting silence. A pod of dolphins bounded toward us with a boisterous performance of loop-de-loops and pirouettes.

"Seems like they're smiling," I said, grateful for the brightness they brought to an otherwise dark day, thinking perhaps they knew we needed it.

June 27 brought more cold and enormous swells.

My head pounded. I had no interest in food. I tried to drink water, but it just sloshed around in my stomach and shot back out. All I could do was toss and turn, sweat and freeze, moan and retch.

Around 1600, I hauled myself on deck, my hair pasted to my face, to check on David. He was standing at the wheel, yet again. The wind vane had been unable to maintain our heading in these seas.

"Good Lord!" I said, alarmed at the realization he had been helming much of the night before and all that day and had had very little sleep the preceding two days.

"I'm fine," he persisted, his eyes droopy, his face burnt from the wind and sun. "How are *you*? That's the main thing."

Inia listed, my stomach lurched, and I launched into another round of dry heaves with such ferocity I thought my eyeballs would pop out.

As he watched me, tears began to stream down his face.

"Dear, if you don't get sleep, you're another seizure in the making," I said, now a sobbing, quivering mess myself. "And I'm useless. We could both die out here if —"

"I've got it!" he said, like a light bulb had turned on. "Sweetheart, we'll be all right." He wiped his eyes with his coat sleeve and furled the genoa. "We're gonna heave to," he said, letting out the mizzen boom to starboard.

According to an instructional video on storm tactics we had watched at home, this procedure enables sailors to essentially park a boat on the ocean. David lashed the helm hard to port, angling *Inia* to the waves. We then saw the "slick" as she slid down them, just like in the video, and, as also promised, the chaotic motion almost immediately subsided. *Inia* hove to beautifully.

Since leaving the Gaspé shore, we hadn't seen a single other vessel. The risk of crossing paths with one was slim and, under the circumstances, it was a risk we were willing to take.

Without concern for watches, we went below and crashed for the night.

Around 0300 on June 28, we were up and out on deck. David looked like a new man. My seasickness symptoms were starting to abate such that I knew I'd be fine in just a matter of time. We had turned the corner.

The breeze was now gentle, from the east. The sea had settled. With neon plankton glowing on its coal black surface, it was lovely.

After raising all the sails, David reset the self-steering system, with the tall, narrow wind vane meant for use in light air.

"We should call it Bobby," I said, watching the skinny vane frantically flip and flop. "It's like it's new at this, and eager to please."

David laughed. "Then what do we call the other vane?"

"Robert, obviously. It's stout and strong, decisive, the pro that takes over when the going gets rough."

Once Bobby had us heading south on a beam reach, David made himself a hearty breakfast: scrambled eggs and precooked bacon topped with hot salsa, on a bagel. I went bagel only, not about to tempt fate.

He then updated Cameron and Leslie about our lack of progress.

> I wish we had a better report, but this is the reality. We are looking for the right wind to get us down to 42 north so that we can zip along to the Azores. Now I am questioning the advice we had (and took) to go the St. Lawrence. We will keep you posted.
>
> Current position is 45 degrees 10 minutes north, 57 degrees 6 minutes west.

Static blared over the VHF. It startled us both. We had not heard another human voice since leaving shore, four days before.

A loud, clear broadcast followed. It was a bulletin from a Canadian warship, warning it would soon be conducting live munitions testing. According to its coordinates, it was in our vicinity. David flew below. While he attempted to establish radio contact, I spotted the menacing gunmetal-grey structure bearing down on us off our port side. My heart quickened. Were we about to be blown to smithereens by our very own navy?

I listened in.

"Canadian warship, this is sailing vessel *Inia*. Uh, we heard your message about munitions testing. And, uh, we want to let you know we are visible on your starboard side. Over."

"Sailing vessel *Inia*, this is the Canadian warship. Roger that. We see you out there. Rest assured, you are not, repeat not, in any danger. Our weapons' testing will be in the thousand-foot range, and it will be directed straight up. Over."

David looked up at me. Yes, I had heard right. But no, he wouldn't be suggesting they should look up the law of gravity.

"Thank you, Canadian warship. This is *Inia*, over and out," he said, and we moved on.

At around 1430 that afternoon, I felt a couple of drops of rain. David did, too. Then a few plopped on the lazarette cushions, then a dark line formed on the horizon. This was no ordinary spring shower. David reduced sail and together we prepared *Inia* to heave to, much faster this second time around, after which we ran below for cover.

David set our waypoint in the GPS to track our movements. *Inia* jerked. Rain pinged off the cabin roof. The sky went black. Then explosions of thunder and lightning detonated all around us and the storm hit in full fury.

Soon winds were screaming through the riggings as the ocean frothed and churned and breaking waves roared over the hull. Below decks, the gimballed lamps banged back and forth. Papers fluttered from the nav station table. A cupboard door sprang open; pans slid, cans rolled, a bag of rice fell out and split.

The pandemonium set my stomach off again and sent David and me crashing against bulkheads as we moved about, handhold to handhold, to restore order. It was hard work to stay upright, too hard. With objects stowed, I arranged cushions on the cabin sole, secured myself against the main berth with a bucket by my side, pulled the comforter up, watched, listened, and vomited.

A rogue wave hit *Inia*'s hull like a wrecking ball, setting off a fierce metal clanging overhead.

"What d'you suppose *that* is?" I said.

"Don't know, but it doesn't sound good!" David said, working his way to the stairs to investigate.

"Stay low," I said, worried things were whipping about. He poked his head out the companionway, letting in the cold wind and spray.

The bilge-pump light began to flash.

"Looks like we're taking on water!" I yelled, scanning the floorboards for signs of seepage.

David descended the stairs, drenched again. "Visibility's pretty much nil out there," he said, drying his face with a towel. Then he manoeuvred from stem to stern to inspect the cabin hull. "There aren't any cracks or leaks that I can see."

"But the bilge —"

"It's likely just storm water. Sue, remember, *Inia*'s made for the ocean. She's made to ride this thing out. We're gonna be okay!"

He was right. At ten tons, she felt stable and sure in these wild seas, and her inch-thick hull was withstanding the abuse admirably. She was a tank, a warhorse. We were in capable hands.

The gale continued for several hours, during which time the cacophony grew familiar, predictable, even monotonous. Same with the motion. It was our new normal, to which I surprisingly adjusted.

Around 1930, the wind weakened and the rain lightened, signalling the storm's passing. David went topside to survey the aftermath. The sum total of damage was a jib block that had broken free. The bolt securing it to the deck had snapped from metal fatigue. Miraculously the block was still at the end of the jib sheet. He reattached it with a spare.

By 2000, we were under sail again.

Seeing that Bobby was handling the weather, I tidied the cabin and went to bed, back on the main berth, and lay wide awake. Although I was pleased with how we had fared in the storm, I found myself questioning how I was going to cope for another whole week, maybe two, and seriously considering calling it quits in the Azores. If not the Azores, Portugal. David's dream of crossing an ocean would have been realized, which was the main goal, and we already had the requisite storm story to bore people with until the day we died. Who needed more adventure? Certainly not me! Maybe we could tootle into the Med instead, hang out there for the winter. That idea was appealing. Yet, for some reason, I kept it from fully surfacing.

∿

June 29, 0400, we were becalmed and awoke to dense fog. After sunrise, all was still grey. Not light grey or dark grey; right in the middle, the total absence of colour, shade, or tone. There was no difference between the sea and the sky, no horizon, no sense of depth or distance or destinations.

"It's as though *Inia's* weightless, suspended, floating in nothing," I said.

David looked around. "Yeah, it does sorta feel like that."

"And it's just you and me."

He smiled. "You got that right."

"We're the only living beings in existence."

"Hmm. That's a bit, uh …"

"Going nowhere in this nothingness," I said.

He got up and stretched. "Can I get you a bowl of cereal?"

"Sure. Shreddies, please. I like it, this feeling of just being."

When he went below, I noticed I felt rested for the first time in days, and content. On second thought, how could I not see this adventure through?

When David returned with two bowls, I continued. "It's the whole let go and let God idea. There's a certain serenity —"

"Great. I'm really glad to hear that, Sue, 'cause according to my calculations, at the rate we're going, we could be out here for a month."

"You're joking, right?"

He dug into his frosted mini-thingamajigs with extra gusto.

Early evening, we went below. I read, David listened to a Portuguese CD with headphones on, and, with our alarm set, we took turns doing look-abouts every twenty minutes, supposedly the time it takes for a freighter spotted on the horizon to mow you down.

～〜～

June 30, 0230, with ongoing stillness, David chose to motor, partly to make progress, partly to top up the house batteries.

Fully recovered, I was eager to communicate with the outside world. I plugged the laptop into the modem attached to the high frequency radio at the nav station, then began to compose my message to my friend Laurie:

> So, we've now been at sea for a full week. And it's
> been pretty wild.... Cold, fog, unexpected storms,
> sea sickness, we've become good at heaving-to,
> it's not particularly fun but it works and feels safe
> under the —

"Sue, come quick! And bring the camera!" David yelled.

I rushed on deck. The dense, fishy air made my eyes water, my nostrils sting. A whale, hovering twenty feet off our port bow, had just cleared its blowhole. As *Inia* got closer, the beast swelled above the surface, waved with its massive fluke, then disappeared.

I went back down and finished my email by telling Laurie about the whale just now, and about all the dolphins that squeaked and squawked and jumped clear out of the water and about how this had continued to be an amazing experience.

Then I studied the propagation graph to determine what radio wave to use. At this time of day, in this weather, a strong signal was coming from Belgium. I set the dial to its frequency, listened for chatter, and pressed Connect when the airwaves were free. The usual static was followed by a high-pitched squeal. Success on the first try! I watched the slow transmission of my message, then waited impatiently for incoming mail, as always hoping for news from home.

"Looks like the GRIB files and two other messages. Yay!" I yelled up over the noise of the engine. "One's from Deborah and Bill. I bet they have no idea how much we appreciate their daily notes. We'll have to be sure to tell them! Oh, and the other's from Cameron."

"Cam? What'd he have to say?"

I scanned his email. "Bloody hell! It's about weather. You need to read it for yourself."

David's eyes darted back and forth like Ping-Pong balls.

> Have been looking at some forecast maps. You may be in some dirty weather and tired so I'll condense what they're saying:
>> forecast time 29 June 18:33
>> gale developing approx. 37N 70W tracking
> ENE

48 hrs out: gale (force 8) predicted to be at approx. 40N 55W tracking NE

96 hrs out: same gale expected to be at 45N 40W tracking NE

High building in behind.

looks like some nasty weather due to cross your track; esp. if you've made considerable SE progress since last night

best wishes: hope you miss most of it.

"Well, the good news is, we haven't made considerable southeast progress. Dismal's more like it," David said. "Ironically, that might've kept us out of harm's way!"

He compared Cameron's weather info with the GRIB files, then pointed *Inia* a bit more south, just in case.

July 1 was still cold on the ocean, but sunny, with the return of moderate winds. We sat outside in our snowsuits and Rimouski toques. *Inia* sailed close-hauled.

"It seems our storm avoidance tack is a success," I said, listening to her beat a steady rhythm as she cut through the waves.

"And it'll get warmer as we go more south," David said.

"Can't wait." I looked down at dried saliva and coffee stains on my jacket front and the grimy knees of my insulated pants. "Do I stink?"

"Do you —"

"Be honest. Am I starting to smell bad?"

Except for occasionally changing my underwear, I was wearing the same layers underneath I had continuously been in since leaving shore, since we hadn't packed for this constant cold. And, for the sake of water conservation, other than brushing my teeth and washing my face, I had abandoned routine hygiene completely.

"No, not really," David said.

"Good to know. I'm doing a little experiment. My aunt Kathy used to say that North Americans wash too much. We inadvertently destroy the natural oils that nourish our skin, that keep it young and healthy," I said. "And she had beautiful skin. Not a blemish or a single wrinkle."

"I mean, not *too* bad," he added, straight-faced.

"Very funny." I swatted his shoulder. "Same's true for hair," I said. "So, excellent!"

Late afternoon, I made a special meal: boil-in-a-bag pot roast and gravy, fresh carrots, frozen peas, and Yoder's mashed potatoes.

"Happy Canada Day," I said, resurfacing with two overloaded plates.

"Strange, I forgot all about it." David spooned hot horseradish on the roast.

"Brian and John wrote," I said. "They both sound good. Brian went to a Sonny Rollins concert and had a great time. The opening act, a guy named Amon Tobin, made a balloon squeal into guitar mics while using a distortion pedal. He said it was awesome."

"To each his own," David said, laughing. "Who'd he go with?"

"Didn't say. Maybe, hopefully, he's met someone new. It's about time," I said. "And John just got back from a full day of shows. They played at a fundraiser for cancer in a downtown parking lot in the afternoon, then did a wedding reception on the back of a flatbed truck on a farm at night. He said everyone was up doing the Hillside twirly dance to their music the whole time."

"Ahh! The Hillside twirly dance," David said with a nostalgic smile. "Just think, Hillside's less than a month away. Weird that we won't be there this year, but nice that John'll still be going. That's got to be one of the best summer music festivals in the world."

"I don't think he's missed a single one in fifteen years. The boys all loved that weekend as much as we did. That's what made it fantastic," I said.

"Remember Ben singing that silly Buffalo Sabres song? The entire car ride home, he sang it over and over and —" David caught himself and looked out over the water.

"And when the three of them couldn't stop laughing about the song with the refrain 'My mama's got a heart condition'?" I looked out, too. "Song-writing rule number one: don't sing about your mama's heart condition. It *was* funny at the time...."

We sat quietly and ate.

"We don't even really know where he is," David eventually said.

"I know. And he hasn't the slightest idea where we are either," I said.

Before hitting the sack, David decided to download the latest GRIB files and saw that Cameron had written again. Twice.

Message number one:

> Looks like you missed the gale with "complex low" (phew!) — but, unbelievably, there is another forming at about 37N 71W and tracking ENE (give us a break!)

Message number two:

> Glad to hear you're seeing some friendly whales and dolphins. That must be exciting. Good luck today.
>
> Still seeing a chain of lows heading offshore in the high 30s N and tracking ENE then increasingly NE.

The lows are expected to merge into a gale
at about 40N 52W absorbing another low to
the NE and becoming a storm.

I don't know what the answer is to getting
across that chain of lows ... there seems to be
an endless supply forming along the track mentioned above.

I guess that's how weather works ... it just
keeps coming.

"What'll we do?" I said.
"Deal with it," David replied.

July 2 was storm-free. In fact, it was again calm — dead calm.
Glassy seas. Not a whisper of wind.

We had been offshore for nine days. In ideal conditions,
we would have been closing in on landfall by now, but with
1,100 nautical miles to go, we weren't even halfway.

We re-evaluated our supplies. Food-wise, we still had a
few items in the freezer as well as eggs, cold cuts, lots of cheese,
yoghurt, veggies, and some wilting salad ingredients in the fridge
and, of course, canned food stashed all over the place. We'd be
fine for a few more weeks, as long as we rationed it out.

"We'll have enough water, too, so long as we continue to use
it sparingly," David reported. "But, let's collect rain water if we
get the chance."

"Good idea," I said, thinking *when* not *if* there'd be rain. "My
skin'll soon be like a baby's bum," I added, smiling.

"It's fuel that I'm most worried about," David said. What
was left would take us a third of the way across, at best. And we

needed to be concerned about power. From that point on, we'd run the engine only to boost the batteries, an hour a day, two max. Hopefully, that way, there'd be enough diesel left to get us into port.

And then there was the Cameron and Leslie concern. When we had arranged the rendezvous, we had all been convinced that, barring a disaster at sea, the risk of us not arriving on time to do the crossing to Portugal with them was minimal to none. Now, David and I weren't so sure, and we were just sick about it. I reluctantly sent them a heads-up and suggested they develop a Plan B. I saw there was yet another message from Cameron.

> There's a gale expected (what else is new) 24 hrs — way down south, 35N 65W tracking NE.
>
> Good news: 96 hours out all atlantic lows expected to dissipate/become stationary and relatively innocuous.
>
> It looks like a good time to make your easting. If you've got some wind — go go go!

"Can't, can't, can't," David said. The two of us scanned the tinfoil-like surface of the water and listened to *Inia*'s restless clanks and creaks. In every respect, we had to be able to sail.

Below decks, I made another substantial meal, this time a soggy salad, rice, and beef curry using leftover beef from the night before.

Afterward, David spent the evening sitting at the nav station, staring at the electronic screens, turning dials, pressing buttons, as though maybe he could effect cosmic change. I took out the crossword puzzle book but couldn't concentrate.

Around 2200 I thought I heard faint ripples against the hull. David cocked his head. It wasn't my imagination. Out the companionway, we could see texture on the water. Hallelujah! Wind!

Back on deck, up went the main, out went the genoa, and on we went.

Inia made such great progress throughout that night, all the next day, and into July 4 that I regretted writing Cameron and Leslie. It felt entirely premature. I sat down at the nav station intending to tell them so, but I smelled smoke.

David was motor-sailing to top up the battery charge and was apparently oblivious to the smell. My cursory survey of the cabin confirmed the stove was off, the lamps were out, and the kerosene heater that never worked was still broken. I went topside to inform him. On deck, I couldn't smell a thing. Yet, as I climbed back down the companionway there it was again, acrid, like burnt plastic. There was a hissing sound, too, seemingly coming from underfoot.

When David removed the stairs panel to investigate, steam billowed out of the engine compartment and wiring began to spark. Our once-shiny green Volvo engine was now speckled like it had a bad case of acne. Salt water was everywhere.

Inia's engine had a raw-water cooling system, which meant it was cooled by the water she was floating in, as opposed to by a coolant. Long-term exposure to salt water is brutal to all things mechanical. After the yacht broker, Mike, had told us she had "never tasted salt water," we learned she had, in fact, binged on the stuff, twice: once in Florida, another time in Newfoundland. When David confronted him with this disturbing revelation, he said he had meant *Inia* had *virtually* not tasted it and he insisted that her subsequent time in fresh water would have flushed salt from her cooling system *eons* ago.

Now here we were, in the middle of the Atlantic Ocean, dealing with a hole in the cooling system caused by salt-water corrosion and we couldn't motor, or even turn on the engine to top up the batteries, because of it. Although we had solar panels and a wind generator, they required sun and wind to generate energy. We often had one or the other, seldom both, sometimes neither. They weren't sufficient on their own to meet our energy demands.

Since refrigeration was one of our biggest draws on power, David raised the temperature. From now on we'd eat whatever was closest to spoiling. Wasting food was out of the question.

While he set about figuring out a temporary repair to the engine, I strategized about food. Our cabin looked like it had been ransacked. The stairs panel lay on the starboard settee. Cushions from over storage compartments were piled beside it. A tool box, bins of spare parts, tubes of adhesives, baggies of materials, and boxes of hardware were strewn over the floor. And the contents of the fridge and freezer covered every inch of countertop.

The bread dough was beginning to thaw. I doubted the ambient temperature was warm enough for it to rise, but I greased a large roasting pan and put the two unrisen loaves in the oven, out of the way, just in case.

All day long, between monitoring *Inia*'s course, plotting our position on the paper chart, and tweaking the wind vane, David tried to patch the engine hole. He used clamps and seals and plugs, alone and in combination. Nothing worked.

I began to read *Marine Diesel Engines* hoping to find the solution. "Well this is depressing," I said, sitting amid the mess. "Says here 'scale and salt deposits can only be removed chemically.'"

"Mike was cocksure and dead wrong," David said, moving all the junk off the main settee to wherever else he could find space, to prepare the area for sleep.

"But *was* he so sure?" I said as we opened the berth together.

"It's a moot point now." He tossed the bedding and pillows on top.

I helped him spread out the sheets and blankets and, after setting the watch alarm, we crawled in under them.

I lay staring at the salt-covered engine. "Still, I can't help but wonder if he knew," I said, deciding now was not the time to tell him the head's flushing lever could maybe use a lube.

July 5, David flipped off every switch at the nav station. He turned the fridge off, too.

Until we could recharge the batteries, we'd use our handheld GPS and VHF radio. Energy consumption would be restricted to navigation lights, radar if need be, and the collection of weather data via the laptop.

I emailed family and friends to let them know we were about to "go dark," not to worry.

"Don't that beat all!" I exclaimed, discovering the bread dough had risen. I removed the bottom oven panel and lit alcohol in the dish at the base of the burner assembly. Once the kerosene was warmed by it, I turned the oven dial to max and shoved the loaves in. David, kneeling a foot from me, continued to try to plug the problematic engine hole.

Soon the aroma of baking bread was wafting through our upside-down cabin, and in less than an hour, presto, we had two perfect loaves. The two of us wedged ourselves among the precarious piles and ate thick, warm slices covered with melting butter, washing them down with warm milk. And all was momentarily right with the world.

While David refocused on the engine, I squeezed in beside him and cooked the rest of the thawing contents from the freezer, frying what meat was left, boiling the baggies of vegetables.

Dinner was chicken breast, broccoli, and rice. It hit the spot.

July 6, our house battery power was now under fifty percent. The laptop monitor kept flashing "Charge Is Low," as if we had to be told.

"We might have to make a pit stop in Flores," David said. It was the closest island in the Azorean chain, one to two days closer than Faial, our intended destination. It would have stores, likely mechanics, too.

"That's assuming we ever move again," I said, looking out over the stillness. "But what about Cameron and —"

"They'll beat us to Horta. And there's no way we can cross to Lisbon in time for them to catch their flight home."

"You mean —"

"It's over."

Despite trying our damnedest, our joint venture with our friends was not to be.

As morning emerged, the sun rose brighter. It was generating solar power, for which we were grateful. And it was generating heat, for which we were ecstatic.

After a breakfast of dry chicken strips on bread, David and I shed our foul-weather gear, stale toques, and sour thermal underwear, and exchanged jeans for shorts and fleeces for T-shirts, at long last. Our arms and legs were bluish white, thinner. David's belly had disappeared.

"You look hilarious," I said. His hair was sticking out at unnatural angles. Then I looked at my reflection on the mirror-like ocean surface beyond the gunwale. Grease and salt held strands of my hair wherever I moved them. We both laughed.

"Hey! Now's our chance!" David said, excited. He disappeared below and returned to the cockpit with towels, a bar of soap, and shampoo. "Let's wash!"

"What d'you mean?" I said, giving myself spiky devil horns.

"Let's have a shower," he said. "Together," he added.

"Shower? Together?" I repeated, now a unicorn.

He pointed to a solar shower bag that, unbeknownst to me, he had set out on the bow before leaving shore.

"Dear, it's broad daylight!"

He looked around at the empty ocean, grinned, and held his free hand out for mine.

"And I'm over fifty now and, as you know, I've given birth, not once, but three times," I said as he led me to the bow. "And that surgeon who did my appendectomy was more like a butcher. And, unfortunately, I let my gym membership lapse. So, we're talking scars and flab, a bit of cellulite and —"

"You're beautiful," he said, lifting my T-shirt up over my head.

"My dad used to say his parents were so modest they'd hide in a closet to change their minds. So, it could be partly genetic, too." I stepped out of my shorts and panties.

With the shower bag hanging on the main mast, David reached up, opened the valve, and, using the hose, gently sprayed water on my head, my back, my front. The water, warmed by the sun, was soothing as it cascaded down my bare skin. I shampooed, giving my scalp a slow, deep massage, while he hosed himself down.

"Feels nice, eh?" he said. We sudsed and splashed and sprayed each other, I with increasing abandon.

"It's more than nice. It's intoxicating." I blew soap bubbles off my hand. "I've never felt so —"

"Shit! We've got company!" David said, pointing to a dot on the otherwise empty horizon.

It was only the second vessel we had seen in the two weeks out. This time, though, we were without wind, without an engine, without a stitch of clothing on. And it was heading straight for us.

We scrambled to get dressed. David opted not to radio them, saying that if they were ill intentioned, telling them that we couldn't move would be advertising our vulnerability. Instead we sat tight and watched the ship grow until we could discern it was a commercial vessel, and grow until we could read its name, and grow until we could clearly see crew milling about on deck.

"What if they're simply unaware of us?" I finally said, imagining I could now even hear them talk.

At that David jumped to his feet, and, just as he did, the ship made a dramatic ninety-degree turn to port.

"They were probably armed, too, but with high-powered binoculars," David said, as we watched it fade into the distance.

Your just deserts, Suzie Q, Grandpa was probably up there saying.

July 7, David and I sat inside looking at each other and at the ongoing stillness.

"I got it!" he suddenly exclaimed. He rummaged in a parts drawer and held up a tube labelled 3M 5200. "Fred called it the mother of all sealants! I'm thinking this is it!" He cleaned the area around the engine hole with acetone, cut a circle of inner tube, and affixed the rubber patch to the engine with the magic goop.

After sixteen hours of calm, cat paws appeared. Although we needed wind, in a matter of hours we again had too much of it. David clambered topside to reduce sail. When he returned below, he reported that a jib sheet had chafed from friction and a snap shackle had broken off the starboard gate.

"Brother! What next?" I said, once again thinking of the stiffening head lever.

I crossed from the main settee to the galley, gripping the ceiling handholds, almost tripping over a lip on the middle floorboard. I tied myself to the counter with the galley strap, slapped together a couple of sandwiches with the last of the bread, and crossed back over, catching my toe again. Then I sat down beside David on the settee to eat. We ate in silence for a while.

"I never noticed it before," I said, referring to the raised floor edge. "It's a hazard, especially in this craziness." I handed David my plate, then knelt on the cabin sole and lifted up the floorboard to investigate. "Don't see anything," I reported, looking around the top of the holding tank for the cause. I reinserted the board with care, but the lip remained. When trying to force it down by stomping proved futile, I stressed that we should be mindful of this new risk for falls. "The last thing we need is a broken bone out here," I said, plunking myself back down beside him to finish my lunch.

As soon as I did, there was a whistle, then a rumble, then an explosive bang. The floorboard blasted off, a hose shot up, and putrid brown sludge spewed out in every direction.

When it had ended, we both remained motionless.

"Shit!" David said.

And it was. Urine too. Feces and urine, *our* feces and urine, were plastered all over the floor, the ceiling, the walls, the upholstery, the bedding, the curtains — and us.

No wonder the head handle required more muscle and the floorboard was lifting. The holding tank was full. Each successive flush built up pressure in the system. My theatrical stomp was enough to loosen the bursting hose.

I gagged at the sight of dripping sewage everywhere. "Can we go any lower? I mean, can we possibly be any more disgusting?" I asked David rhetorically.

Fearing a water shortage, he cautioned us to use it sparingly, and only on ourselves, in the clean-up. We used boat scrubs and spray disinfectants to wipe the surfaces. All soiled laundry was shoved into a giant plastic bag and stowed in the V-berth. It'd have to wait until we were ashore.

David then brought out a Home Depot pail from the quarter berth. "This is our new toilet," he announced.

"No way," I said. "I mean it! There's no damned way."

"It's what blue-water sailors do all the time. They refer to as the bucket-and-chuck-it procedure." He wrote a large WC on the side with a permanent marking pen, explaining it stood for "water closet." "That's so we don't get our toilet mixed up with our rainwater pail."

"Bloody ingenious," I said, surveying the chemical-scented squalor. "At least the engine's fixed," I eventually said. "That's a positive."

"Oh, I wouldn't exactly call it fixed, not just yet," David said. "The sealant takes five days to cure. We'll know for sure then. I'm certainly hopeful though."

"Five whole days! That brings us to the twelfth. We'll have landed by then!"

David put the WC pail in the head.

"Dear? Isn't that right?"

"I'd love to say yes, but ..."

We still had almost 800 nautical miles to go.

By dark we were in another force 8 gale and hove to for the third time. By morning, when conditions abated, we had back-tracked 21 nautical miles.

David replaced the broken jib sheet with a spare and tied the gate closed with nylon twine. As before, *Inia* moved on relatively unscathed, and my body recovered. But this time my spirits struggled to bounce back.

This voyage was far more than either of us had bargained for. The weather was nothing like on the Pilot Charts. Yes, we had had averages of force 4 winds and four-foot seas; that's if you averaged the gales and dead calms, both of which impeded progress. Our supplies were running low. And, despite David's best efforts to prepare, there had been one mechanical breakdown after another. I knew he, as captain, felt responsible for it all. I saw the constant worry in his eyes. I also anticipated a natural reluctance to give up.

I therefore broached the subject of ending the trip in Portugal delicately. "You'll have crossed an ocean. Realized your dream. Succeeded, and not without challenges. Just think: no more leaky engines or exploding toilets. And imagine warm sun on a sandy beach. Goodness knows, you'll have earned it in spades! So how about it?"

Rather than jumping at this out, he responded with complete conviction that what we'd been experiencing was a teensy spell of rotten luck, nothing more. He had no desire to stop whatsoever. Looking into the distance, he imitated Lloyd of *Dumb and Dumber*: "I want to keep going; to discover places where the beer flows like wine; where sailors flock like the salmon of Capistrano."

We both broke out laughing uncontrollably.

In the serious silence that followed, I thought about him with love, admiration, and total incredulity. And I reminded myself that landfall was a ways off. Perhaps he'd come to his senses yet.

On July 9, 10, and 11, it was wet out, winds were blustery, seas rough, skies like steel wool. This was the series of lows Cameron had warned us about. David adjusted our headings and plotted our meagre progress. The wind generator whirred around the clock, producing power to handle our skeletal electronic needs. We collected pails of rainwater from the cockpit, ate what was left of the perishable food, and whiled away the days below decks.

I attempted to knit the sweater I had started at home, but after dropping every third stitch, I put it back in the bag, frustrated, feeling stupid for even trying. After that, I mostly read and did crosswords. For the first time since moving aboard *Inia* I also thought about the Guelph cottage we'd purchased. I discreetly drew pencil sketches of how we'd renovate it and imagined how we'd decorate it and yearned for the day we'd call it home.

David practised Portuguese. *Ah bay say day eh ef* ... The alphabet? I asked. *Sim*. That's good, dear. *Obrigado*. Great. *Muito obrigado*. How's our speed? *Não entendo*. Okay, stop it. *Eu não falo inglês*. That's enough! *Desculpa, não falo inglês*.

On the evening of the 11th, when David downloaded GRIB files, he saw that the new gale Cameron had warned us about was on its way.

By 0100 on the 12th, *Inia* was scaling fifteen-foot waves, breaking through their crests, and crashing down their other sides.

David put on his full foul-weather suit and climbed out into the torrent, in the pitch of night, to set about heaving to for the fourth time. "C'mon, goddamn it!" he yelled, harnessed in the cockpit, yanking on the genoa's reefing line. When he returned below he announced the genoa wouldn't furl entirely; something was sticking.

"Now even our pets' heads are falling off," I said, forcing a smile. He grimaced.

"It's another line from *Dumb and Dumber*," I explained feebly.

"There's stress on the forestay. Sue, we could lose the roller furling," he said.

We lay awake listening to the sail snap, the generator squeal, the wind roar.

When the sky went from black to charcoal grey, David looked at his watch. "It's three thirty. It'll be twilight soon. Let's go."

We raised the storm sail and set up the heavy-duty wind vane. With the genoa luffing, *Inia* proceeded on a downwind tack.

"We really should try to get some sleep now," I said.

When we went below, he turned around at the base of the stairs. "I'll be right there. Want to make sure Robert's handling this okay," he said as he headed back out.

I crawled back under the blankets, exhausted, worried. How much were all these repairs going to cost? Could we afford them? Even if we could, did I want to deplete our savings for potentially months more of *this*? Selling in the Azores started to seem like the thing to do.

Then the wind generator went quiet and David cried out "Fuck!" I sprang up from the bed and vaulted out into the rain to find him balancing on the lifelines, stretching out over the roiling seas — no harness, not even his life jacket on — one hand holding on to the boom gallows, the other manically whipping the end of the mizzen halyard about. It had gotten wrapped, many times over, around the blades of the wind generator, and he was determined to undo it.

"Oh my God! Get down from there," I screeched. A massive wave rolled up from astern, *Inia* jerked forward, David teetered, and I began to cry. "Jesus! Now!"

He continued the frenzied lashing until the rope untangled and flew free.

"How could you!" I yelled, hot tears running down my face, as he descended into the cockpit. "You broke our cardinal rules!"

"I know," he said, retying the halyard to the cleat on the mizzen-mast. "And I shouldn't have. I'm sorry."

"Look at it out here, you stupid jerk! If you had fallen overboard I wouldn't have had a hope in hell of even finding you!"

"It was a mistake."

"And, almost as horrifying, I'd have been left alone out here to fend for myself! I *need* you to be safe," I said, sobbing. "Did that even occur to you? Even for a second?"

He stood there looking dazed, sad, spent.

"Sue, I really don't know what got into me. And I am so, so sorry." He wrapped his arms around me.

We hugged, standing in the cockpit, in the rain, in the dark.

"I love you," I said. "But I don't think I can do this anymore."

"Things will get better. I'm sure of it."

"Let's go to bed."

Before the sun rose, we were burrowed under heavy blankets as *Inia* plowed on.

Late that afternoon, I was awakened by music — Vivaldi's *The Four Seasons* — and the smell of mac cheese. Rays of brilliant sunshine were beaming down through the companionway.

"Rise and shine!" David said, holding plates covered in neon-orange mounds with canned grey-green asparagus spears on the side.

The temporary patch on the engine had held; the house batteries were recharged, so was the laptop; the wind had settled to a force 4 from the southwest; and the seas had calmed right down. *Inia* was now sailing a lovely broad reach under full canvas, pointed right to the Azores.

"I said to myself, what the hay!" David said about the CD-playing extravagance. We climbed out the companionway with our meals.

"Wow," I looked around as *Inia* soared through the sparkling ocean and the orchestra played on. "It's like we're in heaven — mac cheese aside," I joked. "No, actually, mac cheese included. I love it, to be honest. This, right here, right now, is what I imagine heaven to be like!"

July 13, the favourable weather continued. *Inia* did 140 nautical miles in twenty-four hours, her best day yet. In light of this progress, we decided to continue to our original destination, the island of Faial, now only 300 nautical miles away.

July 14 marked three weeks out. It became overcast and choppy, but I didn't care. We were getting close. I wrote to tell the world so.

> Next time I write, it'll be from a nice internet café. I'll be clean and warm and dry and still, and sipping something cool.

We hove to from 1600 to 2000 to rest up for our final push.

July 15, 0630, with 71 nautical miles to go, I emailed Cameron and Leslie.

> Although we will likely be in the area tonight, it'll probably be too late to come in. If so, we will stay out on the water until dawn.

They were in a hotel near the harbour and planned to move aboard when we arrived. I looked around, shocked at how lax my housekeeping standards had become. With spaghetti sauce, burnt cheese, and grains of rice baked onto the stove top; globs of toothpaste-spit in the sink; dirty rags, underwear, and damp towels piled in the corner of the head; and splashes of pee dried on its floor, our home wasn't ready for overnight guests!

Still in David's large T-shirt that I wore as a nightie, I began collecting garbage to be disposed of on land.

"Sue, you gotta see this," David yelled.

Ahead were fifteen to twenty dolphins dancing in a circle, with as many seabirds swooping above them, all yacking and laughing. I put on my life jacket over the T-shirt and went to the bow to watch. It felt like a surprise party and we were the guests of honour.

Then we spotted a boat sailing along, a pleasure boat just like ours, and we knew we were almost there.

With four large bags — two of garbage, two of laundry — stacked in the V-berth, I washed the cabin floors, wiped down the galley and the head, and sprayed Febreze on all the upholstery to give at least the illusion of freshness.

In an attempt to make ourselves look civilized, too, David filled our biggest pot with water and tied it to a burner to heat.

"Dear, that's a lot of water," I remarked.

"It just occurred to me I never had to switch the valve over. We're still on the first tank."

"The first tank?"

"The first tank."

"Over three weeks on less than thirty-eight gallons?"

"Well, we've had soups, and some rainwater, but essentially, yeah."

His skin was tight on his cheekbones. I had felt a constant pastiness in my mouth and had tasted a constant tinniness. Then there was the darkness of our urine. In our obsession to conserve, we had needlessly become dehydrated.

"Good God!" I filled two large glasses with water and stirred in powdered iced tea. "Here, drink up!"

When he stripped to wash, I was taken aback by his twig-like limbs and protruding ribs. He had shed twenty pounds at least.

I went to get clean clothes for us each to change into. There weren't any. Every article of clothing in the V-berth cupboards was saturated. Salt water from the all-too-frequent breaking waves had found its way in.

"Cameron and Leslie will be thanking their lucky stars when they see us," I said, the two of us putting our smelly clothes back on.

"Why's that?" David said.

"Well, we look like —"

"Like we've been at sea?"

"Yeah, but for ten years."

"A year, two at most." David smiled and went on deck.

I turned on the fridge and put the bottle of Dom Pérignon in to chill for our arrival. Although we wouldn't have technically crossed an ocean, we would have done an ocean crossing. "Same diff," I tried to tell myself.

Then I joined David outside with a can of almonds and two more iced teas, and we started to look for land.

After sunset, yet another low-pressure system rolled in.

"What the hell happened to the Azores high?" David sighed. "We're supposed to have sun and a *lack* of wind around here!"

By dawn our distance made good was a paltry 12 nautical miles. Because of rain, visibility was reduced, so we kept our navigation lights on — the radar, too — and donned our foul-weather gear.

At 0930, when I was below checking the screen, David hollered, "Land ho!"

"'Land ho,' really?" I rushed back up, giggling. "I mean, are you really supposed to say *land ho*?"

"Who knows, but I've been practising it for forty years," David said, laughing, too. "So could you indulge me? Please? Just this once?"

Like a mirage in the haze, a grey thickness appeared then vanished. But it appeared again and again, each time a little darker, for a little longer, until it became solid, clear, permanent, and very real. It was the island of Faial.

I wiped away tears and steadied my hands as I typed an update to Cameron and Leslie.

> Subject: I should have known better!
> After I wrote yesterday a strong easterly wind (and rain) developed. So we had to tack through the night and made very little progress. At least we didn't go backwards!
>
> We still have about 20 miles to go. We are motoring at about 5 knots and the engine is co-operating at the moment. If all continues to go well we should be there in about four hours from now. If we're late, don't worry.
>
> See you soon.
>
> Sue
> PS We can see Faial clearly now and have got to say it's a welcome sight.

The uniform greyness slowly transformed into a three-dimensional landscape of rust and black volcanic peaks, rolling hills of green, skinny ribbons of road with speck-like cars flitting along them.

Cameron replied:

> Glad you have Faial in sight. We're keeping a
> lookout. Have a small fresh snack, bottle of wine,
> and a gift we promised to deliver on landfall. See
> you sometime later today. Will risk all and go
> ahead with dinner reservations tonight. Hope
> you are with us!!

Around a point of land, along the water's edge, was a charming European village with clusters of whitewashed buildings with ornate iron balconies and terracotta roofs. Beyond two breakwaters, large yacht basins appeared, one on either side of us, both brimming with sailboats of every size and state of wear, flying flags of every colour, many rafted three deep. This was Horta, famous Horta, the most-visited port by ocean sailors from around the world. And straight ahead on its main pier were our good friends Cameron and Leslie, ready and waiting to catch our dock lines a universe away from home.

SIXTEEN

I JUMPED ASHORE, still wearing my puffy red overalls.

"Whooaah," I said, landing on the dock like a drunk tossed out of a bar. David followed, catching his toe and lunging toward me, looking similarly loaded. We swayed as Leslie snapped our pictures, then bobbed and lurched our way to the customs office.

"*Bom dia!*" David said to the customs official.

"Port of origin?" the uniformed man said, his eyes and hands on his keyboard's home row.

"*Nós* … uh … *nós estamos* … no, wait, wait … *somos* —"

"Canada," I said.

David continued. "Yes. *Somos do Can—*"

"Boat registration, please," the official said.

"Certainly." David unzipped the document case and handed the man the papers. "I mean, *com certeza!*" He smiled over his shoulder at Cameron and Leslie.

Back out on the docks, Leslie commented, "Hey, Dave, you're not bad!"

"Been practising," he said. "Locals appreciate it when tourists make an effort."

"We shall certainly see," I said, and we all laughed.

Then Cameron and Leslie headed off to check out of their hotel, and David and I reboarded *Inia* and motored her through the crowded marina to our assigned spot, rafted against a forty-five-foot steel sloop from France moored on a breakwater pier.

After climbing across our neighbour's bow with sacks of laundry and toiletry cases, David and I walked to the marina facilities, scanning the crazy quilt of graffiti that covered every inch of the dock and breakwater wall. Boat names and country flags, primitive sketches and sophisticated works of art, sailing quotes galore.

Land is for Boats to Visit.

Rough Seas make good Sailors.

It's a Sailor's Life for Me.

"They say it's bad luck to cast off from here without leaving your mark," David said.

"Hmmm," I said, still privately questioning the whole "casting off from here" idea.

After the laundromat monitor scheduled our turn with the machines, we went for showers. The women's shower room was pleasant, a hint of lavender in its bright, steamy air. I stripped, stepped into a stall, and let the soothing spray beat down on my head, my face, and my body, surprisingly now lean and toned. Then I washed, slowly circled to rinse, and circled some more.

As I re-emerged onto the patio, a warm, gentle breeze blew my fluffy hair, caressed my tingly skin. David was leaning against the breakwater, waiting for me.

"You look all shiny and new," I remarked.

"I feel it," he replied. "I can't remember feeling in better shape."

"Me neither!" Looking around, I saw we weren't alone. The wiry physiques of the sailors up and down the docks suggested that ocean sailing was a physically healthy endeavour. "Wanna get fit without even trying? Then the North Atlantic Method's for you!" I said, smiling.

Cameron and Leslie arrived at *Inia* with their luggage, a grocery bag, and two boxes for us. "You were gone, but not forgotten!" Leslie said, handing David the big box full of mail. "And this is from your cousin Mike," she said, giving me the smaller, gift-wrapped one. "He went out of his way to make sure we got this to you."

We opened the parcels in the cockpit while they went below to organize their space.

"Same ol', same ol'." David sighed, setting aside the three months of bank statements, bill payment summaries, and once-in-a-lifetime offers.

"That Mike's such a sweetheart. He sent us a care package," I said. "There's money here, euros, to enjoy our stopover."

"Seems he's also psychic," David said, chuckling.

"I know! And a bottle of rum, our rations on the high seas, as he put it."

"Aarrrrgh!"

"Look, a plaque of Saint Christopher, too."

"Saint who?"

"He's patron saint of travellers. Mike had it specially blessed. We'll have to mount it ... that's *if* we ... no, never mind."

Cameron and Leslie joined us in the cockpit with a hodge-podge of hard Azorean cheese, spicy sausage, crackers, grapes, and pickles. I unwrapped the pewter wine goblets and brought out the champagne we had been given as a going-away present by my family. We hooted festively watching David pop the cork and the champagne bubble over. The sun sparkled on us as we toasted the crossing, landfall, the sudden improvement in the weather, each other, and life.

After dark the four of us walked to a waterfront restaurant for dinner and were seated at a window table with a gorgeous view of the lamp-lit marina and the black ocean beyond. The waiter brought out a plate of olives marinated in oil, chopped parsley, and garlic, with a basket of crusty bread. David requested *uma garrafa de vinho tinto*. Cameron and I ordered Portuguese steak with peppercorn sauce; the others, *bacalhau*, cod, lightly floured.

"So, how was it? Really, what was it like?" Cameron said, spooning olives onto his plate.

"Amazing," David said.

"Wild," I answered at the same time. "Don't get me wrong. Yes, there were amazing parts, lots of them, and I'm glad to have had the experience. But it was wild, wilder than ever I imagined it could be."

"We saw dolphins and seabirds and whales, beautiful sunrises."

"You'll have to excuse him. His memory's shot to hell, salt water on the brain," I said, laughing. "Dear, tell them about the head, the mizzen, the genoa."

"No question, we did have a few problems, but —"

"Cameron, knowing what I now know, I believe it worked out for the best for you guys, honestly."

"But there was nothing we couldn't handle. And *Inia* was fantastic, a real pro out there."

"True, all true. Nevertheless, we're rethinking the year ahead," I said. "We might stop here. Depending on what the repairs cost, we might have to. If not here, then Portugal. Or maybe we'll take *Inia* into the Med. In any event, there's no way I want to cross back over. I mean, what's the point?"

"For the experience," Cameron said, dipping bread into olive oil.

"None of us wants to be in calm waters all our lives," Leslie said, putting an olive pit on the edge of her plate.

If I was hoping for understanding and support, I was sitting at the wrong table. Rather than relief that our joint venture was scuttled, there was unmistakable disappointment on Cameron and Leslie's faces, and David was more eager to carry on than ever.

"What's with you people?" I said. "Correct me if I'm wrong, but I don't think gale-force winds are on Maslow's hierarchy of needs."

"How's the steak?" David asked Cameron.

"Excellent," Cameron said. "And the fish?"

"Wonderful!" Leslie said.

"A bit salty, but great," David said.

"Just to be clear, *I'm* the one who's normal here," I said.

The next morning — and it was morning — the marina patio was packed with sailors from around the globe sitting under red umbrellas at the white plastic tables, drinking beer. David and I joined them.

Andy, Paul, and Thomas, three buddies, were heading to the Caribbean from England. Harold, an eighty-two-year-old guy, recently widowed, had bought a Cape Dory in the States and, with the help of paid crew, was delivering it to his home in Spain. Jason, a quirky Australian, was wandering the world's oceans alone. Marcel, a fellow Canadian, was on his way to Portugal from Nova Scotia, his fourth time in fifteen years — this time, though, with his twenty-something-year-old daughter. They had arrived in Horta the day before us.

"How was your crossing?" David asked him.

"Terrible!" Marcel responded. "Nothing like the others. Wouldn't you know it! I talk my ex into letting my daughter come with me and we get freak weather. Storm, storm, calm, goddamn storm."

"Us, too!" David said. "We crossed above forty-one and got hammered."

"With the same bloody series of lows!" I said to Marcel.

"It took us nineteen friggin' days," Marcel added.

"Don't feel bad, it took us twenty-three," I said.

"No shit!"

"Yup! Twenty-three," I repeated louder, leaning back in my chair, my chest expanding. "And speaking of shit, you'll never guess what happened." I launched into the head saga with gratuitous detail.

Everyone within earshot howled with laughter.

As stories continued to fly back and forth among us and these seafaring men, it became evident that both the weather and the equipment failures David and I had experienced were atypical. Our inaugural crossing was a baptism by fire by everyone's standards. But, I had to admit, we weren't harmed by it. On the contrary. We *did* handle everything that came our way, discovering strengths we didn't know we had. And with only each other to rely on, we experienced respect and love and trust and true partnership, unlike ever before. I grew. We grew together.

As I listened to the ongoing banter, I felt a surprising bond with these windswept strangers on the patio. We shared a deep understanding of the vastness of ocean and sky; of the many moods of Mother Nature, her calms and tantrums, her brooding silences and mind-blowing screams; of the ever-changing landscapes of water, from gentle meadows to forbidding mountain peaks; of experiencing the highest of highs and lowest of lows, the joy of solitude and the melancholy of being alone; of feeling in control of one's world one instant and at the mercy of the gods the next; of feeling ever present, in the moment, fully alive — an understanding you could only acquire through being "out there." Then it occurred to me: David and I were no longer just an accountant dad and an occupational therapist mom on a boat. We had become blue-water sailors, too. I was sitting among my peers. And I welled with pride at the thought.

Still, though …

When Cameron came over to the patio, David and I were describing the merits of heaving to to the others.

"It's a lifesaver, really," I said to Harold and his crew as I stood to leave. "You guys should try it!"

On the walk back to *Inia*, Cameron grinned. "That's the point. That's why people do these things." He added, "That's why you'll go again."

"Ol' Salt Sue," David teased. "I believe you even said the S-H-word."

"You two can be so annoying!" I said, giving David another whack.

Ⴐ

After a breakfast of custard tarts, *pastéis de nata*, and coffee at a dark, smoky café, we found Mid Atlantic Yacht Services, where we arranged for a sailmaker to repair the clew of the genoa, scheduled a visit by a diesel mechanic to address our cooling system problem, bought new jib sheets to replace the chafed ones, and, discovering the electronics men in Whitby hadn't wired *Inia* for shore power in the Azores or Europe, dropped another unexpected five hundred dollars for a step-down transformer. Then the guys went back to *Inia* with the purchases and Leslie and I hit the grocery store, stocking up on staples, snacks, and exotic ingredients for special meals during their stay.

Following a delicious dinner of piri-piri chicken, rice, and Cobb salad, Cameron and Leslie cleaned up the galley while David and I walked to the main pier, bought a long-distance calling card, and took turns phoning family at an outdoor booth. We finally made it, believe it or not, we're fine, storms and all, but yes, we're thrilled to be on terra firma, we said, to universal sighs of relief and congratulations.

Brian said summer had come late to Victoria, but it was really nice out now. Better late than never, I said. Yeah, he said. And he had just watched a video, of "Canon in D," and wondered if we had seen it. Nope, we hadn't been watching music videos, I said. He was certain we'd love it and would send it as soon as he hung up.

John didn't have much to report, either, other than that the Hillside Festival was less than two weeks away, and he was counting down the days.

"I guess that's everyone for now," I said, closing up our address book, thinking of Ben and hearing my friend Charna's voice: *time and space*. I added *patience and faith* to the mantra.

David said there was one other person on his list, his seventy-nine-year-old aunt in Portland. I leaned against the phone booth while he made the call. Chin quivering, he left her a message: "Hi, Aunt Caroline. We've landed at Horta in the Azores. Came in yesterday, July sixteenth, and today's the seventeenth. It's now eleven p.m. Horta time, which is the same as Greenwich, and Sue and I are fine. We have rested overnight and have got ourselves oriented in town today, doing just fine. Had a very interesting crossing, not necessarily easy, but interesting, and in some respects very rewarding. Both Sue and I are proud to have made it, and are feeling very good. Anyway, I thought I'd give you a call.… We love you. I love you. The sailing stuff came from you, and, uh, we've completed the first part of our big adventure. Okay, bye for now."

Over the next week we explored Horta's narrow winding cobblestone streets, secluded beaches, and volcanic peaks with our
friends, stopping each afternoon for a beer and marinated olives,
or *cerveja* and *azeitonas,* as David insisted on calling them to the
busy waiters. With the temperature consistently in the low twenties and the pace slow, it was a perfect place to recharge our
personal batteries.

Within a day or two, the trials at sea had dimmed, as had
my reticence to do the passage to Portugal. While Cameron and
Leslie went to an internet café, David and I stood at the breakwater, looking at boats heading off for different ports of call
around the world.

"I guess we'll need to get painting," I said.

"I'll go get the stuff." David scurried off before I could say
another word.

By the time he returned with cans of boat paint, brushes,
rags, and Varsol, I had found a small faded spot on the wall. He
knelt on the ledge in front of it and went right to work.

"What's that?" I said, looking at the irregular beige shape he
had slapped on.

"The background," he said. "You need a background."

"So … and … what'll we put on it?" I asked, holding a brush
and can, glancing over at the team of eager-beaver artists beside us.

"It has to dry overnight."

"And then? You have no idea, right?" I said. "Shouldn't we
have designed the thing first? God, now we've got this beige blob
that we have to make sense of."

He closed the can of paint.

"Looks great," I said to our neighbours as we walked around
their masterpiece in progress, adding, "Ours has to dry overnight."

The next day we stared at the blob for an inordinate amount of time.

"Okay, all right," I finally said, timidly painting a few black wavy lines. "That's the ocean."

David painted a stick sailboat on top of the waves for *Inia*.

Using the boot stripe paint, I made a big red sun on the horizon. "For brighter sailing ahead."

Then David filled the awkward top left space with a tiny Canadian flag and the year 2007, and wrote "Guelph, Gaspé, Azores ..." along the bottom. "Ta da! Done!" he said.

After gathering the painting supplies, we stood back to look at the result. Just then Cameron and Leslie walked up the dock.

"Great job," Cameron said. "But ... uh ... isn't Guelph landlocked?"

"We portaged," David said, and we all chuckled.

"It's fantastic!" Leslie said.

"For a six-year-old," I said. "Nevertheless, somehow, I do feel luckier."

On July 24, Cameron and Leslie flew to Lisbon for their connecting flight to Canada.

We stayed put in Horta to deal with the remaining essential boat issues and to provision for our 150-nautical-mile jaunt to São Miguel. During this time we met our new dock neighbours, Gjialt and Carrina. The German couple, both about our age, had retired from the oil industry and had just finished a two-year sailing trip in the South Pacific. He was studying for his European captain's papers so that he could do boat deliveries and asked David for help to prepare for his upcoming exam on celestial navigation. In exchange, Gjialt went up our mast using his mountain-climbing gear and installed a bracket that altered the angle between the halyard and headsail, which solved the furling problem.

Then the diesel mechanic came by. He said that, short of replacing the whole cooling system unit, David's patch was the next best fix and what he would've recommended considering the age of the engine.

I could've kissed them both!

By the 26th the marina crowd had thinned. Most boats heading to northern Europe had already taken off to beat the impending storm season along that coast.

Inia was back in shape; our cupboards and fridge were restocked. We were technically ready to go, too. However, David said that the jet stream had dropped south and there were gales to the north, so maybe we should wait a few days to let things pass before heading out. I concurred, even though we were going east. The truth was, we needed a bit more time. Departure was as much about mental preparedness as anything else.

Over the next few days we picnicked at the beach, listened to music in the park, and exchanged embellished stories and belly laughs with another couple of stragglers, American Marlboro-Man Carl and his Canadian wife, Kate, a pixie fifteen years his junior. After taking an early retirement, Carl had set sail alone from Seattle in his unadorned Tartan 34. He met Kate in South Africa. He liked to say he had to go halfway around the world to find the love of his life. They had been living aboard the Tartan, sometimes sailing, sometimes not, ever since.

July 30, David and I woke up and decided this was the day to go.

Gjialt, Carrina, Carl, and Kate all came over to see us off. "Here, take this." Carl handed me a book.

"Great, I think," I said, showing the others that it was a troubleshooting guide for every obscure problem one could possibly encounter at sea.

"But, after such a rough first crossing, you're bound to have smooth sailing ahead," Carrina said while the men undid our dock lines.

"Oh, absolutely," Kate chimed in.

"You guys are right," I replied, now believing it, too. "But if we ever come down with a skin rash from swimming with snails, I'll now know what to do." I laughed as the men gave us a shove off.

~~~

Weather continued to be atypical. David helmed and I moaned and vomited the entire thirty-hour rock-'n'-roll passage to São Miguel.

Ponta Delgada, the capital of the Azores, was more urban than Horta, with a waterfront of modern hotels, high-rises, malls, movie theatres, supermarkets, speedways, and construction crews with sky-scraping cranes building more.

We were again initially rafted to another boat. This time, though, it was a hundred-foot Swiss yacht with paid staff barking at us to take off our shoes before scaling its massive freeboard and sliding across its polished mahogany deck. At check-in, we were relieved to hear a transient vessel had just left, so they were able to give us a dock of our own.

"I know, I know," I yelled over the jackhammers, while David and I undid our shoelaces to cross back over to reboard *Inia* so we could move her.

As we approached our assigned slip, a shirtless man with a thick gold chain around his neck and designer sunglasses perched on his gelled head jumped off the adjacent boat, a Beneteau 37.

"You should dock stern in," he said, catching the bow and spring lines.

"And you should fuck off," David muttered, dog tired, squeezing *Inia* into the tight space.

After tying *Inia* down, we went below and slept until morning.

∿

After a breakfast onboard of yoghurt with chopped bananas and mangoes, David set about recaulking the chain plates and I carried our anchor onto the dock to paint it white so that we could see it in the murky rivers of southern Portugal.

"Great, here comes more advice," I said, as a skinny young guy with fine blond hair and angular features sauntered toward us.

"Nice boat!" He had an eastern European accent. "What kind is it?

"It's an Alberg," David said.

"You sail?" I asked him.

"Been at it for seven years now. That's our boat there." He pointed to a bare-bones twenty-seven-footer. A delicate woman with long almost-white hair stood in its cockpit.

"I'm Nick. That's my girlfriend, Dagmara." She smiled sweetly and waved. "We're from Poland. She doesn't speak English," he explained.

"We're Dave and Sue," I said, standing up and waving back to her.

Nick walked back and forth alongside *Inia*. "Full keeled?" he asked.

"Yeah, she's an ocean-goer," David said.

"Nice. Very nice. You sailed her across from Canada?"

"We did," I said, stretching my lower back. "Twenty-three *looong* days on the stormy North Atlantic," I slipped in unnecessarily. "How 'bout you guys? Where've you been?"

"Let's see, Australia, South Africa, Venezuela, the Caribbean, pretty much everywhere *but* Canada," he said.

"Wow." I felt myself slump. "I guess you've had a few longish passages, too."

"A few. Our longest was seventy-two days."

"Geez Louise!" I said, duly chastened.

"Seventy-two days!" David said. "What kinda trouble —?"

"No trouble. It was by choice," Nick explained. "When we got to the Galapagos, neither of us wanted to put in. Since we had enough food and water, we just kept going."

I looked at him, his wisp of a mate, his tiny boat. "But you seem so —"

"Normal?" he said with a hardy laugh.

"Yeah, I guess that's —"

"Dag and I love passage-making," he said, and I could see he meant it.

We stayed in Ponta Delgada for a week to reseal the hatches, paint the lock boards, and fix the port gate, during which we enjoyed daily chats with Nick. He was charming, funny, and a wealth of information about our potential sailing options ahead — as well as completely normal.

During our stay we also found the real heart of the city. A few blocks inland, in the historic core, was a town square abuzz with musicians belting out fado tunes on a gaudy bandstand, teenagers competing in high-stakes foosball matches, and streams of people weaving through the artisan booths and sizzling food stands around the periphery, in the midst of which David planted himself and attempted to speak Portuguese to anyone who looked at him sideways.

"Did you hear what the guy just said to me?" he said, yanking me out of the pedestrian traffic. "He said *Brasil*! That's the problem! I've been studying *Brazilian* Portuguese."

"Dear, I really doubt he thought you were from —"

"That's it! I can hear the difference. The Portuguese here is clipped, less melodic."

David was disappointed, but undeterred. We headed straight for the waterfront mall. While he went off in search of material to learn continental Portuguese, I made calls to family from a pay phone in the atrium.

He returned carrying a bookstore bag. "Success! Found a great handbook of travel phrases and a better dictionary. Oh, and I picked up a paperback," he said. "What's wrong?"

"Everything!" I said.

Everyone had unsettling news. My mom thought she might have had a heart attack during the night. No, she didn't call anyone for help. No, she didn't tell my brothers or any of her friends either. Why? She didn't know. Yes, she'd make an appointment to see her doctor, not to worry. Brian said his new job was more assembly-line work than carpentry. And his co-workers boxed for fun. He speculated, half laughing, that they punched each other in the head so that they could hang in there 'cause you'd have to be brain-dead to do this job for long. In any event, he was back to reading the want ads, but he'd stay until something better came along. No need to worry. And Hillside was, in a word, disastrous. John and his girlfriend split up over the festival weekend. He was sad but okay. I needn't worry.

I couldn't help but worry. About the only damned thing I could do was worry. I was certain there were other problems I'd worry about, if only I knew of them.

"It *is* all unsettling news," David acknowledged. "But being in Guelph wouldn't have prevented any of it." He reminded me that, no matter where we were, we couldn't protect my mom and the boys from life any more than they could us, nor solve their problems any more than they could solve ours. *Accept the things you cannot change, change the things you can, so on and so forth, blah, blah, blah!*

After dinner I curled up in my usual reading spot under a port cabin light with *Oryx and Crake*, and David got cozy in his corner with his new paperback. He was totally engrossed, as if it were a John Grisham novel, only it wasn't. It was *Winnie-the-Pooh*, in Portuguese. The colourful cover was a picture of Pooh Bear carrying packets of seed, Tigger holding a hoe, and Eeyore a bucket of water, all of them standing on soil between tilled rows and planted carrots. *Vamos Criar … Um Jardim!* was the title.

"So, what's the *plot?*" I asked, as a joke.

"Not sure. I think it's about gardening. The suspense is killing me!" he replied, his eyes glued to the page.

August 7 was bright and sunny. With our preparations all done, it was time to be on our way.

I phoned my mom and the boys to let them know. My mom reported she'd seen her doctor and it had been a false alarm. And she promised she'd call someone for help if there was a next time. Brian said he was looking into doing bike tours around Victoria. Tourism was big there. And it'd be cool to be paid for doing something he loved. And John said the band just had another fantastic show. People were up dancing like mad. Someone videotaped the whole thing and posted it online. He'd send us the link. David was right. Barring an emergency, there was no reason for us to be home.

He emailed everyone else about our departure.

One of the challenges of being ashore is to get up the inertia to cast off the dock lines for the next passage. Daily life in the harbour is pretty nice. We have had a great week in Ponta Delgada, but the time has come for us to depart again. The weather looks reasonable. We are heading for Cascais Portugal today. It will be about an eight-day crossing.

Last minute, I hammered the Saint Christopher plaque to the wall of our nav station.

"They say, 'Look at Saint Christopher and go on reassured.'" I stood back and studied the image of the robed man above our marine radio. David looked at it, then at me.

"Oh, be quiet. It can't hurt," I said.

SEVENTEEN

ON AUGUST 7, at 1430, we backed *Inia* out of her slip and turned her toward the open sea of the North Atlantic. Nick and Dagmara stood at the end of the pier.

"*Yeehaw!*" Nick yelled, madly waving goodbye.

His exuberance almost matched mine. Next stop, mainland Portugal. Somebody pinch me!

Although Cascais was our intended port of call, we pointed *Inia* higher to compensate for the south-setting current. In a matter of hours she was clipping along, a broad reach under full sail. As we took in São Miguel's shrinking sunlit shoreline to our north and west, a black line of clouds slyly gathered to the south and east.

"Gotta head back, and fast," I said, pointing out this ominous formation.

David glanced over his shoulder. "That's the absolute worst thing to do. Sea room's what we need."

We reduced sail, hove to, and scurried below. As soon as the companionway door closed, a whistling blow and driving rain hit, sweat beaded on my forehead, and a squall erupted in the pit of my stomach.

"The forecast was fine. We double and triple checked," I said, curled over a pail secured between my knees on the main berth, throwing up bits of orange in slimy gastric juices.

With his feet braced against the nav station bulkhead, David studied weather data on the laptop. A new marine bulletin was warning that cyclonic activity was moving into the vicinity of the Azores and advising all vessels to remain in port.

"Cyclonic activity? You're saying we're in a cyclone?" I lifted my head out of the sour fumes. "Is that not a hurricane?"

"I meant *extra*-cyclonic activity. So —"

"Like in *The Perfect Storm*?" I said, as *Inia* plummeted from the crest of a wave like an elevator in free fall and the salt shaker whizzed by my ear.

"Well, not necessarily."

"Not necessarily?" I retched again and flopped prone on the bed.

After several hours the histrionics ceased. The system moved on as quickly as it had come.

"Come to bed," I said, woozy.

"Soon. I promise."

As *Inia* carried on in lighter winds, I writhed on the main berth under blankets damp with perspiration and, watching David flit between resetting the wind vane and scanning the horizon, I drifted back off into a very deep sleep.

August 9, the third day out, I finally resurfaced. Fresh air was due.

"You look almost human again," David said, standing at the helm, a dry half-eaten ham sandwich on the lazarette.

"Ever beautiful out!"

"Other than the lack of wind. We're into a massive high-pressure system. Unfortunately, that means motoring."

"How're we doing?"

"Only about 200 nautical miles so far," he said. "Hey, look, we've got company again." He pointed to a pod of frisky dolphins bounding toward us on our starboard side. "They're happy you're on the mend, too."

Our ocean friends continued to frolic alongside *Inia* until one jumped clear out of the water and did a final bow, after which they turned en masse and disappeared into the sparkling horizon.

We moved along, listening to the hum of the engine and the trickling of the gentle seas. Then *Inia* lurched to a stop with a high-pitched squeal and a clamorous clatter below decks.

"What the hell …?" I scanned the clear blue sky and placid ocean in search of an answer in the eerie silence that followed.

"Whatever it was, it yanked the wheel right out of my hands," David said. He turned off the engine and headed below to investigate. "The transmission's searing to the touch," he reported as he climbed back out. He circled the deck, looking down beyond the gunwales. "I don't see anything," he said. He tried to turn the wheel again; it wouldn't budge. "Something's definitely fouled our rudder and prop." He returned below and tossed our mesh bag of snorkelling gear up into the cockpit.

"You can't be serious," I said, through the companionway. "You can't just hold your breath!" He climbed back into the cockpit wearing only shorts, and I told him he'd freeze. When he proceeded to put the mask on his head, I reminded him that *Inia* was ten tons and that the prop was underneath her. He flinched and worked his toes into the flippers.

"Believe me, this is the very last thing I feel like doing!" he said. "But we simply can't be without steerage." He tied one end of a rope around his waist and the other to a cleat. "This is so we won't get separated. I need you to haul me up when I give you the signal. The ladder's loose, so hold on to it. All right?"

"All right."

"Ready?"

"Ready as I'll ever be."

He secured the mask over his eyes and nose, descended the ladder, and pushed off. After treading water for a moment to get his bearings, he inhaled and disappeared into the opaque depths.

As *Inia* bounced along in the ocean current, I sat at the gate, gripping the ladder uprights, swallowing the queasiness.

No one back home has any idea. They're going about their busy days. I guess that's good. After all, if they knew, what could they do to help? Not a thing. That's the harsh reality. David and I are so damned alone. It's truly just him and me in the middle of the ocean, a flimsy rope keeping us together. Unbelievable!

David loathes ocean swimming at the best of times. He says the pretty little fish around corals reefs are food for sharks, ipso facto, so are the snorkellers. Ipso facto, that's his favourite part. I love his goofiness! And he's convinced the open ocean is full of their bigger, hungrier relatives skulking in the shadows, waiting to eat him alive.

He could've called a mayday. Others would have under the circum-stance. But no. Here he is, underwater, all by himself, in the bloody North Atlantic. Why? Because the safety of his vessel and the welfare of his crew are at risk. Inia and I are in the hands of a consummate blue-water captain. Good God! The line is still slack!

Then his goggled eyes rose up. I pulled the rope hand over hand while he groped aimlessly until he hit the ladder's bottom rung. Dangling half in the water, coughing and sputtering, he blurted that we had snagged a massive rogue fishing net and he needed a knife.

I handed him the Swiss Army knife from the nav station ledge. He pried open the tiny blade, repositioned his mask, and returned to the sea.

When he popped up again he announced, with a hint a hope, that he had cut a thread.

"You're goin' all MacGyver on me," I said.

Once his breathing had settled, back down he went, again and again, more encouraged with each successive dive.

His growing optimism was catching until I spotted a big red blotch on the top of his head. Realizing human blood is a magnet for sharks, I decided not to tell him. Why scare the living bejeepers out of him, likely unnecessarily? No, instead I'd prepare. But how? If I saw one approaching, would I be able to pull him up fast enough? I doubted it.

"It's slow going," he said, resurfacing. "One strand at a time."

"Persistence should be your middle name."

What to do? Can sharks hear? Would screaming like a banshee scare one off? I doubt that, too. Maybe I could stab it in the eye with our butcher knife, or whack it with the boat hook. Exactly what kind of force is needed to bludgeon a shark to death? I wondered as I continued to lift and lower him, relieved he was still alone and intact each time he came back into view.

Close to an hour after snagging the net, David exploded out of the water's surface shouting, "It's gone! It's over! We're free!"

"Thank the Lord!" I said, this time pulling him all the way up.

As he approached the top of the ladder I saw that the head blotch wasn't blood after all. It was red bottom paint. "Looks like your skull met up with *Inia's* hull down there."

"Might have, didn't notice." He clambered aboard and kicked off his flippers. "Too scared to."

We hugged and watched the loosely woven amorphous mass float up and away. "That took enormous courage," I said.

"To tell you the truth, I've never been more scared in all my life."

"I know."

When David went down to have a better look at the engine, he didn't come back up.

I found him lying motionless on his side in the narrow quarter berth with his head buried in the engine compartment, muttering to himself.

"Dear, if there is one thing you can't do aboard *Inia*, it's hide," I said, tapping one of his legs. "What's wrong?"

He shimmied out, sat up, and took a few long deep breaths.

"What is it? We're in this together. You need to tell me — everything."

"Okay … well … here's the situation. The engine's off its mounts and the propeller shaft's now out of the gear box. So we no longer have propulsion. And if it moves out any farther, the prop'll block the rudder. I clamped rubber around the shaft to prevent that from happening. But if it doesn't work, we could lose steerage, too."

"Oh, honey, why wouldn't it —"

"And … we're taking on water."

"We're what?!"

"It's a thin steady stream from the stuffing box," he said, as the electric bilge pump began to hum.

"How can this be happening to us? We've more than paid our dues. Everyone said so."

"I'm going to try to stem the flow. Write down how often the bilge light goes on." He slid back into the cubby hole head first.

I stared at the indicator light and contemplated the complete unfairness of the cosmos while David tried putty and various tapes and silicone, all without success.

"The pump went on again after about forty-five minutes," I reported when he wriggled out.

"Good. Looks like it might be all we need. If not, we've got the two manual pumps."

"But what if —"

"If worst comes to worst, we throw the life raft over and climb in."

Conventional sailing wisdom is that one should get into a life raft by stepping up — *up* being the operative word. In other words, abandon ship only if it's sinking.

I soberly gathered everything we'd need for that worst-case scenario: our EPIRB, our ditch bag, our watertight container of boat documents, a pen, a notepad, emergency contacts, and our foul-weather gear. I lined them up along the main salon, within easy reach.

David went over the life raft deployment procedure and how to call a mayday, reminding me to press the Man-Overboard button to get our exact "lat and long."

"The EPIRB's built-in GPS would track the life raft after that," he explained. "Sue, I honestly didn't expect —"

"It's not your fault," I said. "And we're as prepared as we can be, thanks to you. There's comfort in that."

We climbed up the companionway stairs. To our delight there were ripples on the water. We raised the sails and turned *Inia* around.

"If this breeze continues, we should be back in São Miguel in two, maybe three days," David said.

"Then ... why not keep going to Portugal?"

"Sweetie, it's triple the distance."

"As long as we're floating, going three days in one direction or a few more in another makes no real difference in terms of our safety, right?"

"That's true."

"And Portugal would be a better place to deal with these boat issues."

"You're probably right."

"And we'd likely have more favourable winds going that way. Isn't that so?"

David studied my face, then smiled. "Prepare to come about," he said, reaching for the port jib sheet.

Firming up the starboard jib sheet, I responded, "Ready to come about."

"Coming about!" he declared, turning the wheel hard to starboard.

As *Inia*'s bow crossed through the gentle breeze and her sails slowly refilled, we winched in the lines and cleated them, and continued on east, Portugal bound.

∿

August 10, four days out, with 600 nautical miles to go, the wind again died, and we now had no ability to move without it.

"Do you know what today is?"

"Another damn day of calm." David sighed.

"It's my dad's birthday," I said. "My brother Steve used to say that in times of trouble, my dad could always be counted on to pull a rabbit out of the hat. This might sound hokey, but I feel his spirit with us right now."

"Okay, so, Larry, do your magic. Now's kinda one of those times!" David said, looking skyward. Then he went below, returning minutes later with a book. Since focusing on print still made me queasy, he offered to read aloud.

"That'd be nice," I said. "But *Life of Pi*? Really?"

"What's wrong?"

"Well, you know, it's about being stranded. On a life raft at sea."

"Yeah, but with a *Bengal tiger* and an *orangutan*!"

"I guess," I said.

Story time came to an end when three whales the size of hills paid us a visit and put on a show, breaching, lunging, and slapping the flat seas with their immense flukes.

When the performance ended David made dinner: a one-pot meal of basmati rice, onions, green pepper, chickpeas, and stewed tomatoes, with generous pinches of oregano and hot chilies. "It's fusion. All the rage," he said, handing me up a plastic bowl of the concoction.

"Smells heavenly, and I'm pretty sure it'll stay down now." I blew on a steaming forkful. "And this too shall pass," I added, looking out over the stillness, both of us aware I had no real ability to forecast weather.

David picked at his dinner, hunched over, heavy eyed, then set his almost-full bowl aside. At my insistence, he agreed to take the opportunity to catch up on sleep for when wind returned.

"I hope I can remember the fetal position," he said, opening the main berth.

He can always make me laugh.

Around 2000, a light breeze did develop. I woke David up. He set the sails and the wind vane, then returned to bed. Twenty minutes later, Bobby began to flop about like a fish on land.

I opened the aft hatch and stared down at the stainless-steel wind-vane quadrant, wishing I had the slightest inkling as to what to look for, during which *Inia* drifted into the wind, causing her sails to flail, her hull to bounce, and David to cut short his much-needed sleep.

He climbed into the cockpit, strain on his face.

"I tried to figure it out," I said.

"It's okay," he said, shining a flashlight into the aft hatch. "A control cable's broken," he announced, instructing me to take the helm.

"But I couldn't. I didn't know what to do."

"You were right to wake me up," he said. "Besides, it's a two-person job."

After gathering spare cable and tools, he slid into the trunk-sized lazarette to splice and thread new cable through the self-steering system.

Two hours later he re-emerged and mentioned that he felt tension between his shoulder blades and a throbbing behind his eyes. "It's fixed," he said, taking deep breaths — in through his nose, out through his mouth.

"Please go back to sleep."

"I can't."

"Just try."

"Not now."

"Can I get you anything?"

"Peace of mind would be nice," he said.

That this unrelenting barrage of major issues was taking a toll on him was understandable, but so, too, was it disconcerting. As long as he was able to cope, I felt we'd be okay. But what if he no longer could?

He busied himself studying the chart. I whiled away the night taking pictures of glowing plankton, a tern perched on the bow pulpit illuminated by the running lights, the perfectly trimmed mainsail against the starry sky. We hardly talked.

In the morning twilight, David quietly gathered his sextant, clipboard, and nautical almanac and stepped up onto the lazarette, a stopwatch around his neck. Conditions for sight-taking were ideal. Steadying himself against the boom gallows, he aimed the sextant at various celestial bodies in quick succession, recording their altitudes and the times.

While I was peering through the camera's viewfinder, congratulating myself on my superlative photography skills, he looked up from his sight reduction calculations. "Nailed it," he said with an irrepressible grin. "We're definitely on the Atlantic."

"Phew!" I said, realizing he was back in the saddle.

Throughout the day, Bobby kept us pointed right at Portugal. David and I took turns napping.

Late afternoon I wrote to family. A note was overdue, an explanation deserved.

> Hi from 37 degrees 34 minutes north; 20 degrees 48 minutes west.
>
> Our apologies for not updating you sooner, but we've had a few challenges on this leg to deal with already. David's been busy resolving problems and I had three days of either sleeping or vomiting from a new bout of sea sickness.
>
> We've again had not too great sailing weather.
>
> Our biggest problem was that while we were motoring during a calm on the 9th a huge submerged unmarked fishing net got seriously caught in our prop and wrapped itself around our rudder. So David had to spend about an hour in wavy seas.
>
> Unless we have wind, we can't move. Today there's a nice breeze but calm is forecast.
>
> On a positive note, I'm feeling fine now (the symptoms seem to magically disappear given time), the weather is beautiful, we've been visited by two huge groups of dolphins today

(15–20 at a time), and we saw whales in the distance, surfacing and diving, making spectacular
splashes in the process. It's pretty exciting to see!

We'll keep you posted on our progress, or
lack thereof.

Before pressing send, I erased all mention of taking on water.
That detail would wait until we were back on solid ground.

August 12, six days out, the pump was bailing every half hour.
Inia was crawling along at a snail's pace. Yet I didn't mind. Late
afternoon, David read more of *Life of Pi*. Although I was no
longer sick, I loved the intimacy of being read to. As I lay on my
back watching tufts of fair-weather clouds drift along, I listened
to stories of mid-ocean catastrophes and lifeboat rations with
detached fascination. We'd make landfall someday, I was certain.

David was optimistic, too. He updated family.

> We're doing fine, and … knock on wood … we
> should see good winds (no calms) from here to
> the continent.

August 13, as David had predicted, *Inia* had perfect winds to
make her northing to above Cascais. Anticipating landfall, he
wrote to Fred.

> Do you have any miraculous ideas on how
> we could somehow reconnect the shaft to the

transmission so that we could run forward and reverse, if even just to get into the dock?

Any thoughts would be appreciated. We'll send you a postcard from Portugal.

Thanks very much.

Midmorning, my appetite returned with a vengeance. Fat, fluffly pancakes were in order. While David relaxed outside with a mug of coffee, I whisked together flour, baking powder, salt, and enough milk for a thick but pourable mixture; lit the kerosene stove; oiled the camping skillet; and began production. As I ladled out the last of the batter, the flame fizzled. I divvied up the pancakes, smothering each stack with melting butter and a generous drizzling of real maple syrup. Maybe the flame had always been fickle. No, I would've noticed. If I hadn't primed the pump enough, I wouldn't have been able to cook at all. That wasn't it. And we had enough kerosene to last us to Timbuktu.

David was savouring the pancakes. The weather, the progress, the reprieve from worry — he was enjoying it all. I wished the moment could last.

"Something's funny with the stove," I finally said.

He gulped down his last forkful and went below to have a look.

"The gasket's cracked," he announced. "No big deal. We have plenty of rubber scraps onboard."

For the entire afternoon, he sat at the drop-down table and, with unbelievable patience, cut little circles of thick rubber, thin rubber, and medium-thickness rubber, retesting the kerosene pump with each. None created sufficient seal.

This was, in fact, a very big deal. We could no longer cook.

I reassessed our provisions. There were many stove-dependent ones: dry mixes of sauces and soups, bags of rice, bins of pasta, baking ingredients, frozen meat, eggs, coffee, tea.

Regarding canned goods, I had bought most of our current supply in Horta's supermarket, acting worldly and familiar with foreign cuisine. Reality was, if I liked the picture on the label, into the cart it went. So, when David, with the help of his Portuguese-English dictionary, determined we had a stash of blood sausage and pigs' feet, I was disappointed but not surprised.

"I certainly have no intention of ingesting links of congealed blood or anything's toes, neither hot nor cold," I declared with indignation, deep down suspecting I could be eating the cans' contents, along with my words, in the not-too-distant future.

Early evening, Fred wrote back.

Egads!!!!!
Okay, the only way to get "drive" back will be to remove the burrs and scoring from the coupling & shaft with a fine file and emery cloth.

You will have to reinsert the shaft with a "key" in the keyway & align the dimples with the pinch bolt holes.

Once everything is back together you may have to drill through the shaft & coupling & thru-pin the whole assembly to achieve a solid drive. This may weaken the shaft but it could last a long time. Let me know how it works out. Good luck.

"No shame in getting a tow in," David said, closing up the laptop.

"None whatsoever," I said.

I propped up a couple of fluffy pillows against the cockpit bulkhead and sat out to watch the flaming sun set.

"We've just passed the four-hundred-mile mark. We're half-way," David said, joining me with two glasses of wine, on our otherwise "dry" crossing.

"Cheers to this wonderful adventure!" I said.

The night sky was magnificent: brilliant stars, the Milky Way, blackness to infinity and beyond.

August 14, while doing a routine check of the leak, David discovered the clamp he had applied to the propeller shaft was rubbing against the gear box. The shaft had been pushed in by the full night of following seas. It was just a smidgeon; nevertheless, it was movement in the right direction. He repositioned the clamp accordingly.

August 15, the wind strengthened to 25 knots and swung to the north. David again wrote family.

> We are having an exhilarating ride with speeds 7 knots, sometimes above. We are approximately 275 miles from our destination. Current position is 38 degrees 58 minutes north, 15 degrees 19 minutes west.
>
> It's still too early to predict the exact day of arrival, but we are expecting good distances with these winds.

As *Inia* cut through the water, we talked about landfall. I could hardly contain my excitement. The Cascais harbour was protected from the untamed Atlantic. It had the towing and repair services we'd need. It was also a stone's throw from historic Lisbon. Sightseeing was still at least part of this adventure, after all. And, being due east, it was the closest port of entry to us, a singularly compelling feature.

But the breeze continued to build throughout the day and, as it did, so too did it veer. By night we had a powerful blast out of the northeast. Coupled with the strong south-setting current, *Inia* was being forced southward, losing another minute of latitude, a nautical mile, every time we checked.

While the two of us chewed potatoes, corn niblets, and ham, all canned and cold, with machine-like interest, I insisted the winds would change. David showed me the GRIB files, which indicated otherwise, but he allowed I could be right.

～～

August 16, the winds did change, but only in intensity.

The sea state, which is affected by the length of time the wind blows in one direction and the distance of uninterrupted water, or fetch, over which it does, was growing at an alarming rate. By morning, *Inia* was heaving spasmodically, almost broadside to monstrous seas.

All aspects of living became dangerous, taxing work.

I again pulled down berth cushions, pillows, and blankets for a makeshift bed on the cabin sole. This four-by-six-foot area became our safe haven and our only hope for rest.

As the day progressed, the canvas weather cloths that we had installed in the Gaspé to provide shelter from ocean spray began to tear.

Scanning the horizon for freighters became an exercise in futility. The odds of cresting with another vessel while looking in its direction were minuscule. And in the troughs, all we could see were walls of water. Radar became important like never before.

When we realized we were hungry, I tied myself down with the galley strap and slapped together two sandwiches with the last of the bread, a lone tomato, and some wilted lettuce leaves.

"Fantastic," David said.

Maybe it was knowing there'd be no more bread, tomatoes, and lettuce until landfall. Who knows? But I agreed.

Then a freak wave hit, my stomach spasmed, and my sandwich shot back out.

"I wouldn't have eaten had I had any idea," I said, guilt-ridden, exhausted, totally fed up.

David said he was wearing out, too, and suggested we both try to sleep. We were still far from shore. Again, fatigue was a bigger threat than other boats.

As *Inia* ploughed on, sounding like a freight train barrelling down a mountainside, we lay nestled under the heap of blankets on the floor, arms and legs entwined, warm, secure, safe. I could feel the tension seep from my body and David's limbs fall away.

Then he twitched. "Do you hear something?"

"You'd have to be stone deaf not to."

"No, something inside, scratching," he said, always on the alert for unusual sounds. "There it is again!" he exclaimed.

We both lay still to listen.

"Heard it," I said. "It's more of a scuttling sound. Coming from the head."

By the time it dawned on me that it was the bucket we were using as a toilet, and that it hadn't been emptied for some time due to the wildness, and that it too would have difficulty staying upright, and, moreover, that the door of the head was wide open, it was too late. Out it flew and over it toppled, splashing its contents all over our bed. And us.

Crawling over each other, we sponged and sprayed, flipped the pillows, rotated the blankets. Then we hugged and reclined, hoping to pick up where we had left off, but with the cabin now wet and smelling like a pine-scented porta-potty, a good night's sleep would continue to elude us.

Around 0430 on August 17, David announced we had edged south of Lisbon and, according to weather data, conditions showed no signs of abating.

"There's a thing called a nortada," he said. "It's a strong persistent wind system from the north. If that's what we're in, and I believe it is, we should heave to and set the alarm. We'll need rest to handle it."

He went above decks to set the mizzen and lash the rudder. I stayed on the floor cushions with the blankets tucked high up under my chin. Watching the oil lamp's frenzied toing and froing, I thought about what he hadn't said. He left out that getting to Lisbon under sail was virtually impossible unless there was a major wind shift.

As exhausted as he was, as unbearable as this tack had become, as futile as it would have been to carry on, he was willing to continue to try, just for me.

When he returned below, I pulled back the bedding. "Thank you," I said as he slid in. "But it's not necessary."

"Your heart's set —"

"We'll fly there some day," I said. "We must be getting awfully close, though. I hear music, big band music. Did you see cruise ships out there?"

"Nope. And didn't hear any music either."

"Dear Lord!"

"Yeah, I know. Last night I could've sworn I saw a gnome curled up on the bow. We do need sleep."

In a matter of minutes, I was dead to the world.

At 0700 I awoke to formidable ocean peaks, the same strong winds from the same damn direction. David snored beside me. As much as I hated to, I gave him a nudge. With Lisbon a mere 92 nautical miles away, we nevertheless altered course and headed south. And *Inia* took off like a rangy demon.

As her propeller spun faster, she took on water at an accelerated rate, and the electric pump began to squeal. The flag halyard broke loose. Our Portuguese courtesy flag was now flying thirty feet straight out to starboard. And the weather cloths continued to shred.

With waves now on our quarter, I strapped myself to the galley and combined ingredients to stretch out our diminished cold-food reserves. Chopped onions, carrots, and cabbage, mixed with mayonnaise became combo one. Mashed canned tuna, more onions, and what was left of the mayo was combo two. And combo three consisted of the rest of the onions, canned kidney beans, chickpeas, and green beans. Back on deck I announced that we'd essentially be eating from these three Tupperware tubs until we made it to shore — assuming that'd be in the next couple of days, of course.

David shrugged. "Who cares? We can always crack open the blood sausage. And maybe I'll harpoon us a marlin, for sushi."

"You're ridiculous."

"I'm just saying we're not going to starve out here. Only if you catch me sprinkling salt and pepper on your arm should you start to worry."

"Ridiculous *and* warped." I laughed.

Then a gust of wind pulled the corner of the storm jib out from under the lashings. David harnessed himself to a jackline and inched bow-ward on his hands and knees, through the howling winds and breaking waves, to secure it.

No sooner did he return to the safety of the cockpit than one end of the starboard lock board broke free and the six-foot-long two-by-six began to wallop the bow. So back into danger he crept.

Jesus bloody Murphy!

August 18, our twelfth day out and our third of continuous force 7 to 8 winds, we entered the shipping lanes just after midnight.

"Shit! Two freighters off our starboard beam, a third to port, all less than three miles away!" David exclaimed, the glow of the radar screen reflecting on his glasses.

I sprang from the floor. "Yikes." I stared at the grainy images with him, watching them stealthily manoeuvre from one side of us to the other.

"We're being circled. It's deliberate," I said, imagining a band of pirates, my heart racing.

David went out to take a look, then rushed back below.

Reconciling what he observed above decks with what he was seeing on the radar screen, his shoulders collapsed. The ships weren't even moving. It was *us*! Robert had lost control under the strain. *Inia* was in the midst of doing an unintentional one-eighty.

When we went on deck to get her back on track, we saw that the halyard of our radar reflector had chafed and broken off. The large aluminum ball was now flying straight out to starboard with our courtesy flag.

Over the course of the night, both weather cloths continued to tear, the fitting for the jib halyard that Gjialt had attached to the top of the mast broke off, and the mizzen halyard got tangled in the wind generator yet again.

Sunrise marked over seventy-five straight hours of chaos.

We expected to make landfall later that day. Imagining an end to the constant motion, the wet, the nausea, the unrelenting mechanical problems, the numbing exhaustion, and the cold beans and cabbage was thrilling. Unless we were prepared to eat cat food in retirement, it was time to put a stop to the financial hemorrhaging, too. But I couldn't bring myself to broach the subject this time.

"Whatcha thinking?" David said.

"Nothing much."

"We're almost there."

"Yeah, almost there."

"It'll be great."

"Can't wait."

The conversation continued to move along in awkward fits and starts until David said, "Well, my dear, we've crossed an ocean and I'm grateful. It's been an amazing adventure. Pretty rough, too — and I'm truly sorry about that.... I think this might be the end of the road. We'll likely have to sell *Inia* in Portugal. But we've got a great little house to go back to, to fix up. It'll be fun. And I'll find a new job of some sort. That'll be exciting."

I was taken aback. He was saying exactly what I was thinking. It was sensible and rational and long overdue. Why then was it so disturbing to hear him say it?

Then it occurred to me: This trip had very little to do with sensible thinking. It was inherently irrational from the get-go. It was about a boyhood fantasy, an impractical goal with intangible rewards. David was the dreamer of this nonsensical dream. Had he been more logical, we would have stopped long ago or, more likely, we would have never left home in the first place. But now, out of the blue, he had become Mr. Voice of Reason. I guess I was caught off guard, that's all.

I said neither of us could think straight in this bedlam. We agreed to postpone "the talk" until after landfall.

Midday, we spotted land. It was a glorious sight indeed.

Under a brilliant blue sky, *Inia* rounded Cabo de São Vicente. Once protected by this westernmost point of mainland Europe, we sailed on euphorically over smooth seas, along Portugal's magnificent southern shoreline of rugged cliffs, jagged stone outcroppings, caves, and miles of sand beach, careful to dodge dastardly fish pots as we did.

David emailed the Lagos boatyard.

> We are the sailing vessel *Inia*. Our motor is disabled. We are about an hour from your entrance canal. We do not have a mobile phone. We will try to contact you on VHF 09. We will monitor VHF 16. Your help is greatly appreciated.
>
> *Inia* is a 37-foot yawl.

At around 1530, David radioed the marina. "Marina de Lagos, this is sailing vessel *Inia*. Over."

"Hello, *Inia*. Marina de Lagos. How can we help? Over."

"We're approaching the bay outside your channel entrance. We need a tow in. Over."

"Be at the beach in four minutes. Over."

"Four minutes," I exclaimed. "Precise or what!"

David trimmed the sails. We tacked to avoid vessels entering and exiting the channel and windsurfers flitting about and scanned the shoreline to spot the tow boat.

When four minutes had long since come and gone and no help had arrived, David called again. "Marina de Lagos, this is *Inia*. Over."

"*Inia*, this is Marina de Lagos. How can we help? Over."

"We're at your beach, waiting for a boat, a boat to tow us into the marina. Remember? Over."

"The marina's full. Over."

"Noooooooooo!" I said.

"But our engine isn't working," David explained to the receptionist.

"Come to main dock. Over," she replied.

The channel, cluttered with fishing skiffs, was long and narrow, and a strong afternoon breeze was blowing out of it. Entering under sail was out of the question.

"It's a cruel, cruel joke," I said.

Then David flipped through his dictionary. "Engine's broken. *Motor é quebrado.* Help. *Socorro!*"

After tacking in the bay for two and a half hours, the Polícia Marítima came to the rescue. With their monster of a Zodiac, powered by a pair of humungous outboard motors, they towed us in.

At launch, just three months before, *Inia* had been radiant. But she'd been under constant siege by the elements ever since. With her salt-stained canvas, peeling woodwork, ripped weather cloths flapping in the wind, crusted metal, rust dripping from every conceivable seam, she was war ravaged — that's what she was.

The channel was in the heart of Lagos, with a boardwalk of cobblestone and palm trees running alongside it. As we were unceremoniously dragged along this waterway, passing the hordes of onlookers and gleaming multimillion-dollar yachts, *Inia* wore her combat wounds as a badge of honour and moved on with dignity. David and I held our heads high, too.

This was our victory march.

EIGHTEEN

ONCE *INIA* WAS TIED to the pontoon, the *polícia* marched us into the marina building. The receptionist watched us walk by and looked at me with apologetic doe eyes. I flashed a conciliatory smile in return.

The uniformed constable got right down to business. The local boatyard was next door; we could stay where we were until it reopened Monday. Good, great, we said. We'd be billed for the tow in. These rescues weren't cheap. Yes, of course, we said. And we had to surrender our ship's papers. If we lacked regard for our own safety, that was one thing. However, he wasn't about to let the likes of us put this historical seafaring nation at risk. Only when *Inia* was deemed seaworthy, which would be decided through an inspection for which we'd be charged an additional to-be-determined amount, would we be free to re-enter Portuguese waters. David swallowed hard and handed over the documents.

On our walk back to *Inia* I pushed all unpleasantness aside. "Dear, we just got ourselves across the Atlantic Ocean. We've got some serious celebrating to do!"

Unshowered, unchanged, and unconcerned about it, we walked over the bridge toward the ancient city centre. We wound up in a tiny, almost-empty restaurant off the beaten path. The waitress, happy to have business, closed her glamour magazine and brought over the customary plates of olives, cheese, and rolls the instant we sat down.

David ordered wine in Portuguese. She smiled.

And we toasted Saint Christopher.

The next day, vessels on the reception dock were bucking and pitching in the funnelling winds. A forty-foot sloop with an older couple dressed for a monsoon sidled up to the forty-one-foot span between us and the boat ahead. I rushed to grab dock lines while David fended their stern off *Inia*'s bow. After we all exhaled, we exchanged introductions.

John and Freda were from England, late sixties, newly retired. This landing marked the exciting completion of the fabulous first leg of what was certain to be a sensational multi-year sailing adventure.

"We're from Canada," I said.

While David resumed pulling down the chafed halyards, I cut off the torn weather cloths and watched the couple bounce along to the marina office. The contrast in our circumstances and moods was stark.

Midafternoon, Freda returned carrying bags of groceries and announced dinner would be aboard their vessel, *Quyver*, at six, and "no" was not an option.

After depositing the scraps of rope and canvas in a garbage bin, David and I went to the marina for long, hot showers, our first in two weeks. He emerged in khaki shorts and a crisp butter-yellow shirt and I in my favourite flowered sundress, and off we went anew.

As we approached their shiny vessel, the scent of slow cooking floated up from their galley. John welcomed us aboard with glasses of Cabernet. Freda served cheese appetizers, followed by plates of oven-roasted lamb with mint sauce, small new potatoes, a fresh tomato, parsley and vinaigrette salad, and warm soft rolls thick with butter. We sat out in their cockpit, savouring this unforgettable meal, sipping wine, and talking sailing into the night.

"We'll eventually make our way into the Pacific Ocean via the Panama Canal," John said, adrenalin almost squirting out of him. "How about the two of you?"

"Yes, do tell us, where to next?" Freda said.

David and I waited for each other to answer, then talked at the same time. "Well, we've got some mechanical ... money ... problems ... shit ... issues ... to iron out ... to address."

"So maybe nowhere," I said.

"Who knows?" David said.

As stars came out, a warm night breeze enveloped us, and once again, only a day after landfall, I began to magically morph. David did, too. By the end of the evening, listening to us, you'd think the net incident was hilarious; the nortada was like a carnival ride; the water coming onboard was a minor nuisance, no worse than a leaky bathroom faucet.

"So then Sue says, 'If we're gonna sink, what's the difference if we're heading back to São Miguel or carrying on to Portugal!'" David said.

"Well, see, the bilge pump was working, so my thinking was what the hell! Why not keep going!" I said.

"And here we are!" we said, smiling like idiots.

Freda and John noticed the change. "I've heard it said sailing's like childbirth. You forget the pain. I'm thinking perhaps it's true," Freda said with a laugh.

Past midnight, we meandered back to *Inia*. Instead of sensibly retiring for the night, we opened another bottle of wine. We sat side by side, our backs propped up against the main berth bulkhead, a blanket over our knees, and looked around at our tired cabin.

"So …" David finally said.

"So …" I said. "Well, your sister says we should feel very proud of what we've accomplished. She says they're proud of us."

"That's nice."

"My mom expects we won't want to set sail again for a long time, if ever. She pointed out we now 'have that option,'" I said. "In case we didn't notice." I grinned.

"Very thoughtful of her."

"Helen wrote. She said she can't believe what's happened to us and that she'd be completely done in if it were her. And Judy said that whenever she feels she's having a rotten day, she thinks of us and it no longer seems so bad."

"I'm not sure I like that one," David said with a chuckle.

"The point is, no one would question our decision to end the trip here." I added, "And then, of course, there's the money part." Although the costs of repairs were not yet determined, we both knew they'd be sizable. Even if I hadn't been looking for a practical reason to stop, I had a very big one.

This was my opportunity. It was essentially up to me. I knew that all I had to do was give the word and the trip would be over. But I was reduced to a puddle of tears at the very thought.

"Dear, we just can't —"

"I know, and I understand."

"No, I mean we can't stop." I began to sob.

"Uh-oh," he said, trying to tuck me in.

"It's not the wine!" I said, resisting momentarily before passing out.

But the following morning, over coffee, I felt no different. Somehow, somewhere along the way, David's dream had become my dream, too. Despite all the debacles and disasters, no matter what the cost, suddenly I felt, in every fibre of my being, that I had to see the entire voyage through.

"Let's have a list of repairs ready to hand the boatyard manager first thing tomorrow," I said.

To describe David as jubilant would be too mild a word.

Most boatyards don't allow live-aboards. It was our good fortune this one did. Colleen and Roger had booked flights to meet us in Lagos mid-September. A month of marina fees at the height of tourist season would have been prohibitive, especially now. Living on the hard was a fraction of the price.

On August 21, *Inia* was hauled out of the water by a massive travel lift, without forewarning — with us still onboard. I peeked through a porthole as we were being carried, swaying twenty feet above the ground.

Once the contraption jerked to a halt, I popped out to a cacophony of electric tools squealing and grinding, animated chatter in Portuguese, and smells of diesel and fish detritus heavy in the concrete boatyard heat. A man propped a ladder at our gate. David and I climbed down and met Hugo, the affable bilingual yard manager. Beyond him a crowd was gathered at the boatyard crane, where a monstrous sea creature with bowling-ball eyes, spiky steel-blue fins, and a spear-like snout was being disembowelled.

"It's a marlin," Hugo said. "Three metres, around two hundred and thirty kilos."

I watched, aghast, as its voluminous slippery innards spilled out.

"What? I *so* could have!" David said in my ear.

"You are *so* full of it!" I whispered back, giggling.

We followed Hugo along a corridor between two long, low buildings and rows of disabled vessels cheek to jowl. Amid answering calls on his two cellphones and responding to employees' sundry workplace crises that couldn't wait, he gave us a brief tour of our new neighbourhood.

The building to our left, where we were headed, was the business headquarters and a well-stocked chandlery. A string of workshops was in the building to our right. Engine overhauls, carpentry, fibreglass repair, painting, you name it, they did it there. At the end closest to the marlin were the men's and women's washrooms. Senhora, the boatyard owner, lived in an apartment at the other end.

Sitting in Hugo's disorganized office, we told him our engine story and handed him the detailed list we had prepared. He scanned it too quickly to read it and slapped it down among a million similar-looking scraps of paper on his desk.

"*Tá bem*," he said. "Our head mechanic will be right over. We'll have you shipshape and outta here in no time." He then excused himself, explaining he had to take this other call.

David and I let ourselves out. We walked through the boatyard gate, past a smoking outdoor café deep-frying sardines, and down the hot, dusty road to the marina.

While I scoped out the laundry facilities, David phoned Fred in Toronto.

"Shit!" he said, hanging up. "According to him, the net likely damaged the prop, the gears, the bearings, and the cylinders."

"Really?"

"As well as the mounts. And he believes there could very well be other internal damage that wouldn't be immediately detectable."

"Oh no! So?"

"So, he suggested *not* to repair the engine. For reliability on the ocean, we need to replace it — that's if we intend to carry on."

"Okay," I said. "All righty then."

"It could easily be over ten grand. Insurance might help."

"Okay ... so ... yeah ... certainly worth touching base with Lloyd."

We went back and relayed Fred's comments to Hugo.

"*Tá bem.* Our guy will look her over. We'll have you ship-shape and outta here in no time," he repeated while waving to another customer and answering another call.

After talking to him, we found *Inia.* She had been moved onto a cradle. With her stern facing the chandlery entrance, her bow almost above Senhora's home, there was no busier, noisier, more public spot on the yard.

We decided to hit the washrooms before climbing aboard, only to discover there were line-ups of men and women all carrying shampoo, soap, and towels. There was one toilet, one sink, and one shower in each washroom for the entire yard's use.

"Did you notice how crazy busy the marina was?" I said to David. "Besides, it's too snooty for my liking."

"We'll be just fine here," he said as we got into the queue.

~

The next morning David went to the chandlery to get stove parts. We couldn't afford restaurant meals all the time, and we'd soon be hosting our friends. The ability to cook was essential.

I followed him down the ladder with a basin filled with plates and coffee cups to wash and saw a pair of skinny legs beyond the hull of the kelly-green steel double-ender beside us. As I approached, the legs retreated. When I retreated, they advanced. I doubled round and landed face to face with a blushing blue-eyed elf.

Chris had been living on his boat in southern Portugal for ten years. He didn't sail far. He said he just liked the live-aboard lifestyle: the self-sufficiency, the simplicity, the solitude — particularly the solitude.

"I understand," I said.

"Sorry, that came out wrong," he said. "It's this place, it's driving me bonkers."

"I can see why." The two of us watched mechanics with engine parts and painters with rollers dart by.

"Just wait'll you meet the *senhora*. She hovers day *and* night. Speak of the devil." A stalky, stern-faced woman in her midsixties charged past us, barking in Portuguese at a man, three boats down, for leaving a paint tray under his cradle. "You don't want to get on her bad side," he added in a paranoid whisper.

"Yikes! Fortunately, the manager said we'll be outta here in no time," I said.

"Hugo said that, did he?" Chris responded with a grin. "He must be talking Portuguese time. I've been in the yard for three months waiting for a small part."

In the afternoon, when it got too hot to do any more tidying of *Inia*, David and I went for a beer. South Bar, on the second level of the marina complex, was modern, with lots of windows overlooking the state-of-the-art harbour and lots of yachties braying about their state-of-the-art sails and winches and lives.

"Unbelievable!" David said.

"I know. Who needs a five-hundred-dollar gadget to read the wind?"

"I'm talking about the news."

I looked at the TV above the bar. "FINANCIAL CRISIS" was emblazoned on a red banner on the bottom of the screen. The newscaster followed with a report: *BNP Paribas terminated withdrawals from three hedge funds … a complete evaporation of liquidity … housing markets plummeting … Could be the worst financial disaster since the Great Depression.*

"Oh my God!" I said.

"You didn't know?" said the bartender, who was watching the broadcast with us. "It's been in the headlines for weeks."

The Australian man sitting on a barstool beside us looked up from his computer and said, "If it's not the market meltdown, it's the McCann story."

David and I exchanged blank looks. "We have no idea what you're talking about," I said.

"Really? You haven't heard about Madeleine McCann? The four-year-old from Britain? Early May she went missing from Praia da Luz, a resort near here. Her parents, both doctors, left her and her two younger siblings alone at night while they went off partying with friends. She vanished and hasn't been seen since. The parents insist she was abducted. Others, myself included, believe they drugged her to make her sleep, she died from the drugs, and they disposed of her body to hide the evidence. What've you guys been up to for the last three months? They say it's the most heavily reported missing person's case *ever*." He closed up his laptop to leave.

"Apparently not following the news!" I said. We got up to leave, too.

On our walk back to *Inia*, we saw a weathered poster of the missing girl — blond hair; pink cheeks; large, wonder-filled eyes — with the heartbreaking caption "Have You Seen Me?" Then another poster, and another.

At home, we would've been glued to CBC and newspapers to get the latest on this little girl's tragic disappearance, the financial crisis, climate change, global terrorism, the shrinking middle class. Underway, however, our preoccupations were only wind and waves and *Inia* and each other.

"In some ways, life's easier out there," I said.

∿

August 23, while David hung around *Inia* hoping to meet the mechanic, I called John and Brian.

John announced he had received the sheet music for his fourth-and-final-year audition. "Just think, I'll be all graduated by the time you guys get home," he joked.

I struggled to respond. John had started playing clarinet when he was eight. Until he went to university, I drove him to weekly lessons and listened to him practise for hours on end. I got to know every piece, where he'd play softly and crescendo and breathe. And I attended all his recitals, feeling his disappointments, celebrating his successes, watching him grow. Naturally, things changed after he left home. But what didn't change was his resolve to be a musician. Despite all the distractions and detractors, no matter how many people hinted he should get a "real job" or how often he heard he was destined to starve, he continued to believe in his dream. It took immense courage. So if there was one thing that killed me to think about, it was that I'd miss his graduation.

"Believe me, I know," I said.

When I called Brian, he said he had a new idea. "So here it is, my idea," Brian said. "As you know, I want to stay fit."

"Yes, and it's great that you do."

"And what I like to do for fun is outdoor stuff, adventure sports, that sort of thing, right?"

"Mmm-hmm, right."

"And I've been thinking about what other line of work I'd like to get into."

"Good. That's good."

"So, I'm gonna join the military."

"The military!" I gasped for air as horrific images flashed through my mind of our loving son wearing camouflage and toting an AK-47.

"They'll put me through job-skills training *plus* give me a free gym membership."

Of his legs being blown off by land mines.

"Mom? You still there?"

Of his easy laugh being forever silenced by the trauma of war.

"Yes, yes, I am."

"Sure, there's a chance I could die, but that seems to be a small negative with all the pros that go with it."

"Good Lord, Brian!"

"Just kidding," he said. "But seriously, Dad always says there's an element of risk in everything that's worth anything, right?"

"Yes, right. I suppose he does say that," I said.

The walk back to the boatyard was a blur. I understood the boys needed freedom to choose their own paths in life and to find their own spots in this world, but I never once imagined military paths or military spots. This was horrible news.

Back at *Inia*, David reported that the head mechanic, Mauricio, had finally had a look at the engine and he confirmed Fred's suspicions. The force of the net caused extensive damage. Considering its age, Mauricio doubted they could even find parts to repair it. Replacement was our only option.

"And my estimate was low, in fact way off," David said. "It's more like fourteen thousand euros."

"That's over twenty thousand Canadian!"

"Close to twenty-one."

"Holy macanoli!"

"And there's no guarantee insurance will come through for us."

"Since when has it ever?"

"And it'll affect us, too, the financial meltdown, I mean."

"Yes, I realize that. Well, I'd much rather have spent our savings on an experience of a lifetime than to have watched it vanish while sitting on our couch at home. Dear, order the engine."

Then I told David about Brian.

"Oh no!" he said. "Well, at least he's not robbing banks."

"You sound as though you think that'd be worse."

"Sue, I don't like it either, but lots of people have good careers in the military. And if that's what he wants to do, we can't stand in his way."

He went below and fired off a note to Brian:

> We are interested in hearing more about your plans. Are there many options, i.e. navy, army, types of jobs, etc.? Do you have to go through some sort of basic training?
>
> We'll look forward to your next update. In the meantime, hope things are going well and that you are able to sort things out to your satisfaction.
>
> We love you,
> Dad

Hugo ordered our new diesel and said it'd arrive in a week to ten days. Perfect timing. We'd be in the water for Colleen and Roger's visit mid-September.

While we waited, we established a routine. Mornings, while it was relatively cool, we focused on *Inia*. David arranged fabrication of new weather cloths, repair of the mizzen sail, and replacement of the head's through-hull fitting; I lubricated the winches, redid the bright work, and applied a fresh coat of bottom paint; and together we recaulked all the chain plates. Afternoons we visited the world-renowned beaches, hiked on the ocean-front trails, shopped for our evening meals in the local markets. I soon settled into this daily mix of ordinariness and exotic tourism and grew to love life in the yard.

September 14, still no engine, still in the yard. Colleen and Roger arrived. The original plan had been for them to stay with us on *Inia*, but that was envisioning we'd be in a charming marina. Now that we were on the hard — climbing up and down a ladder, lining up for a single washroom a football field away, peeing in our bucket at nighttime — although the invitation still stood, the appeal didn't. They respectfully declined and booked into a luxury ocean-front hotel.

Dinner aboard was the very least we could do. David and I bought a *cataplana*, a steel cooking device hinged like a clam shell, and shopped for shrimp, fresh produce, spices, and wine to entertain Portuguese-style. And we cleaned like mad.

Prior to their arrival, I lowered and unfolded the teak table, set it with handwoven placemats and napkins, and lit our wall-mounted paraffin lamp, transforming our utilitarian cabin into an intimate dining room. As an angst-ridden Portuguese CD played in the background and hot peppers, onions, and celery sautéed on the stove, Colleen and Roger descended into our home.

"Smells wonderful!" Colleen said as they slid into the port-side seat at the table.

"It's a cataplana," David said, pouring us all a glass of wine. "A local way of cooking seafood." He laid out nibblies, including a bowl of the marinated olives. "This is another Portuguese tradition," he said, sliding into the starboard bench across from them. Once the veggies, shrimp, garlic, and tomato sauce were steaming over a bed of rice in the cataplana, I sat down beside David on the seat closest to the galley.

"Cheers to good friends," David said.

"To good friends," we all responded.

"Here we are, together in Portugal, just like we planned last New Year's," Colleen said. "Hard to believe!"

"Well, it hasn't all gone exactly as we planned," I said, laughing. Then I noticed the kerosene flame flickering brightly.

"But, I'm happy to report we haven't been bored," David said. While they chuckled, I slipped over and turned the stove dial down.

"To tell you the truth, at times I would've appreciated a tad of boredom," I said, sitting back down.

"These are great!" Roger said about the olives. "You could've just bought a recipe book in Guelph though," he joked.

The flame grew higher.

"But yeah, you're right, Colleen," I said, rushing back to the stove, intentionally blocking their view with my body while I shut the valve right off. "It *is* hard to believe … us all here … here together." Then flames shot up, down, back and out, and I shielded my forehead with my arms. "Honey, I could use a hand with —"

"Jesus!" David shrieked. He jumped to his feet, grabbed the fire extinguisher, pulled the pin, squeezed the handle, sprayed the base of the blaze, and snuffed it out, all in a matter of seconds.

"Phew! That was close," I said, my eyes watering, trying to suppress a cough.

Without a word, Colleen and Roger slid through the blanket of white chemical powder and scurried single-file through the floating ashes up the companionway. David followed them out. I went last. The four of us hacked and sputtered our way down the ladder, then stood in the yard, our faces speckled with the flour-like residue.

"We look like blinking mimes," I said, giggling.

"Colleen and I'll go buy pizzas," Roger said, the two of them using their napkins to wipe the powder off each other.

"Thanks, Roger, but no need," I said. "We just so happen to have bought two little alcohol burners last week."

"Any topping preferences?"

"Roger, I said 'no need.' We can still cook the cataplana."

He and Colleen looked at each other like I had lost my mind. "We might be a while," he said. They linked arms and walked off.

"What the hell!" I said to David, watching them go. "We've got a perfectly good dinner underway here!"

"They're just trying to help," David said, climbing the ladder.

"If they want to help, they can help by eating our perfectly good dinner," I said, following him up. "We don't need a damned pizza."

We looked around. The cabin was coated in white, like fresh-fallen snow.

"You gotta admit that was scary," he said. "Fibreglass is highly flammable. *Inia* could've caught fire."

"But she *didn't*," I said. Armed with rags and pails of soapy water, we began to clean up. "She could've sunk, too, but she didn't," I continued, scrubbing maniacally. "We could've drowned, but we didn't. You could've been eaten by a shark, but here you are! So it was scary, so what! It's over. The fire's out. *Inia's* fine. We're fine. The food's fine. What the hell's wrong with them?"

"Nothing's wrong with them."

"Oh, so *I'm* the problem. Just great. You think I've lost it, too!"

"No, not at all. But Sue, I do think you've changed."

"I'm proud of this place, this life, us. Tonight was important to me." I started to cry.

"I know," David said, wiping the pasty streaks off my face.

For the rest of Colleen and Roger's two-week holiday, we toured the Algarve in their rental car, shopped for hand-painted pottery, and shared meals together, always out. As we played tourist, the yard workers began the engine installation.

Late September, after our friends had left, we returned to our boatyard life. David, itching to be part of Team *Inia*, loitered around the base of the cradle, waiting for each workday to begin.

"*Olá!*" he said to a mechanic who came to align the prop. "*Bom motor! Boa hélice!* Aaand, let's see … *bom eixo, eixo da hélice!*"

"*Sim,*" the mechanic said, avoiding eye contact.

"*Olá!*" he said to the canvas maker. "Good job! *Bom, bom trabalho!*"

"*Sim. Obrigado,*" replied the canvas maker, checking his watch.

"*Olá, bom dia!*" he said to the gangly diesel apprentice carrying fuel filters over. "*Como está?*"

"Dear, honestly, they all have work to do," I said, carrying a bag of laundry down the ladder. "And deadlines to —"

"*Bom dia, tá bem!*" the young man answered back, smiling broadly. "And you?" he said with effort.

David was as surprised as I was. "*Tá bem, tá bem* as well!" he said. "*Eu chamo-me* Dave. This is Sue."

"*Olá, Dave, Senhora Sue. Eu me chamo Edson,*" he said. "What's the flag?"

"Canadian. We're from Canada, far from home."

"*Brasil's* my home. Far, too," he said.

Edson was not much older than our sons, but he had a wife and two daughters. They still lived in Brazil. He took a grease-stained picture of them from his wallet and stared at it longer than we did. Then his toothy grin returned. "But I'm lucky," he said. "The work is good." This boatyard job enabled him to support them financially and to become a top-notch mechanic in the process. Someday, when he had saved enough, they'd reunite as a family. "So, thanks be to God," he said, blessing himself.

From that day on, David prepared assiduously for their daily chats.

And, as the weeks unfolded, we got to know Chris a bit more, too. One day, at the base of our ladder, he divulged there had been a woman once. She was bipolar. He could have lived with that if only she had tried to help herself. But after thirteen years of attempting to rescue her, he had to walk away. It still hurt.

"Oh, Chris, that's so sad. Maybe there'll be someone else someday, though," I said.

"No. Uh-uh."

"Don't be so sure. You never know. Maybe this afternoon when you're out for your walk —"

"No. She was the one. And, besides, I love my own company," he said, signalling the end to the conversation.

Back aboard *Inia*, I peered down through the porthole at him, still shining the same spot on his hull. "I'm not sure I buy it, his loving being alone all the time. Do you?"

David looked up from his phrase book. "Why would he say it if it weren't true?"

"Denial maybe. Or fear of exposure. Fear that, in a world that exalts individuality, admitting to loneliness might be seen as a sign of weakness. If so, a sailboat's a perfect cover. You say *solo-sailor* and everyone thinks of a strong man, a brave man, a man that needs no one. Yet he could be the very opposite." I looked at Chris again. "Is it possible to polish right through steel?"

After tossing our kerosene stove into a scrap-metal heap at the far end of the yard, we bought a flimsy robin's-egg-blue camping stove, clamped it to the galley counter, and strung a ten-foot piece of hose from it to a portable butane tank in the cockpit. This would serve for all our cooking for the remainder of our trip.

Once a week, on Friday nights, we treated ourselves to dinner out at the Marina Café, the café of our landfall dinner. Since it was never busy, the waitress, Karine, taught David practical words and phrases in Portuguese and she seized the opportunity to practise her English. We learned she lived with her boyfriend, Alex, who was a crane operator. They danced the samba and they were madly in love.

October was the start of the rainy season. A heavy downpour on the 1st fell as a reminder. Most boats heading to the Canaries had already left and the rest were hustling to go, since the later the departure, the stormier it would likely be. We provisioned to the rafters to be ready to take off the instant the engine work was done.

October 7, in the quiet of a Sunday morning, a female voice called out our names. Karine, wearing snug black leggings and a tight black T-shirt that showed her ample curves, was standing at the base of our ladder. Beside her was a tall, lean man in baggy yellow Nike shorts, massive white runners, and a sleeveless red T-shirt that revealed sinewy arms. He was Alex.

On their only day off, Karine invited us to their place for lunch. No camp-stove meal, no restaurant food. Today we'd experience real Portuguese home cooking, she insisted.

After giving them the two-second tour of *Inia*, we climbed into the backseat of their white hatchback and Alex sped off into the countryside, CD player cranked, Creedence Clearwater Revival blaring through the open windows.

Their apartment building was a long single-storey wooden structure, door window door window from end to end. We walked to their door across a broken concrete patio, weeds sticking out of the cracks, through a group of six men sitting on cinder blocks, drinking, smoking, and barbecuing chicken in the golden sun. Their unit was a ten-by-fourteen-foot room. An unmade double bed piled with laundry was opposite the door. A counter with a sink, a hot plate, a roaster stacked on a microwave, a fan stacked on a bar fridge, and an economy-size can of cockroach spray ran along the length of the left wall. On the right was a veneer hutch with a CD player and a vast collection of CDs neatly arranged on the shelves. A guitar was propped against the hutch. A white plastic table-and-chair set filled the middle of the room.

I stood at the door in my LL Bean shorts and linen tank top, unsure what to say or do, almost certain this was a bad idea.

"Nice guitar," David said.

"You play?" asked Alex.

"A bit. *Um pouco*," David said.

"*Um pouco*. Me, too," said Alex.

"Sit! Sit!" Karine said. She got a bottle of *vinho verde,* green wine, from the fridge and poured four glasses while Alex rooted through his music and put on another CD, Van Morrison this time. Then together they gathered ingredients, chopped and stirred, sautéed this, roasted that, chatted with us in broken English, giggled at each other's mistakes, sang, bumped and grinded, and poured more wine.

Karine spread a plastic tablecloth with turquoise and orange flowers over the table, and Alex laid out the eye-popping meal: piri-piri shrimp, steak roasted in a garlic vinaigrette marinade, stewed cassava and yams, and a mixed green salad. Then they joined us.

Over lunch, Alex played Neil Young and Shania Twain CDs for us, aware they were Canadian musicians, and then he played Brazilian music. We learned that they, like Edson, were from Brazil, working in Portugal to support three children who were "temporarily" staying with Karine's mother. It had been four years so far. Alex brought out pencil sketches of a house he was designing. It was where they'd someday live all together again as a family, Karine said, beaming. They'd have a big kitchen, a separate room for eating, maybe two bathrooms, definitely everyone a bedroom of their own, Alex said. *Paciência*, they both said.

Here they were, working long, hard hours, living in substandard housing, apart from their children, missing out on their formative years, missing one milestone after another, with no clear end in sight. And for what? For the unselfish betterment of those children's lives. There was no rancour, no ploy for sympathy, not a hint of feeling like victims. Instead they accepted their lot with optimism, courage, and this shocking generosity of spirit. What could have been a depressing afternoon was, instead, an uncomplicated celebration of life.

Alex picked up the guitar, tuned it, and, with a twinkle in his eye, played a few iconic bars, then, in the voice of an angel, crooned "The House of the Rising Sun" in Portuguese.

"My first song," he said when he finished.

"Go, Dave," Karine said as Alex handed him the guitar.

David picked the same opening bars, and we all laughed. Then, neck craned, he sang a heartfelt rendition in English. "Mine, too," he said, putting the guitar down.

To think that, as teenagers, these two men cut their rockstar teeth on the very same tune. Oceans, prevailing winds, world economies, explorers, opportunities, choices, rolls of the dice might have separated our cultures and us — but not completely.

October 8 was Canadian Thanksgiving. David sent an email to Ben, Brian, and John. Then I phoned my mom. She had oodles of invitations to dinner but had declined them all. No, she hadn't been in contact with any of the boys, so she had no idea what they were up to for the long weekend. But she had been young once and she understood they had better things to do than to spend it with her, and she stressed she was glad not to have to cook a damn turkey.

It turned out John spent Thanksgiving alone in Toronto, Brian alone in Victoria, and Ben, who knows how, who knows where. No phone calls were made, no emails exchanged among them. Actually, no one had heard from Ben since May.

Maybe holidays were commercial bullshit and maybe turkey dinners were bullshit and perhaps family was nothing more than a bullshit social construct. I suddenly made myself sick wondering.

October 12, the engine work was finally finished. We charged it to Visa. Then, October 13, Lloyd's of London wrote that they'd cover the cost, minus the deductible. It was like we had won a lottery!

After David paid the port captain's dubious bill in return for our ship's papers, *Inia* was launched. We motored her up and down the Algarve coast to clock the fifty engine hours required for the first warranty inspection.

October 27, on our way back to the Lagos marina, we stopped in Portimão and unexpectedly ran into Carl and Kate. They had just arrived from the Azores. Their departure had been late. Their crossing was stormy. Their engine was shot. And they were a pair of emotional wrecks. We invited them aboard for spaghetti.

Over dinner we shared our engine saga. It was cold comfort. They wanted to continue to travel as long as they had the health, but they were on a modest pension and they had no insurance. So if they had to replace their engine, it would spell the end of the line.

Carl expressed envy of our situation. "A new engine to a boat is like a new heart to a patient. You guys should be good to go for another twenty years!"

I replied that we were not yet retired and that we expected to be back to work by spring. After a pause I added that we had bought a little house to move into on our return, regretful as soon as I said it.

Carl and Kate reacted with predictable dismay.

"Why a house, when you've got everything you need right here? When you can have the world's oceans as your backyard?" Carl said. "The more crap you have, the less free you are. I say sell up and sail!"

"Besides, we have children to get back to," I said.

"Children! How old are these *children* of yours?" he said.

"I don't know why I called them that. We have three sons. They're all in their early twenties. So you're right, they're certainly not children any more. But still, they're young and searching and —"

"Early twenties! Christ, by then I was totally on my own!"

"I know. That was me, too," David said. "I've been pretty independent my whole life. Summers, growing up, I'd often leave the house in the morning and not show up again 'til dinnertime."

"But times have changed," I said.

"They sure have!" Carl said. "What the hell happened? How did our generation, the anti-establishment generation, the generation that embraced freedom and experiential learning and creativity and simple living and uniqueness and diversity, become the most oppressive, money-focused, driven parents of all time? Scheduling play dates for their kids. Christ, since when did play require scheduling? Sitting in on their adult kids' university lectures and writing their papers; paying for their cars and phones and spa sessions; texting them several times a day to ensure they're eating well and being treated right. In my view, it's no coincidence that anxiety's rampant among those kids. If you feed the birds, they never learn how to find grubs and worms on their own, they never gain independence."

"Carl's right," Kate said. "I witnessed that first-hand, in my family. My brother, Jake, quit school and got into heavy pot use at seventeen, and my parents went on this rescue mission that never ended. They died broke and broken, and Jake, who's now in his forties, is a lost cause. My sisters and I are convinced that, had my parents let him take responsibility for himself and learn from his mistakes, the outcome would have been better for him, for us all really. It certainly couldn't have been worse."

"Believe me, we get what you guys are saying," I said. "In fact, part of why we took off was to give our sons space. But, Kate, in your parents' defence, from a mother who's been there, it's hard to know what the right thing to do is, especially if you're seeing your child struggle. I mean, how do you know what's enough help and what's too much? How do you decide when it's the right time to let go? Speaking as a parent —"

"I have four kids. Kate hasn't even met them yet," Carl said. "You were smart to take off when you did. And if you ask me, the best thing you could do for your sons at this stage is to keep on going!"

I sat there, stunned. According to my calculations, Carl hadn't seen his children in at least six years. I believed that our sons needed to be free to live the lives they wanted to live. And I had come to agree with the whole not-feeding-the birds notion. Until Carl's comment, though, it had never occurred to me that their independence could possibly mean no relationship at all. I still very much hoped to be able to watch the birds grow, and to hear them sing, and to see them soar.

Yet why hadn't we heard from Ben? What if he agreed with Carl? What if he felt that, in order to have true independence, he needed to sever all ties with us? If so, if complete separation was what it took for Ben to soar, then, as radical as it was, as unnecessary as it seemed to me, as goddamn heartbroken as I would be, I was prepared to accept that, too.

In any event, I had every intention of moving into that little house come spring.

October 28, with fall in the air, we returned to Lagos and tied up to a pontoon by the boatyard. Mauricio scheduled our engine checkup for first thing on the 30th.

I wrote everyone to say departure was imminent. And I wrote Brian separately to say happy birthday and that we'd be emailing him a hundred dollars for it. There was a message from him:

> 23 in 2 days. The military thing's in the waiting stage right now.
>
> Elsewhere, do you remember the movie *Sleuth*, with Michael Caine and Lawrence Olivier, that you showed us when we were kids? Well they've made a new version. Caine is playing Andrew Wyke this time and Jude Law is playing Milo Tindle. And Milo is a poor actor rather than a poor hairstylist. Saw the trailer. Seems worth seeing. Thought you'd be interested.
>
> Nothing else new here.
>
> I hope you're having fun.

His message caused me pause. Did he really have no other news to report than that there was a remake of *Sleuth*?

October 30, Mauricio inspected the engine, and everything checked out fine. While David went to the chandlery to buy spare parts and supplies for routine maintenance, I ate dry toast and swallowed Stugeron, a new seasickness medication, and then stowed items below.

David reboarded with astonishing news. Hugo had refused to take any money for the labour or the parts or the time on the pontoon. They were free, *gratuita*. He said David's effort to speak Portuguese was truly heroic and, even though productivity would likely go up after we left, David would be missed by everyone in the yard. Then Senhora ran over with his-and-hers T-shirts as mementos.

The good news was we were ready to go; the bad news was we were ready to go. We bade a fond farewell to all the staff. I was gripped with nostalgia as we motored over to the gas pumps on the reception dock where, two and a half months before, our Portugal experience had begun.

Just as the gas attendant finished topping up our diesel, a fifty-foot sailboat, flying an Atlantic Rally for Cruisers (ARC) race flag and filled with puffy-chested men dressed like a bowling team, cut through the crowd of vessels waiting to refuel and headed straight for the gas pumps. With a collision all but certain, the attendant yanked *Inia* forward; I, with a boathook firmly grasped in both hands, stood like a sentinel midships; and David engaged the motor and slipped *Inia* past the imposing bowsprit in the nick of time.

"The bastards," he said, anxiously steering toward the centre of the channel.

"Assholes," I muttered in solidarity.

And we were off!

NINETEEN

MADEIRA IS ANOTHER North Atlantic archipelago. We were headed to islands Porto Santo and Madeira, the two biggest in the chain and the only ones where humans live. The others were home to monk seals, petrels, and other protected species.

As soon as *Inia* was beyond Cabo de São Vicente and no longer in the lee of Europe, I upchucked the toast and Stugeron in the lively cross swells and went to bed.

That evening I awoke to a loud bang, became airborne, then crashed into the hard edge of the starboard settee.

"Rogue wave, but I'm okaaaay!" David yelled down.

As I lay there amid the blankets and books that had travelled with me, nursing my bruised hip, I had to chuckle since, truth be told, his welfare hadn't even crossed my mind.

I grabbed a blanket and joined him in the cockpit. Since it was past the autumnal equinox, it was already dark at 1900. Throughout the night, freighter traffic was heavy from every trajectory. Next to these massive, brilliantly lit vessels, *Inia* was like a tub toy with a bauble for a mast light. David made several attempts to inform approaching ships of our position, but none of his calls were acknowledged.

At dawn we veered southwest.

Daytime, the ocean was dark blue-grey tinged with bronze, the air a light mauve. The sun, in its south declination, was low and at an angle relative to our northern latitude, not only creating the longer nights, but also this subtle change of palette and glow. Despite the absence of the typical hallmarks of fading gardens and dropping leaves, it was unmistakably fall. With seas gently pushing us along, I soon recovered and felt content to be underway.

November 2, midafternoon, we spotted a faint stick barely darker than the sky on the horizon to the south. The sailboat's skipper radioed that they were off our port beam. David called back to say we saw them and asked where they were headed. They didn't bother to respond to his call either. Since we maintained the same relative bearing throughout the night, it became evident they were shooting for the same island.

November 3, with the rising of the sun, dramatic cones of black and brown and grey appeared above the ocean's surface.

I wrote family:

> We are currently at 33 degrees, 15.8 minutes North and 15 degrees, 50.0 minutes West. It's a beautiful sunny morning. We're sailing 5 knots on relatively calm seas.
>
> We've just spotted Porto Santo.
>
> It's been a perfect passage — no storms, no calms, no mechanical breakdowns, of any kind. However, we haven't docked yet so there's still opportunity.
>
> We'll keep you posted.

Early afternoon we rounded the uninhabited island of Ilhéu de Cima, then passed between two concrete breakwaters due west to enter the Porto Santo marina. Since the spur walls were high and *Inia*'s freeboard low, David called the marina on the handheld VHF for assistance docking. The marina manager ran to the end of a pier, waved us in, and caught our lines.

The four-and-a-half-day passage had been beautiful and was over in the blink of an eye. If our circumstances had been different, I felt I could sail on for years.

After tidying *Inia* up, we strolled the scenic sidewalk along the beach to Vila Baleira, the island's only town. White plaster buildings with red clay roofs, palm trees, and rhododendrons in bloom surrounded the large town square. Nuns in full habits shuffled silently back and forth across the communal space. All was quiet and clean and slow.

"Ahoy, fellow sailors," men yelled from behind, like shattering glass.

It was the crew of the sailboat we had been travelling in tandem with throughout the previous day and night. They said they had tried to radio us. Did we not hear them? We said we had, loud and clear, *and* we had responded.

"Did you not hear *us*?" I asked needlessly.

This passage hadn't been problem-free after all. Although we could receive messages via our VHF, unbeknownst to us, we weren't reliably transmitting them. Apparently, none of the other vessels had heard any of David's calls.

How many shipping lanes had we crossed, how many ports had we entered, how many skippers had David attempted to hail with this malfunctioning radio? And, oh my God, what if we had used it to call a mayday? The consequences of mistakenly believing we were being heard could have been dire. We, again, were lucky.

But, what exactly caused the transmission problem? Was it the antenna? Or had our new radio gone on the fritz? Too bad we didn't discover the problem before our stay in the Portugal boatyard, where we had access to experts and time. There was no radio servicing in Porto Santo, and the weather window to the Canaries was continuing to close.

On our way back to *Inia*, we popped into the marina office and asked the manager, Nelson, for a restaurant recommendation for our landfall dinner. He handed us a business card for the best place in town — his. And there was transportation to it — him. He'd pick us up at 2000.

At 2000 on the dot, a shuttle bus came to an abrupt stop at the end of our dock. Nelson, having changed into his driver's uniform, jumped out, slid open the side door, helped us in, and carted us off.

The restaurant was simple, lots of shiny wood, white linen, lantern lighting. A waiter ushered us to a table that had been specially set. The meal was Madeiran fare: an appetizer of *lapas grelhadas*, tidal mollusks pried off rocks, grilled, and served in their shells, and, as our main course, *espetada*, barbecued skewers of seasoned beef suspended from a stand in the centre of the table.

Still disturbed about Thanksgiving, I raised the topic of Christmas. Maybe, given the opportunity, the boys would like it to be a family affair. Maybe, sometimes, they still could use our help. And just maybe now was one of those times.

We had racked up more reward air miles after paying for the engine on Visa. However, having learned the hard way that we couldn't know for sure where we'd be when, we didn't dare arrange flights for them to meet up with us. And since we were behind schedule, we couldn't afford the time to fly back to Canada for the holiday. So we'd explore the possibility of their getting together with each other.

When dinner was done, the waiter brought us a box containing our cleaned *lapas* shells as a souvenir and pointed out each had a different *arco-íris* inside. Rainbow, Nelson translated.

"A rainbow's hope and love," I mused aloud, still thinking about our family.

"I guess," David responded.

Then the cook came over with a bag of laurel.

"Laurel! Dear, think about it. Laurel symbolizes triumph. Does it not?"

"It seasons beef. Soups, too. We call them bay leaves at home."

"Okay … so … nevertheless, we'll make Christmas happen back home in some shape or form."

David agreed that Thanksgiving would not be repeated.

The next day, David refocused on the radio issue. The more he thought about it, the more he suspected the antenna. Since an antenna requires more power to transmit a message than to receive one, and the farther the transmission, the greater the power demands, it seemed like the logical culprit. But the only way to know for sure was to check it — at the top of our fifty-four-foot mast.

"I wouldn't have a clue what to look for," I said, glancing up into the stratosphere.

"Then I'll go." David began to strap his one-hundred-and-seventy-pound self into our bosun's chair, a canvas diaper-like sling.

"But, who's gonna —"

"You, of course," he said, attaching the sling to our main halyard and explaining that all I had to do was turn the winch handle.

I couldn't decide which end of the deal was worse.

When I turned the handle and David's feet lifted off the deck, I panicked. "This is lunacy! We need to get help."

"You won't let me fall."

"But, dear, what if —"

"You just won't."

"Good God."

I continued to turn the handle, with my left hand, then my right hand, then both, and inch by vertical inch David ascended to the top of the mast, where, swaying with the motion of the water, he inspected the antenna.

"You can lower me now," he eventually called down. "Gravity'll help."

"Exactly!" I yelled, momentarily paralyzed by visions of him landing splat on the deck.

"I'm ready!" he said. I wrapped the halyard a couple more times around the winch. "Any time now!" Then once more around the winch for good luck. And around both hands. "Sue, please. It's getting dark out." Then I braced my legs against the opposite lazarette and lowered him with care. "I've now got a permanent wedgie," he announced when his feet eventually touched down. "But the antenna looks fine." He disentangled himself from the contraption.

We went for a long walk on the white sand beach, then returned along the sidewalk. On our walk back, we spotted *espetada* stands made of wrought iron and hand-painted pottery in a store window and impulsively bought two. As we carried on with the cumbersome boxes, a pickup truck pulled over and the elderly driver offered us a ride.

Manuel had a fishing boat in the marina. He said he owned a house in town but spent most days aboard. He had health issues. Water was solace. If he fished, that was a bonus. He had watched me raise David to the top of the mast.

"That's love," he said with a booming laugh.

"Stupidity's more like it," I said, laughing too. Then I told him about our equally stupid purchases. "They're big and breakable. We really should get our heads examined."

"Oooooh, *espetada*," he said, his eyes glistening. He parked and we walked down the dock together. "The secret's good meat. Fat, but not too much. Lots of crushed laurel and garlic. Rub with coarse salt last minute and cook fast over a hot fire. Then serve with potatoes, a green salad, and, of course, a nice bottle of wine ..." His voice trailed off. "Enjoy it while you can." He stopped at his boat, then turned to David. "Why were you up the mast anyway?"

When David told him, Manuel's face brightened again. "I know a thing or two about radios."

They devised an experiment to isolate the problem, to be conducted in the morning.

After breakfast, Manuel set up a second antenna externally. While David walked and talked on our handheld VHF, Manuel and I listened aboard our respective vessels, and we both heard him, confirming the antenna was working just fine. Then we both responded to David, and he heard Manuel but not me. So, contrary to what we had expected, our new onboard radio was the guilty party. Manuel arranged for an electronics guy to have a look at it on the island of Madeira.

That afternoon we made one last trip into town, via the beach strip, to visit a stone museum that, five centuries before, had been the home of Christopher Columbus. On our return trek, Manuel zoomed past in his truck. Seeing us in his rear-view mirror, he slammed on the breaks, reversed, and told us to hop in.

On the ride back, he said, "Aah yes, Columbus. Porto Santo's claim to fame. The funny thing is he wasn't from here, and he wasn't even Portuguese. He was from Genoa, northern Italy. While in the sugar trade, he stopped over on business. Next thing you know, he married the governor's daughter and made it home. I imagine it was pretty much the same here in his time: everyone knows everyone, crime's almost non-existent, the pace is slow, the weather's stable, one knows what to expect one day to the next, one year to the next. That's why everyone falls in love with this place."

"But, then he chose to head off into the wild unknown," I said. Both of us glanced at the whitecaps and the ocean surge.

"True, that's true," Manuel responded.

When we got out of Manuel's truck, men were screaming and leapfrogging one another on the high wall opposite us. Onlookers on our dock told us a skipper had tried to catch the dock lines of the sixty-foot Australian ketch that had followed his boat in, but he was elderly and frail — and sloshed. Once the crew realized it, they jumped ashore to take over and he engaged in this frenzied tug-of-war with them.

"Where's his crew?" David asked.

"Doesn't have any," they said.

We watched as the Aussie captain flung his peer precariously close to the wall's edge.

"But —"

"Yes, he arrived like that."

"From —"

"England, we think."

Once the ketch had been secured, two of its crew scooped up the floppy man and dumped him into his vessel and he disappeared below.

I lay awake, wondering why he was alone and why he was in such bad shape and if he was all right and what if he wasn't. Would anyone know? Would anyone care?

At dawn David walked around to the wall. He was about to check on the man when he caught a glimpse of his unshaven face and red-rimmed eyes looking out through a porthole. Realizing he didn't need, or likely want, attention right then, David came back to *Inia*, and the two of us refocused on our own business, the business of departure. It was time to be moving on.

This time David ordered me to take the wheel. November 10, at 0940, with Nelson's help, we cast off. After making a tight turn in the small basin, I waved to Manuel, who was standing at the stern of his fishing boat watching us go. Then I steered *Inia* between the large breakwaters and past the lovely beach strip and pointed her southwest.

TWENTY

OUR TRIP TO MADEIRA, 21. nautical miles, was a pleasant day sail. In contrast to spartan Porto Santo, this island is lush with green terraced gardens and waterfalls cascading from its highest peaks.

We had hoped to go to the marina in Funchal, Madeira's historic commercial port and capital city, but it was full and booked up for the foreseeable future. So we headed to a more modern facility on the east end of the island, built to handle the overflow.

The marina, Quinta do Lorde, was nestled in a bay by a volcanic cliff with a solitary white church on top. There was a multi-coloured complex along the base of the docks. The office and a café with a patio sat on either side of it.

After paying exorbitant dock fees, we discovered that aside from washrooms and a few washers and dryers, there was nothing behind the colourful exteriors. The facility was still under construction; the buildings were empty. There was no grocery store, no public phone, no mail service, and nothing of interest nearby. A load of laundry cost $15.00, internet $7.50 a pop. We felt cut off from the world and duped, but also stuck because of the radio.

We went to the café and paid for Wi-Fi access to update family. Wanting to float Christmas ideas by them, we let Brian and John know we'd be calling — that is, as soon as we found a phone.

Brian wrote back to inform us he no longer had a phone himself. He added,

> But, if you need to call, pick a date during the week and a time (either 10 a.m. or 2 p.m.) and phone me at work. I'll wait at the Cash 'n' Carry area.

As we sat outside at a table for two by the water, under the stone ridge of black and gold, with the sun beating down and waves lazily rolling in, my mood began to improve. There was no denying this was a stunningly beautiful spot.

"What the hell! I ordered a fuckin' double!" an old man sitting alone bellowed, his speech thick.

The bartender, stunned by the outburst, smiled nervously and held up a shot glass, indicating the drink had been measured, and then resumed serving others. That he dared dismiss the patron, and so publicly, seemed to only infuriate him more.

"I know what a double looks like, and there's no goddamn way this's a double," he railed, scanning the patio for allies and admirers until his eyes met mine. Holding his glass in one hand, dragging his chair with the other, he shuffled over to our table. "Gotta good one for ya's. How come bathroom windows in airplanes have frosted glass?" He chuckled as he lodged himself comfortably on his seat. Then he downed the Scotch and snapped his fingers for a refill. "I'm James and I'm sailin' the worl'."

"I'm Dave. This is —"

"Jus' retired. Was forced out. An open-'n'-shut case of age discrimination."

"Oh, that's too —"

"Then doesn't the missus up 'n' leave." He drank the new drink in one big swallow and slammed the empty glass down on the table. His eyes started to roll independently, his body to reel. "Gave her everythin' she ever wanted, a mansion with a tennis court, luxury cars …" He picked at a food stain on his shirt and belched a tune, forgetting we were there. "To hell with the good-for-nothing ingrates," he eventually said. "Gonna sail the fuckin' worl'." He looked around the patio. "Hey, gorgeous, you with the nice … heh heh heh, " he said with a sloppy, wet grin to the young disgusted waitress. "Tell the loser behind the bar, a round for me and my friends here," he added. "Name your poison," he said to David and me.

"Oh, thanks," David said. "Really, thanks … James, is it? But we really must —"

"Shit!" James said, jumping to his feet, steadying himself with the table. "Cancel that, darlin'. Got a chicken cookin' aboard."

We waited for him to go, then followed a safe distance behind, watching his white bony legs struggle nobly to keep him upright as he passed dock after dock.

"Damn," we said together when James turned. His boat was across from ours, a few slips closer to shore, directly in our line of sight.

As we passed it, we recognized the name and realized that James and the man who, the day before, had caused the kerfuffle on the high wall in Porto Santo were one and the same. That he had safely navigated to Madeira, let alone down the pier, was truly miraculous.

The next morning, David and I were awakened by opera music coming from a large, comfortable motor-sailer across from us. As it blared, the captain swabbed his deck and sang along, pleased to share his discerning taste and superior sound system with the rest of us. Turned down a few decibels it would have been lovely, but as it was, we couldn't hear ourselves think.

We hid in the back of *Inia* planning a bus getaway until the sun disappeared behind the opera man's tall frame as he loomed over us from the dock.

Graham, in his late fifties, was Scottish. Certain the drudgery of working was going to kill him, he had unilaterally decided to stop doing it. His wife of thirty years didn't take to the whole house-husband concept and took off for the hills.

Having spent his youth in the Merchant Marine, he had acquired an affinity for the sea. He decided to sail the North Atlantic — a similar route to ours, over a similar period of time, but beginning and ending in Scotland, and doing it on his own.

Graham was carrying an armful of books to swap right then and there. He explained he also had an affinity for great literature, adding he was equally passionate about music, which we had probably already deduced. Actually, he was a lover of the arts in general. History, too; after all, you can't know who you are if you don't know from whence you came, right? But science, oh science, it captivated his imagination like nothing else could.

"I guess you could say I have an insatiable hunger for knowledge. Knowledge and adventure. To quote Thoreau, I want to suck out all the marrow of life," he said, gazing into the distance. "Can't help it, it's just the way I am."

And my need for space grew.

~

Monday, November 12, we hiked up the steep hill to the roadside bus stop and took a bus to the closest town of significance.

The driver travelled this mountainous route like the bus had two pedals, "stop" and "go like there's no tomorrow," careening down hills and banking corners at breakneck speeds.

Machico was a down-to-earth, midsized town. We strolled along its tree-lined pedestrian mall by the sea, visited a few shops, and bought food in its modern grocery store. Then, even though the short jaunt between islands couldn't seriously be classified as a passage, we decided to call it one, and stopped for a landfall meal at a busy diner.

The plain establishment was filled with local regulars who watched as the waitress showed us to a table and handed us two cracked, stained menus. The female cook, built like an NFL linebacker, stared over the saloon-style kitchen doors and snapped, "*Cozido à portuguesa!*"

"*Cozido à portuguesa*, it's good," the waitress strongly suggested, pointing to the other tables at which everyone was eating the exact same thing.

We closed our menus. Minutes later, the waitress set down two empty plates, a platter piled high, and a large serving spoon.

David served us both, then dug in. "Mmmm, it's essentially a stew," he said, smiling nervously at the glaring cook.

I forked through the peculiar shapes of meat. Suddenly they began to piece themselves together like a 3-D puzzle. It was a stew all right, a pig appendage stew, like in the cans from the Azores. I whispered to David that he had just bitten into a sow's snout. He spat the spongy chunk into his napkin. We paid up and made a hasty exit.

Back at the pedestrian mall, at 6:00 p.m. our time, 10:00 a.m. Brian's, 1:00 p.m. John's, we made phone calls from outdoor booths.

Brian was waiting at the Cash 'n' Carry.

"What are the odds of meeting two single-handed sailors?" he said. "Presumably one does the starboard jib sheet, the other the port." He laughed.

I said how bad the joke was, laughing too, then asked him how things were going.

"Good, pretty good, nothing new to report," he said. Again.

Then I brought up Christmas and asked what he thought of getting together with John. He replied that he'd love that, but … well, it wasn't in the cards. He didn't want to go into detail, but the long and the short of it was, his cash flow was "a bit of a problemo at the moment." He couldn't afford to travel to John or, to be honest, to have John visit there.

"Oh dear," I said. "But, Brian, what if —"

"Mom, don't worry. I'm getting things under control. I just felt you needed an explanation."

"Good to know," I said. "But what I was going to say was, what if it was your present?"

"Sweet. That'd be sweet," he said.

John loved the idea, too. He said exams ended December 14. Max Galactic would be playing on the 20th. It'd be awesome if Brian arrived in time for their show. Did he mention they had landed a gig at the Opera House? Capacity 850. Oh, and he had written to Ben.

"Ben! You wrote Ben!" I said.

"The school orchestra's going to Montreal in a few weeks. So, I thought just maybe … but he hasn't —"

"Don't be too hurt if he doesn't —"

"It's been two years, Mom."

"I know."

Then I phoned my mom to tell her about Brian and John. "And Ma, I have a big favour to ask."

"Shoot!" she said.

"Would you cook just one more turkey?"

"But, the guys don't want to spend time with little ol' granny, do they?"

"And pie. They need your pie."

"I'd be happy to host Christmas! Delighted, actually."

Back at the boat, exhausted from the day in town, we settled in the cockpit with a pot of tea.

Within minutes, James showed up, again half lit. He was delighted to discover we were dock neighbours and insisted we meet another kindred spirit across the way.

"Just peachy," I said to David as we followed James over with our tea.

The boat, a plain twenty-one-foot double-ender with rye bread spread out on its canvas to dry and long johns flapping on a makeshift line, was flying a Finnish flag. Its skipper — a hunched man wearing a plaid shirt, oversized pants held chest-high with suspenders, a hat with earflaps, and thick glasses that magnified his eyes — was playing guitar on the back of his boat.

"Permission to come aboard?" James asked him.

"Permission granted. Welcome," the man replied warmly.

"*Hyvää päivää*," I said, tucking into a corner of his cramped cockpit.

"*Hyvää päivää*." He smiled with long teeth and receding gums. "*Oletko Suomalainen?*"

"My mom's from Finland. Those are the only words I know."

Raimo was seventy-seven. After retirement, with his family grown and gone, he had set out from Finland to solo-circumnavigate the world in this teeny vessel, having secured a magazine deal to chronicle his journey. Halfway around, though, he met a woman in Venezuela and became a father once more. With the writing contract not yet fulfilled, he carried on for what would become a twelve-year odyssey. Madeira was his last stop before heading back to South America to live out the rest of his life.

"Do you know Samuli Paulaharju?" I asked Raimo.

"Of course. He explored Finland's remotest communities above the Arctic Circle on foot. My generation grew up reading *his* tales of adventure."

"He's my great-grandfather!"

"Well, well, and here you are. Seems you've inherited his pluck, *sisu* we Finns call it!"

"Actually, appliqué's my —"

"She sure has," David said.

As darkness descended, Raimo suspended a light bulb from the mast boom and picked up his guitar again. Reading from brittle sheet music held on a makeshift wooden stand with clothes pegs, his voice thin with age, he sang "Unchained Melody." It was clear he wasn't just reading the lyrics, he was feeling them. He was singing to his Venezuelan love, his Venezuelan darling.

James's gaze grew troubled, Raimo's remote, and I wanted to cry. "We fell in love listening to Willie Nelson's *Stardust* album. That song's on it" was all David could think to say.

November 13, after a longer bus ride, this time to Funchal, David and I sauntered back to the marina, gnawing on the fruit of a philodendron we bought at the city's outdoor market.

"It's mild, mildly citrus," I said.

"I can't taste a thing either," David said.

Across from *Inia*, Raimo was dangling from his bosun's chair, halfway up his mast, while James and Graham were watching him from the dock below, discussing how fortunate they were to be free from the shackles of domesticity.

As we approached, Graham explained that a wooden spreader was cracked. There was a favourable forecast for the week ahead. Since weather windows were now fewer and farther between, Raimo felt a sense of urgency to take advantage of this next one. So they were helping him repair it.

Then a compact guy with a crewcut jumped off a spanking-new forty-two-foot Nauticat three boats down and joined them with a canvas tool bag. Graham introduced us. Keith was yet another lone sailor, considerably younger than the others and more circumspect.

Sensing Raimo was impatient swinging up in the sky, David and I boarded *Inia* and let the spreader repair team get back to work. Following a flurry of activity, multiple trips up the mast, and much discussion and debate, the single wooden pole was glued, clamped, and set aside to mend.

Not yet ready to call it a night, the four men lingered on the dock at our bow. I listened through the forward hatch as Graham and James resumed listing the joys of being bachelors again. No having to listen to mindless babble, can piss with the seat up *or* down, no bitching about socks on the floor, can drink as much as I want, fart whenever I want, as loud as I want, they took turns saying, the giddiness growing as each one topped the one before.

"Like the song, 'No Woman No Cry'!" James concluded.

Graham corrected him. "The title is actually No Woman comma No Cry. But yeah, I'm with you. Hell'll freeze over before I get into another relationship."

"I'm going back to that woman in South America," Raimo said. "Can't wait."

There was a collective clearing of throats. Then James said, "Hey! I've got one for ya's. Why do bathroom windows in airplanes have frosted glass?"

"But, James, airplane bathrooms don't — no, never mind," Graham said.

Keith reminded Raimo to leave the spreader for a good twenty-four hours for the glue to set. Then everyone moodily retreated, each to his own boat.

$$\int \mathcal{C}$$

The electronics specialist confirmed that the transmission problem was in the radio itself and he had shipped it to Lisbon for repair or replacement.

November 17, we had been in the marina only a week, but it felt much longer. The minute the office opened, David and I were in it, eager to get a status report. Catia, the multilingual office manager, made several phone calls to Lisbon on our behalf. The news was crushing. There was a compatibility issue between European and American radio software which needed sorting out and it could take weeks.

Back down the docks we slogged. "Mornin', James…. Hey, Keith, how's it goin'?… Yes, Graham, we did pay ten euros for the philodendron fruit. *So what!*… Hi, Raimo, looks like you'll be good to go midweek, eh?"

$$\int \mathcal{C}$$

Below decks, thinking about the trip ahead, I scanned through our sailing guidebook and stopped at the section on the Cape Verdes. We had been dissuaded from going there by several ocean veterans. Unlike the other Atlantic islands, this archipelago is not part of the European Union and it's poor. We were repeatedly told that crime was rampant and sailors were prey. Given a reputation like that, we were initially inclined to pass them by. However, from what I was now reading, this struggling nation had made strides in increasing security in its harbours and hospitality on its shores, and it was pleading for transatlantic sailors like us to just give it a chance.

"If we stop there, we'll have visited every one of the Atlantic island groups," I said to David. "And it sounds very different. And it's Portuguese-speaking. And, besides, once we hit the Canaries, we're pretty much in the vicinity anyway."

"Nine hundred miles is hardly in the vicinity," David said, feigning exasperation as he looked for the charts he'd need to revise our course.

November 20, bonkers from four straight days and nights of rain, and with more of the same expected, we put on raincoats, bused it to Machico, rented a car, and, avoiding boulders that had washed down from the mountainsides and the slippery edges of steep cliffs, toured the island's north shore.

Walking down the hill from the bus stop to the marina at the end of the day, I saw Keith flitting back and forth in front of the complex.

"Do you know what his story is?" I asked David as I waved to Keith.

"No," David replied.

Keith waved back and made a sharp turn down the dock.

"What his plans are? How long he's been out? Where he's heading?" I persisted.

"Uh-uh."

"Don't you think that's odd?"

"Perhaps a little," David said.

We watched him dart off, then decided to go the café for a nightcap before going back to *Inia*. Soon after, Graham walked in with a bounce in his step. He said he had picked up an errant satellite signal by the main building and had spent all afternoon chatting with people back home via Skype for free.

"We Scots like to say we're born with a hedgehog in our pocket," he said with a chuckle. After ordering coffee and a slice of pie, he launched into another joke. "Did you hear about the Scotsman who was heading out to the pub? He turned to his wee wife and said, 'Heather, put your hat and coat on, lassie.' She replied, 'Aww, Robbie, you takin' me with you?' 'Nah, Heather, I'm just switchin' the central heatin' off while I'm oot.'" Graham leaned back in his chair and howled. "To be honest, I miss it already — Scotland — everything about it. The sooner I get going, the sooner I'll be back." He attacked his pastry.

"Do you know what's up with Keith?" I blurted.

Graham stopped chewing and looked at me. "Why do you ask?"

"He spent the entire day yesterday talking on his satellite phone out under his dodger. And today he's running around in the rain like a chicken with his head cut off."

"Not a clue. And if he ain't sayin', I'm not askin'. I do wonder too, though," Graham said. "As an aside, it's called a spray hood, not a dodger. A dodger is the canvas hanging from lifelines. I spent my youth in the Merchant Marine."

The instant we arrived back at *Inia*, James rushed over with a tumbler of Scotch. He needed to talk to us in confidence. After he had clambered into our cockpit, I lit a lantern and the three of us sat out under a tarp.

"It's about Keith," James said. "To cut to the chase, I think he's runnin' from the law."

I looked at David. "Well, I have to say, that never even crossed my —"

"Jus' look at the way he's actin'. And that boat of his, it's mega-bucks. How'd a forty-something-year-old swing that?"

"Maybe he was successful in the stock market," David said. "Or perhaps he was the sole benefi—"

"Drug smuggling, tha's fuckin' how!" James said, his eyes pen-etrating ours. "Such a young guy, throwin' his goddamn life away." He went on to say that he had had a successful career managing an international engineering firm. "Of course, that's before they showed me the fuckin' door. It was an open-'n'-shut case of age discrimination. I coulda sued the pants off the bastards. But, what I'm sayin' is, I'm not broke and I wanna help the kid get his life on track."

"Oh, James! That's unbelievably generous of you to want to help someone, someone you don't even know," I said. "But what if you're —"

"My nephew was a genius, but fell in with the wrong crowd. By the time I found out, he was too far gone," he said, sorrow in his sunken filmy eyes.

The sky flashed a brilliant green, then blackened. The tarp whipped and snapped.

"Sonofabitch!" James pulled himself up with the stanchions, climbed onto the dock, and power-shuffled across to his boat.

I was taken aback. Likely this was Scotch-induced conjecture. Still, though, James truly believed Keith was in trouble. He cared about his well-being. He wanted to help this other human being out. It seemed his crustiness was just that, a hard exterior, armour to protect his big, soft, too-often-injured heart.

We went below. The heavens rumbled and it poured so hard we couldn't see a thing — again.

November 21, more high winds, more rain. After coffee and toast, we sprinted to the marina office, our hoods scrunching our faces. Good news from Catia: the radio manufacturer obtained North American software. Our unit would be repaired under warranty within the week. They agreed to ship it to Las Palmas, Gran Canaria, where we could pick it up en route. We were now free to go. All we needed was the weather.

We splashed through puddles to the café with our laptop. The place was packed with sailors staring at isobars, downloading weather data from all the sites, comparing notes, griping about the endless series of low-pressure systems forecast, and drinking beer.

Keith came over, having had several. "My crew should be here any day now. I'm hoping to be off by the end of the week."

"Crew?" I said.

He went on to say he hadn't intended to sail alone, not at all, never, but his partner had bailed last minute. "So I've arranged new crew through the internet."

"Yikes. That sounds risky!" I said.

"According to the website, she's young, but experienced and looking for excitement," he said.

"Did you say *she*?" I said.

"So, I don't see how it can go wrong." His eyes twinkled.

That explained everything. Keith wasn't on the lam at all; he was on the make and, in light of this imminent liaison, engaging in small talk with the rest of us had been the furthest thing from his mind.

"Well, as they say, nothing ventured, nothing gained," David said.

"And as they also say, there's another ship in every port," Keith said, starting to smile.

"And every sailor knows, only a ship in motion can be steered."

"Oh, for heaven's sake!" I said.

"It's true though," David said. "Think about it. If one's boat's afloat there's life, and if it's moving there's hope 'cause as long as a vessel's in motion it can be steered, and as long as there's steerage, there's possibility."

"I really hope it works out for you, Keith, that's all," I said. "And I always say, no friggin' in the riggin'," I added with a giant grin.

David and Keith looked at each other, then at me.

"Well *that* was inappropriate!" David said.

Then Keith excused himself, saying he had some tidying up to do before his crew arrived.

After Keith left, David emailed family.

> We have had almost a week of low-pressure sys-
> tems passing through with mostly cloudy skies,
> periods of heavy rain, and winds from the south
> and southwest which is contrary to current and
> totally unfavourable for heading to the Canaries.

Just as we were about to pack up the computer, Raimo plunked himself down at a table beside us, ordered a hungry man's breakfast, and told us he'd had a change in plans. "My nephews are flying here from Finland. As soon as they arrive I'm outta here."

"Haven't you seen the GRIB files?" David said, turning his laptop screen around.

"To hell with forecasts. We'll raise the storm and trysail," Raimo said. "I wanna get home. I *need* to get home."

Being caught in heavy weather was one thing, heading out in it another. Poor judgment and impatience were the causes of many a disaster at sea. But Raimo, of all people, had to know that. *Love can be a powerful thing,* I thought as I watched, in silent resignation, this tiny, resolute man wolf down his enormous meal.

Walking down the dock, David noticed Graham's slip was empty.

We rushed to the end of the pier and spotted a lone sail pitching wildly in the distance and knew it had to be him. *Godspeed, Graham!*

November 22, Keith came by to introduce us to Elise.

"She's from Paris," he said. "And she's just finished her Ph.D. — in science, no less. And get a load of this: she wants to travel the world *before* completing her breakthrough research. I guess the scientific community will just have to wait!" He laughed an unnatural amount, unabashedly elated with his new crew.

"*Oui, oui,*" Elise said, batting her lashes and nodding like a bobble-head, as if to say *Yes, hard to believe, but it's all true. I am amazing in every way!*

As pleasing as it was to see Keith looking so happy, I was skeptical about his new crew. And I knew for certain that being able to sustain that level of enthusiasm on a small sailboat at sea would be an epic challenge. It was exhausting just watching him.

Raimo's crew had also arrived. Soon both boats were hubs of activity with mini-tours for the new hands; inspections of the riggings; and the loading of cans of diesel, containers of water, and boxes of food in preparation for the ocean. The rest of the marina watched on in worried anticipation.

When Raimo called over to say they were ready to go, James, with Scotch in hand, appeared out of nowhere to help them cast off.

"I'll manage the bow, you get the spring," he instructed David while casually loosening the line with his free hand. "And hold 'er in tight," he added, taking a sip of his drink.

Raimo started his engine. "We're good to go," he said, kicking it into reverse. David threw his line to Raimo's nephews, then all eyes turned bow-ward.

James was still holding on to the bow line with all his might and was teetering on the brink. A panicked chorus of "Let go-o-o-o" rang out, upon which he loosened his grip, the line fell into the water, the crew hurried to haul it in, David yanked James to safety, and Raimo pointed his vessel out to sea. The three Finns waved a relieved goodbye, and James waved back, dazed and hurt by all the fuss.

When the little double-ender had disappeared beyond the breakwaters, James turned his sights on Keith, who was walking toward us.

"Uh-oh. Ask James for help with something, anything," I said to David.

Too late.

An hour or so later Keith and Elise headed into the choppy Atlantic, too.

Watching them all sail off, I was naturally concerned for their safety. But what caught me off guard was that I was also sad to see them go. Spending almost two weeks together in a foreign country, in relative isolation, in rain, I got to know them, and I got to know they weren't four needy lone sailors. Rather they were men who, through twists of fate, with considerable courage, found themselves sailing alone. Raimo, having fulfilled his writing contract, was returning to South America to reunite with his soulmate; Keith was embarking on an open-ended journey of love and adventure; a finite personal challenge was all Graham said he wanted; and James was flailing about in an attempt to start anew. To use David's metaphor, they were individual ships in motion, each with their own destinations in mind, each changing tacks depending on the weather — like our boys were, no different than any of us really. It had been a pleasure meeting them.

James was still standing on the dock beside us, looking forsaken, like an abandoned child.

"How 'bout we raise a glass in honour of friendship and friends at sea?" I said.

"I'm buyin,'" he said, and the three of us walked to the café.

November 24, the harbour was mayhem. As forecast, a severe system hit from the southeast, the absolute worst direction. Restaurant staff hustled to close patio umbrellas and shut all doors and windows, while dock hands moved the most vulnerable boats closer to shore and reinforced lines on the rest. For the next twelve hours, rain pummelled the marina, massive waves crashed over its breakwaters, spray shot up twenty feet in the air, boats thrashed wildly in the surge, and *Inia* gyrated like a rabid beast on a short leash.

The following morning, in waning drizzle and calm, with the sun poking through the clouds, David and I wiped off a table and sat out under a café umbrella with mugs of coffee, checking the GRIB files for the zillionth time. This time, though, we were encouraged by what we saw. Behind this front and ahead of the next was a sliver of good weather, and a sliver was all we needed.

I couldn't wait to leave, to make progress, to explore new places, but most of all, to be back on the ocean.

Journal entry, November 26:

> At this point, much to my amazement, I'm looking forward to the passages themselves as much, or maybe more, than the stops!!

November 27, after what turned out to be a seventeen-day stay, with the help of two dockhands and James, we cast off from the island of Madeira.

"Meet you on the other side, my friends," James yelled.

"We'll be looking for you," I yelled back, a depressing lie.

"Gotta brush up on my Spanish," David said, lowering Portugal's flag and raising Spain's as we headed to the Canaries.

TWENTY-ONE

ONCE WE REACHED the Canary Islands, local weather systems would no longer rule, since this archipelago is in the latitudes of the trade winds, the winds that Christopher Columbus sailed to the Americas, the winds that caused British sailors to quip that their shortest return route to England was via the Caribbean, the winds that would ultimately take David and me home.

We had been warned that Las Palmas, Gran Canaria, where we were to pick up our repaired radio, was a holiday destination for well-heeled western Europeans, and that the ARC race, with 240 boats registered, was scheduled to start from there at the end of November. To avoid excessive costs and crowds, we headed for the island of La Graciosa, with plans to hang back in the smaller islands in the chain until we were certain the radio was there and the racers weren't, after which we'd put in just long enough to snatch our parcel. Then we would move on south and west.

As we passed Ilha de Deserta, there were three-metre swells and I got sick. Still, I was happy to be underway. We all were.

Journal entry, November 27:

Even Inia seems content to be back "at it." As she
creaks and whirs, she proudly goes about her job,
confident that she's good at what she does … better than most. Life is just about perfect right now.

David collected his sextant, a stopwatch, the 2007 *Nautical
Almanac*, and a spiral notebook to practise celestial navigation
en route. By civil twilight, *Inia* had settled into a rhythm in the
waves, the self-steering was working well, and stars began to peek
through. David yelled down that he had captured Altair and Vega.
I yelled up how great that was and that I was starting to feel better. He said that was fantastic news.

In the morning, David was still running on adrenalin. Despite
dark rings under his eyes, he said he couldn't sleep; he wanted to
take it all in. We sat out together, looking at the water, communing
with dolphins, scanning the sky, tweaking the wind vane, chatting.

Evening twilight of the 28th, he took a single moon sight,
but found the horizon difficult to judge.

"You need to get some rest," I said. "And I can do this."

He looked around. The breeze was steady, the waters calm,
and *Inia* was right on course at 142 degrees. "Looks good," he
said. "And I know you can. But wake me up if necessary." In a
matter of minutes, he was snoring below. Just as I thought, he was
exhausted. Yet if I hadn't offered to take over, he wouldn't have
asked. My needs always came first.

I sat out harnessed in the cockpit as the edge of night
advanced and *Inia* surged on with a comfortable ten-degree heel,
the sea slipping by mere feet below me, the silver riggings twinkling in the navigation lights. I had long since abandoned my
watch kit. No need. The thrill of adventure and the joy of discovery were what interested me now. The winds and the waves and
the stars were entertainment enough.

Around midnight, clouds rolled over the stars. A sudden blow caused *Inia*'s leeward gunwale to dip below the water's surface. I could touch the inky ocean. David had said to wake him up *if necessary.* But it was just a gust, I said to myself. And that's what gusts do, they come and they go; essentially, they *gust.* Waking him up wasn't remotely necessary. *I've come one helluva long way,* I thought with a chuckle as *Inia* righted herself.

Then there was another gust, followed by another. Soon the wind began to whistle and the shrouds to shimmy and shake. *Inia*, with sails taut, at a twenty-degree heel, was bolting like a thoroughbred out of the barn, with me at the reins.

We had agreed that rough weather required both of us on deck. This wasn't what you'd call calm, but we had known much rougher. No, I probably could handle this. More than likely I could. They say, if in doubt, let it out. By letting sails out, I'd straighten us up and slow us down. A wave crashed over the gunwale and green water gushed down the deck toward the drains.

I looked at the GPS. *Inia* was doing 7 knots, sometimes 8. "Whooaa, Nellie!" I said as the ocean roared past. "This here filly's wild and running free." Spray shot over the bow. The wind vane spasmed. I checked the GPS again. "And she's headed north! Shiiit!"

"Daaviid!" I called down. He didn't respond.

I darted below and gave his shoulder a gentle shake. "Dear, wakey-wakey!" I said. He snored even louder and rolled over.

"Wake up, goddamn it!" I yelled, giving him a whack as waves broke in every direction.

He sat up, fuzzy, rubbing his arm, talking about walking the dog. Then he looked around and his eyes bulged. "Jesus!" he said, grabbing his life jacket, then rushing on deck as *Inia* flailed out of control.

Over the next half hour, we worked together to reduce sail, change tacks, and reset the wind vane.

"It was a squall," David said. "You should've woken me up earlier."

"I just thought … you were so tired … and I really wanted to —"

"Far earlier."

"I realize that," I said.

November 29, under a crystal-clear sky and gentle breeze, we were nearing the island of La Graciosa. The literature warned that the waters outside the harbour in Caleta de Sebo were littered with semi-submerged fishing floats. So arrival after dark was to be avoided at all costs.

Sunset was 1755. Since neither of us relished the idea of spending the night tacking beyond the breakwaters, we took turns at the helm throughout the day. By 1615 the four volcanic mounds that compose the island came into view, and at precisely 1752, with three minutes to spare, *Inia* slid between the rusted steel sculptures that mark the harbour entrance.

Two shadowy figures were standing at the end of the pier, waving. Lo and behold, they were Keith and Elise. And they were both still smiling. Then another person jumped off a boat and ran over to help catch our lines. It was Graham!

Although it had only been a week since we'd last seen each other, we greeted with hugs like long-lost friends.

"I have to say, I was worried about you guys," I said.

"It was pretty wild," Keith said. "We flew like a bat outta hell."

"Worried? About me? Pshaw!" Graham said. "Perhaps I neglected to mention, I spent my youth in the —"

"In the Merchant Marine, yes, I know," I said.

"Anyway, welcome to Graciosa," Keith said. "The place's like a throwback to the sixties. You guys are gonna love it."

"Tomorrow night there's a meet-and-greet at the end of the pier," Graham said. "It's a Friday tradition, and always a blast."

"*Always?*" I said. "But you just —"

"It's casual, potluck nibblies, BYOB. We'll let you guys settle in and see you then," Graham said.

"Be there or be square," Keith said, laughing.

"*Oui, oui. À demain!*" Elise added, giggling.

The three of them walked off like they were high on life, or something.

Early Friday morning we sat in the cockpit, sipping coffee, taking in the view. The landscape, with white box-shaped buildings, rust-coloured mountain peaks, and cobalt sky, was exquisitely austere.

As soon as the office building opened, we went in to clear customs. The part-time constable was casual and the process was simple, refreshingly so from my perspective, disconcertingly so from David's. We paid for four nights in the marina. At sixteen euros in total, we agreed the price was right.

Afterward, we walked along the wide sand roads lined with palm trees and cacti, all taller than us, passing islanders wearing straw hats shaped like upside-down flower pots. Some swept sand off walkways, others scoured tidal rocks for food with knives and buckets, and then others touched up scratches on their boldly painted wooden skiffs. We eventually made our way to the village centre, where David picked up a Spanish-English dictionary.

The island had all the basics: groceries, a hardware store, a bakery, a couple of cafés, a pay phone. What was striking was what it didn't have. There were no paved roads and, aside from occasional service Jeeps, no cars, no trucks, no vehicles of any kind. And there was no construction equipment, no heavy machinery, no pounding, no grinding, no industrial hum. On a still day, between the chatter of birds and people, silences were noiseless, the quietest quiet I had ever heard. Keith was right. I loved it there already.

Early evening, we knocked on Graham's hull armed with beer, nachos, and salsa. Out he popped from his enclosed cockpit with a large steaming casserole and a cloth sack of paper plates and plastic utensils, enough to feed an army.

"What's that for?" David asked.

"The meet-and-greet," said Graham.

"But —"

"It's nothing really. I love to cook."

Walking to the end of the pier, we could see fifteen to twenty people milling about under the orangey-blue sky of the setting sun. On top of the wide ledge of the breakwater wall, between candles, a smorgasbord was laid out: cheese and crackers, chips and dips, baguettes and salamis, peanuts, pickles, herring, and Graham's casserole. Bottles of vodka, magnums of wine, and an ice chest full of beer lined the wall base.

A Dutch couple, Luke and Melissa, came over to say hello. They had been travelling the world's oceans for twenty years aboard a steel ketch he had built from scratch.

"Wow! It all must be old hat to you guys," I said.

"If only that were true," Luke said. "The reality is, the school of navigation's never closed. As soon as you think there's nothing left to learn, you're taught another, often costly, almost always humiliating, lesson." He confessed they were awaiting repairs to the prop he had damaged as a result of pilot arrogance among lobster pots. Once that was taken care of, they intended to make their way to the States to end their travels, probably in Oriental, North Carolina, where more of the town lived on boats than in houses.

While David continued to talk to them, I noticed a guy standing to my right. He was skin and bones, with blond feathery hair, a pointy face, hollow cheeks, and a long tense neck, not unlike a malnourished chicken, and he was preening in my personal space. Through a rapid-fire series of clucks, he indicated his name was Ian, he was a lone sailor, he was from Australia, his boat was next to ours, and he had been in La Graciosa for weeks. He added, with a chortle, that he had no intention of leaving this great island any time soon. Then he stuttered off into the thick of the crowd.

After dark, the party got livelier. Stories grew wilder, laughter shriller, bonding of total strangers stronger, deeper, in the candle-lit sea air.

David and I went to the cooler for another beer. A woman in her forties with long frizzy hair, wearing a beaded headband, fringed cotton top, and cut-off jeans, was standing alone at the breakwater wall, gently swaying, sipping a tall glass of wine. Aurora was her name. She had hitched a ride here on a German boat.

"Far out," she purred to us drowsily. "I mean, it's like something in the cosmos has brought me here … us all here, together … like the power of universal love made this magical night happen … don't you think?"

David reached down for our beer.

"Could be," I said. "That's certainly an interesting concept. One to ponder."

"Do you believe in the afterlife and reincarnation?"

"Uh —"

"I do," she said, her eyes misty. "And I believe we must've been good in our previous lives, I mean, to deserve such happiness. Like maybe we were white doves, or panda bears, or, or — "

Just then Keith walked over. "Hey!" he said to us.

Aurora continued without skipping a beat. "I mean, how else can you explain it? Each of us, from far-off corners of the earth, on little boats, meeting up on this little dock, on this little island, in the middle of nowhere?"

· "There's karma and then there's destiny, two different things," Keith said, proud of his spontaneous profundity.

David yanked at my T-shirt. "Nice woman, but if she gets any more relaxed she could very well die," he joked as we slipped away.

Then we met an American couple, our age. He had worked as a sailmaker and, like David, he had planned to set sail once he retired. But, also like David, his timetable had been accelerated. Witnessing client after client abandon the dream because of illness or other life events, he had shut down his business ten years early. They had toured the canals of mainland Europe and the Mediterranean Sea before landing on La Graciosa, where they had been for a month so far. Their schedule was sumptuously open ended.

Behind the Americans, I spotted Elise again. She had spent the entire evening floating from one small gathering to the next, laughing copiously at everyone's jokes and graciously accepting everyone's offers of booze.

As the candles burned low and the crowd began to dissipate, David and I picked up our remaining beer and said goodnight to Ian, who was pecking at cracker bits, and to Keith and Aurora, who were delving further into the meaning of life. Then we waved to Graham, who was flanked by four women, all saying he had gone above and beyond, requesting the casserole recipe and asking him if there was anything he *couldn't* do.

"Well, I don't know how to make glass. Not yet anyway," Graham responded. And they tittered at his quick wit, Elise louder than the others.

"Graham's quite the guy," I said with a laugh, walking down the dock arm in arm with David. "I agree with Aurora. There *is* something magical about the coming together of us miscellaneous souls on this tiny, out-of-the-way island."

"So magical that Elise learned how to speak English!"

"Yeah, I know!"

December 1, we decided a hike would do us good. I packed fruit, almonds, and water, and we set out along the southern shoreline.

The dirt road by the harbour soon melded into rocky sand and desert scrub. We traversed this barren, rugged terrain, combing it for souvenir shells and rocks under the bright sun.

By late morning we had reached Playa de la Cocina, a secluded beach with emerald-green water. Sitting on a boulder, snacking, David spotted a large man-made structure, partly occluded by a mangy shrub, ahead in the distance. When we got closer, we saw it was a canvas tarp supported by tent poles. Closer yet, we saw charred wood from a bonfire, then two beach chairs, then beach towels hanging on a rope strung between the poles, and finally, the occupants of this lean-to, an elderly couple — both of whom were honey brown and stark naked — roasting weenies over the flame of a tabletop barbecue.

"Good Lord! C'mon let's go!" I said, picking up the pace.

"Dear, you're acting like a ten-year-old. It's natural. Nothing we haven't seen before," David said.

"And for goodness' sake, quit gawking!" I grabbed his arm.

"I'm *not* gawking. I *am* wondering why they're not wearing aprons, though," he said, beginning to laugh.

"Oh my God!"

"It's a joke. Don't you get it?"

"Look!"

Up ahead, by the water's edge, there was a three-sided, two-foot-high structure made of stacked stones, and someone's bony white butt hanging out over the top of it.

"Okay ... so, apparently we're on a nude beach," David said. "What's the big deal?"

"Nothing. There's no big deal." I tried my best to walk normally. "I was just caught off guard, that's all. Need I remind you I work in health care? You're right, I *have* seen it all," I said, adding, "And then some!"

"What the hell is *that* supposed to mean?" he said, laughing harder.

Then, seemingly in slo-mo, the butt disappeared and a man poked his head up, craned his neck around, leapt out from behind the stone wall, and began waving both arms high in the air, displaying his full frontal. I looked behind us to confirm what I already knew: there was no one else around.

"Jesus!" David said.

"Pretend you don't see him. Just look down and keep walking," I said. "Maybe pick up a shell or two."

"What if he's just being friendly? Maybe we should wave back," David said, staring at the man as we drew nearer. "If we don't, we run the risk of looking uneasy."

"Which we're most certainly not, so ..."

We both acknowledged the man with reticent waves, immediately after which he retreated behind the stone structure. "See! He was just saying hi," David said.

I stopped dead in my tracks. "And that's because he knows us."

Ian, the lone Australian sailor, our slip neighbour, was the naked man with the spindly wares. There was no mistaking his gait.

"Shit!" David said.

Calling cards were only available at the post office Monday to Friday between 1100 and 1300. We found that out midafternoon Friday.

Nevertheless, Sunday, December 2, was the best day to contact John. Late afternoon, we walked down the dirt road to the outdoor phone booth in the village centre, my shorts weighted with pockets full of coin.

John sounded groggy and said he had just woken up. I told him I'd keep it short. Christmas was a go. Brian's flights were booked. Grandma was looking forward to seeing them. For his present, we thought we'd use reward miles to arrange a trip of some sort for him, too, perhaps during his reading week. Maybe he could even meet up with us. By then we'd be done ocean passages, so there'd be less risk in booking. Food for thought. No pressure, though. We understood his final stretch would be a busy one with his fourth-year recital, orchestra stuff, exams, et cetera, et cetera.

"I'd love that," John said. "Speaking of the orchestra, I'm in Montreal right now, and last night —"

"Oh, that's right. It's this weekend. I forgot," I said. "I guess you had a late night."

"It was much later than expected because —"

"Oh, and the Opera House gig was Friday night. No wonder you're tired. How'd that —"

"Mom, I saw Ben last night after the show."

Ben! My heart pounded. I took an extra breath.

"He emailed me just before I left Toronto."

"So, he got your email, did he?"

"He did."

"And he's been in Montreal all this time?" I asked.

"Yes, seems so," John replied.

"Well, that's great, John. That's really great news." I held the receiver and told David. "I'm thrilled for you. Dad is, too."

"Ask him if Ben's working," David said. "And if he's made friends there. And if he's okay."

"And how, how's he doing?" I asked, feeding the phone more money.

"I didn't recognize him at first. His hair's super-long and he's grown a huge beard."

"Do you know where he's living? How he's living?"

"He has a tiny place. We had pizza there. It's cool, in a Ben sorta way."

"And did he say what he's up to?"

"Still the bike courier thing."

"And, and does he seem happy?"

"Happy enough."

"Good, that's good. And —"

The phone line went dead. We had used up all of our coin.

"Well, at least he connected with John," I said to David on our walk back. "And I *am* happy just to know he's okay."

"Yeah, let's just relish that thought," David said.

∿

December 3, the two of us sat in the cockpit drinking orange juice, watching the sun rise, soaking in the stillness. David raised the unpleasant topic of departure. If he hadn't, I would have. Both of us were keenly aware of the passage of time. With only five months left before we'd be back in Canada, lots of territory yet to cover, and a forced stop on the island of Gran Canaria, from this point on, tough choices would have to be made. Unlike the sailmaker and his wife, we'd now be faced with continual trade-offs; the longer we stayed in one place, the less we'd see of others. As much as we loved this island, we agreed we'd leave the following morning. And we made dinner reservations, this time to celebrate casting off.

The restaurant was casual, dark, almost empty. We were shown to a table off to one side. As my eyes adjusted to the dimness, I spotted Keith sitting on his own in the corner, eating a fish dinner, drinking a half litre of wine. He said he had heard rave reviews about this place. The fish was great. It exceeded his expectations. In fact, it was the best fish he had ever tasted, and he had tasted a lot of fish. Then he blurted, "Actually, I needed to get away from Elise. It's not working out. I've made a change in plans."

"Aurora?"

"Oh, Aurora. It's a good name for someone who's brought strange new light into my life. I wish! But no, I'm sailing on alone from here. And it's okay."

"What about Elise?"

"She'll be fine. She's leaving with Graham."

"Graham! But he was adamant —"

"Yeah, well … ships in motion … possibility … and all that sort of thing," he said with a laugh.

"Well, well, well," I said, as David ordered beer and paella for two in Spanish.

At 0856 on December 4, with the help of Graham, Keith, and Ian, I backed *Inia* out of her slip and took one last glance at this enchanting island, then passed between the breakwaters and pointed *Inia* south-southeast for the 40-nautical-mile trip to Lanzarote, the very next island in the chain.

TWENTY-TWO

A GIANT SEA TURTLE with short, stout flipper-like legs glided by *Inia*'s hull and escorted us to the entrance to Marina Rubicón before paddling back out to sea. The marina facility was modern, the office efficient, the woman in charge dressed for success.

"Look at this!" I said, giggling as David filled out the registration forms. A sign on the desk read "Please Use Clothes and Shoes When Entering the Office."

He chuckled, too.

"It isn't a joke!' the woman said. She proceeded to talk about the island's problem with nude tourists like an animal-control specialist would an invasive species. "They migrate off the beaches into town, where they stroll the promenade, meander through our shops, even jog on our streets."

"Not jog!" I exclaimed.

"And there have been recent reports of them in local banks and businesses, too," she continued.

I peered out the window. "But, I don't see —"

"Too cold," she said.

For once, I appreciated a nippy north wind.

Inia looked small and primitive, like the "little vessel that could," sandwiched between two private luxury yachts. After locking her up, we walked along a boardwalk, passing a maze of expensive boutiques, high-end restaurants, manicured gardens, and souvenir stands all selling the same plastic crap. The only thing we liked about Rubicón was its chandlery. But, expecting Las Palmas to be even fancier, we decided to stay put for a few days to do boat jobs.

Top on our list was to devise a system so we could sail downwind more efficiently, since that's what the entire trade-winds crossing would be. Because of the boat's natural yawing under self-steering, there was heightened risk of wind from behind catching the opposite side of, or backing, the sails. In the case of the mainsail, this would cause a violent swinging of the boom from one side to the other, or an accidental jibe. David tied a line to prevent that from happening. However, backing of the jib continued to be a problem which, although less dangerous, was inefficient and, over time, caused wear. A whisker pole is the tried-and-true solution, but it was expensive — too expensive right then. So he rummaged through bins of stainless-steel doodads and bought a couple of blocks, which he fastened to the boom to hold the jib out.

Over the next few days, he also rewired our broken bow light, replaced worn lines, and trued the rigging, while I shopped for groceries and sent postcards to friends.

December 8, David and I walked around to the restaurant on the boardwalk opposite *Inia* and sat on the patio between groups of Botoxed faces that looked permanently alert. We ordered a pitcher of iced tea and a basket of fries. While waiting for our food to arrive, we overheard the people at the table next to us complaining about the boat with dishtowels hanging from its shrouds. It was *Inia*.

"No one should have to look at someone's dirty laundry over a nice meal out," the old man with a comb-over said to the waiter.

"It's an eyesore!" whined his wife, who wore dangly diamond earrings and had purple hair.

The waiter assured the patrons management would deal with the uncivilized transients immediately.

Then we heard a buzz. It was our wind generator. We tried to ignore it, but the breeze picked up and the grating noise grew louder until patio conversations stopped. Soon all eyes were on David as he stood among flapping dishtowels on *Inia's* lifelines, hugging the boom gallows, frantically attempting to lasso the generator blades.

Meanwhile, back at the table, our order arrived and so did two large birds.

"Shoo!" I said, waving my hand. They chirped and flapped their giant wings in response. As the wind generator continued to buzz and David continued to thrash about in an effort to silence it, the birds stood on the table, flinging half-eaten chips at me, swelling in defiance when I so much as twitched. And the dishtowel protesters began to snicker.

As soon as David returned to the table, the birds took flight. We paid the bill and followed.

"I can't believe how obnoxious that couple was," I said to David on our walk back to the boat.

"Could've been worse. They could've been nude," he said.

We agreed we'd leave Lanzarote the next morning — that was, of course, after untangling the mizzen halyard from the wind generator for the third time.

TWENTY-THREE

ESTIMATING THE TRIP to Gran Canaria would take twenty to twenty-two hours, we departed Lanzerote at noon for a morning arrival.

With wind directly on our stern and rough cross swells, David's pulley set-up to hold the jib out didn't work, nor did the wind vane. So, we motored and took turns at the wheel the entire night through.

The lights of Gran Canaria appeared around 0300, sooner than expected, too early. David slowed *Inia* down and we, along with fourteen freighters, hung out on the ocean until sunrise.

At around 0600 Las Palmas came into focus with neon blue palm trees twinkling along the water's edge, a vast container port sparkling red and gold with men and machinery in perpetual motion, a massive city lighting up the early morning sky.

"Neon blue palm trees, wouldn't you know it!" I said to David.

We entered the harbour alongside a freighter being guided in by a pilot boat. They veered starboard to the commercial docks. We went left to the long Texaco pier where we intended to wait until the marina office opened.

Just as David secured the last of our lines, the gas attendant flew out of the building, arms flailing, yelling at us in Spanish.

"*Se trata de un muelle de gas.* Vamoose!"

"But the guidebook says … *el libro dice* …" David said.

"¡*Sali*! Vamoose! *Aquí no pueden atracar su barco.*" He began to detach our bow.

"There's no space … uh … *no espacio en el muelle de recepción*," David said while undoing our stern.

"¡*Esto es tu problema, no el mío*!" the man spat, hurling the line on deck and heading to where our spring line was cleated.

"But the reception dock's full," I said to David as we re-boarded.

"I told him that and he said it was our problem, not his."

"Did you tell him we haven't slept for twenty-four friggin' hours?" I said, catching the last of our lines.

"No." We watched the man give *Inia* a shove off. "And somehow I doubt that would've made a difference." David stoically resumed helming, round and round the bay.

"I hope you at least told him that we didn't want to stop in his goddamn city in the first place. And that the instant we get our radio, we're so outta here," I said, fighting back tears.

We heard more shouting and saw that the attendant was hollering at us again.

"And that he's a world-class jerk," I continued, watching him do jumping jacks along the dock. "And I really, really hope you said that, in your wife's professional opinion, he and his fellow Las Palmians could take their neon palm trees and shove them —"

"Wait! Sounds like he's wanting us to go back. And he seems to be smiling!"

As David turned the boat around, the attendant ran into his office and re-emerged waving a giant Canadian flag. "¡*Bienvenido, Canada*!" he yelled. Then he and two dockhands caught our lines and tied *Inia* back down. "*Bienvenido*," he repeated. "Welcome to Las Palmas."

"*Muchas gracias*," David said, glancing at me and then at our tired Canadian flag flapping astern.

As soon as the marina office opened, we walked over to register. The desk clerk pulled out a calculator to determine our docking fees. The more numbers he punched in, the tenser I got.

"Based on your vessel's waterline length, it'll be seven euros," he finally announced.

I didn't hear most of what he subsequently said about our radio, customs, the facility, and our slip, still stuck on the seven euros. I had fully expected this marina to be the most expensive ever. But, next to La Graciosa, it was the cheapest — by far!

We slowly motored over to scope out our assigned slip. There were no finger docks or pilings, just one long pier to which boats were attached, bow in, separated by a jumble of fenders. While we strategized how we'd squeeze *Inia* between two rusty steel tubs, an unshaven Finn wearing droopy greying underwear climbed out of his cabin on the starboard one to help. He was my second clue that perhaps this wasn't such a fancy marina after all.

After he had secured our bow to a cleat, he handed David a line on the dock that led to another line that was affixed to a submerged cement block. David retrieved the slimy, foul-smelling rope from the water and tied it on *Inia's* stern. That was all there was to it.

We went below, pulled out the main berth, and crashed for eighteen hours.

December 12, we woke up rested, eager to check out this new place, and also hoping to buy a whisker pole.

Standing on the bow we looked at each other, then around. We didn't know how to get onto the dock. It was too far to step, too precarious to jump. Then we saw a woman leaving a boat. She climbed over the bow pulpit, reached for the cleat on the dock, stepped onto the taut bow line, did a kind of a tightrope walk over the water, and pulled herself up onto the pier.

"Looks straightforward enough," David said. He carefully did the same.

I stood outside the bow pulpit and glanced at the oily green-black water below.

"Just do it. C'mon," David said.

I stepped onto the line. It swung. I froze. It sagged. And I slowly sank between *Inia* and the dock.

"That was a good first try, honey," David said, trying his damnedest to sound sincere.

After clambering back up onto our bow, I waited for *Inia* to drift back out. The next time, what I lacked in style I made up for with undue velocity.

"Whoa!" David said as I hurled myself at his feet.

I straightened my shorts and we proceeded.

The docks were filled with serious blue-water vessels. And along the waterfront, instead of boutiques and galleries, were practical shops all pertaining to ocean travel: diesel mechanics, riggers, sailmakers, electronics specialists, and extreme-weather outfitters. The only hospitality establishment was the no-frills Sailor's Bar, "at 28 degrees 7.58 minutes north, 15 degrees 25.67 minutes west," as they liked to say.

We went into the rigging shop. The rigger said of course they sold whisker poles but they came in various sizes. According to him, the calculation to determine the length was 90 percent of the bottom of the jib, which in our case was 5.7 metres. The few he had in stock were longer, so we ordered one. It would cost five hundred euros and would arrive in four or five days.

Then we located the marina's mailroom, where our repaired radio was waiting.

Afterward, we searched for Marcel, the Canadian we had met in the Azores. He had emailed us a while back from "Pontoon 5, Las Palmas," and that's where we found him, sitting on the back of his boat, minus his crew. His daughter had flown home to Dartmouth for Christmas. We invited him for dinner. He gladly accepted.

Back at *Inia*, David slid along the bow line to board and I followed, a bit more smoothly this time.

While David installed the radio, I went to the marina to get cleaned up. The washrooms were in the middle of the chain of sailing shops, behind solid metal doors. I opened the women's to a blast of urine-scented steam, walked passed unflushed toilets, and waited in line for a shower. After a scowling old woman with long grey hair and sagging tattoos came out of a shower stall, I went in. The enclosure was divided into dry and wet areas by a brittle plastic curtain suspended on a pitted metal rod. I stripped, hung my clothes and towel on hooks, placed the shampoo and soap within easy reach, then stepped onto the wooden grate and closed the curtain.

There were two wall knobs; the right was for cold water, the left for hot. I pushed them in simultaneously, producing a tepid spray. As I stuck my head under it, the cold knob popped out and the water turned scalding. I quickly pushed the knob back in, reached for the shampoo, and began to lather. Then the hot water knob popped out, the spray went ice cold, soap got in my eyes, I knocked the cap to the shampoo bottle off, felt for the knob, and shoved it back in, too. But it popped out again. Then out popped the cold knob, followed by the hot … the hot … the c-o-l-d … hot, cold, h-o-t … hot … cold *and* hot.

"*Heeelp!*" I screamed.

Deciding to cut the infuriating shower short, I lifted the floor grate to get the bottle cap. There it was, floating in a still pool of scummy water, amid a mesh of brown grey black blond long kinky straight curly hairs clogging the drain. I gagged and bolted, finally convinced that, although international, this marina was anything but swank.

Early evening, after we had set the table, our guest arrived. Marcel was tall and fit, with thick white hair, a deep tan, and pearly teeth. He boarded *Inia* with agility, looking at home among yachts, at ease with life in general.

I served cheese and crackers and wine in the cockpit and, predictably, the two men immediately got talking boats. Marcel asked how we stopped the jib halyard from twisting at the top. David said that our dock neighbour in Horta had added a fitting at the top to change the angle, but it had broken off on our way to Portugal, so he had added a pendant at the bottom in Lagos, which effectively did the same thing. David asked Marcel what he thought of his CapeHorn wind vane. Marcel replied that it was finicky downwind. David told Marcel about our issue with our new VHF radio. Marcel said he had just bought himself a single sideband for longer-distance communication.

I went below, lit the oil lamp, and called up through the companionway that dinner was ready.

When David and Marcel had slid into their seats, I placed the bottle of wine and bowls of Thai chicken, steamed rice, and a tossed salad in the centre of the table and joined them. As we passed the food around, we discussed where to next. Marcel said that, as soon as Claire returned in January, he intended to head to the Caribbean, then to make his way north to Nova Scotia. He was an oceanographer on a year's leave and had to get back for work. David told him we had decided to go to the Cape Verdes, then cross over from there.

"Crossing from here or there makes no real difference. Sailing the trades is easy. That's why they call it the ladies' passage," Marcel said, flashing his orthodontic smile.

Then the topic of Christmas came up. Marcel would be hanging out in Las Palmas on his own, which, he said, was fine by him. Having spent five months there a few years back, he had a special bond with the place. "But if you guys are around, maybe we can meet up for a yuletide beer," he said.

"Depends on the whisker pole," David said.

"I'm really hoping to be underway, though. It'd be so fantastic to celebrate Christmas mid-ocean, just the two of us," I said, smiling at David.

"Besides, I could use the time to figure out my new radio," Marcel said, refilling his glass.

"So, you're an oceanographer," David said, to change the subject.

"That I am, and it impresses the hell out of everybody, but the truth is, thirty years of studying wave action is twenty-nine and a half years too many. I'd love to be doing something else, something creative like writing or photography, or at least something that makes a tangible difference to a single other human being. Oh well, the gig pays for the lifestyle to which I've grown accustomed." He strained to smile.

I understood Marcel's predicament of feeling stuck in a thankless job because David had been in the exact same situation. That career train was almost impossible to get off of once it left the station. Fortunately for us, though, David had been given the nudge he needed to jump.

"How 'bout you guys? Clearly you lucked out somehow," Marcel said. "Let me guess. You're retired civil servants."

"I was fired," David said.

"Jesus! Sorry!"

I assured Marcel there was nothing to be sorry about, then changed the subject again.

"So, five whole months, you must really know the place. Do you have suggestions of things for us to do?"

"Let me think," he said. "Well, you have to experience the marina showers. They're unique, state-of-the —"

"Ugggh!" I said, my stomach lurching.

"Oh, so you already have," he said with a chuckle.

I stacked the dishes in the sink. David found our map of the city from under a pile of papers on the nav station. Marcel poured himself more wine, then opened up the map, turned it to the proper orientation, and laid it on the table. We sat down beside him.

"All right ... so ... we're here," he said, pointing to the marina. "You go this way, and along here's a shopping district. Right now it's all decked out in lights. If you need to buy gifts for the holidays, that's where to go." He circled and labelled the area in pencil. "Then, if you walk in the opposite direction, you'll find lots of great little diners." He made small *x*'s along two city blocks. "Look for a place that serves *papas arrugas*, new potatoes stewed in a hot-and-sour sauce," he said, jotting the name of the dish in the margin. "And along here's an amazing beach. I wear sunglasses when I run there so I don't look like a perv — if you get my drift!" He smiled again. "On a practical front, here's a small business called BEM, where you can make long-distance calls on the cheap. And if you're yearning for North American food, here's a mall where you can get pretty much everything your homesick heart desires, except peanut butter. It's the one thing you won't find anywhere on this side of the Atlantic." He scribbled *phone* and *mall* on their respective locations on the map.

"So, you're a hard-core PB-and-J man," David joked.

"Not at all, but it's the best damn cure for seasickness there is!"

"Good to know!" I said, suddenly remembering the jar I had bought in the Gaspé. It had to still be somewhere onboard.

Marcel paused to take a drink. "And speaking of sickness, if you're needing the hospital, it's here, and I can attest the care's second to none."

David and I looked at each other.

"And here, right here," he said, making several concentric circles, then adding stars around them, "here's where, if you get yourself hammered and try to jump off the concrete wall, you can experience compound fractures, a head injury, the whole enchilada."

"You didn't!" I said.

"I did," he said. "The worst part is, I was forever at my son to be responsible. Play it safe. 'Don't be a doofus,' I'd say. Then I — the perfect role model dad that I am — go and pull a goddamn stunt like that!"

"You've made a remarkable recovery, thank goodness," I said. "And really, when you think about it, most of us have done stupid things that could've ended badly. Driving too fast. Swimming when we shouldn't have."

"Sailing tiny boats across big oceans," David piped in. We grinned uneasily. "But, Marcel, with respect to your son," he continued. "Sue and I know how you feel. We have three boys of our own. I can't count the number of 'be careful' speeches we've given over the years, but they still took risks."

"In fact, one of our sons had a similar fall off a wall, except on his bike," I said. "He was into this thing called trials — using urban landscapes as obstacle courses. It's crazy dangerous if you ask me, but there was no stopping him. One day we got this call from the hospital that started with 'Your son's had an accident, but he can wiggle his toes.'"

"They said that?" Marcel said, taking a sip of wine.

"Those were the exact words!" I continued. "When we got to emerg, he was lying on a stretcher with his neck immobilized. A tooth was broken, his top lip was hanging on by a thread, his whole face looked like ground meat. We could barely recognize him." I paused, remembering the horrific scene. "He made a full recovery, too, thank goodness."

"But once they're adults, our kids have the right to live at risk just like we do, and there isn't a damn thing we can do, except hope and pray," David said, adding, "Who knows, maybe, ironically, your 'close call' made more of an impact on your son than any speech ever could!"

Marcel made more stars on the edge of the map. "No, he's dead," he said, raw with grief. "He died snowboarding off-trail." He wiped his eyes with his T-shirt and drained the wine bottle into our three glasses. We sat quietly for a while.

Then I pulled off the starboard settee cushion and rummaged through all the compartments behind it. "This is for you," I said, handing Marcel our jar of peanut butter.

"Oh, I can't —"

"Merry Christmas."

"It's the best present ever!"

269

December 15, David and I walked to the shopping district.

Lights dripped from trees, lined pathways, trimmed buildings, and were draped across every street. Candy canes, teddy bears, snowflakes, and bells lit up storefronts. Blue and gold angels adorned the night sky.

David and I split up to buy gifts for each other. As I watched him walk off, it wasn't lost on me that the last time we made this shopping arrangement was that fateful Christmas, that Christmas when he had a soul-destroying job and a fractured spine, when our family was splintering, when my world was falling apart and life was so damned bleak. But now, just two years later, the boys were carving out their unique paths and reconnecting with each other, the two of us were on this amazing adventure and were looking to a future wide open to possibility on our return. It seemed we *had* lucked out somehow.

I joined the crowds of Christmas shoppers wandering in and out of stores and bought a pottery wine pitcher, a handmade bowl, candy, and garland and baubles and bows, smiling like a fool at complete strangers, feeling joyful to my core.

December 18, our whisker pole arrived. It was a full metre shorter than what we had ordered. The holidays were approaching. Businesses would be shutting down. Exchanging it would mean staying put until January, which neither of us wanted to do. But crossing back over the Atlantic would be a nightmare without a downwind system of some sort. So, what to do?

We walked up and down the docks, studying everyone's set-ups for sailing the trades. Then we went to the Sailor's Bar, where there were as many opinions about whisker poles as there were sailors.

"You don't need a whisker pole. Just tie the jib end to something."

Tried that.

"It's not an exact science. Any pole that'll hold the sail out'll do."

Why would the rigger say —?

"Five hundred euros is highway robbery."

Yeah, we know but —

"It *is* an exact science, and the J-measurement, the distance between the mast and the forestay, is the proper length."

But the rigger specifically said —

My head was about to implode when a wizened old salt, sitting in the corner, smoking a hand-rolled cigarette, spoke up. "The ninety percent measurement is pretty much the same as the J-measurement, assuming the calculation's using a regular jib, which, of course, it should be."

"Of course," David and I said.

We had erroneously measured our larger genoa. It turned out the whisker pole was accidently perfect.

December 20, after David and the rigger installed the hardware to accommodate the whisker pole, the two of us slipped into preparation mode: checking the ditch bag, the lights, the engine, filling water; charging the handheld devices; sorting the charts; stowing the books. Since we had done it so many times before, it had become a highly choreographed dance.

Last, we went by taxi to the supermarket, HiperDino, where, along with the standard fare, our final provisioning included fixings for a turkey dinner. Then we stopped at a hardware store and bought a roasting pan, C-clamps, and a spool of wire to tie pots and pans to the camping stove so we could cook it.

We were set for Christmas on the Atlantic.

After the taxi driver helped us carry the carload down the dock, David passed boxes and bags over the lifelines to me on deck. The Finn in the grey underwear sat in his cockpit, drank beer, and watched us. "You're not leaving tomorrow, are you?" he finally said.

"Yeah. Why?" David said.

"It's Friday."

We both looked at him.

"So ...?"

"No one leaves on a Friday. It's bad luck."

"Says who?" I said.

"Heavy rain's forecast Saturday," David said.

"Then you wait 'til Sunday."

David and I snickered.

"Suit yourself," he said, scratching his groin.

We finished loading the boat in silence.

"Okay, so Sunday it is," David said as soon as we were below.

Saturday, December 22, with our documents wrapped in a plastic bag, we made the long hike to the customs office through teeming rain. I sat on a bench and flipped through a magazine while David went up to the wicket, where he was greeted by a customs official with a large gut, a booming voice, and an enormous attitude.

We soon learned that the simplicity of the administrative process to clear customs in Caleta de Sebo that seemed too good to be true was. La Graciosa wasn't even a port of entry. Unbeknownst to us, we had been gallivanting around the Canary Islands illegally for almost a month.

David looked over at me, terrified, then turned back and began to grovel in a halting English–Spanish blend, eventually wearing the official down. He said he wouldn't go so far as to make our entry into the country legal, but he'd stamp our exit which, by then, was all we needed.

We were free to go. Actually, he ordered us to go — within twenty-four hours.

Thinking of the time differences, we stayed up until 2200, then walked to BEM. Beyond the ordinary storefront was a long narrow room lined with phone booths. Families huddled around some, individuals hunched in others, with different languages being spoken, universal emotions being expressed, humanity filling the air.

David and I crammed into a booth together and, with the phone receiver held between our heads, we got in touch with everyone on our list — everyone except Ben, since we didn't have his phone number, and Brian, since he wasn't at the Cash 'n' Carry — to say that we'd be on the ocean over the holidays, that we'd be okay, that we were actually excited, that they needn't worry, that we hoped they'd have a fantastic Christmas, too, and that we loved them all very much.

Back at the marina, I told Marcel we were leaving in the morning. He insisted on treating us to a beer, and he and David devised a loose call schedule to keep in touch on the ocean via radio. Then David and I took a final leisurely stroll down the colourful docks of Las Palmas, shimmied across *Inia*'s bow line like a couple of experts, went below, and tried in vain to sleep.

TWENTY-FOUR

ON DECEMBER 23, I released the bow line and exchanged a longer than desired goodbye with underwear man while pushing alongside his vessel to back out. David detached the gooey green stern line. *Inia* floated over it, and we left Las Palmas. I wondered if, hoped that, we'd someday return.

Beyond the concrete breakwaters, David called Marcel to test our repaired VHF radio. Marcel heard him perfectly.

Soon, long waves pulsed on our quarter. We had entered the main shipping corridor between the Canaries and Africa, and freighters were everywhere. *Inia* was like a lone Mini Cooper on a highway filled with Mack trucks.

By evening I was headachy, sweaty, needing to crash. As David sat down at the nav station to prepare for his scheduled call to Marcel, I drifted off to sleep.

I was awakened by a loud crackly "Ho, ho, ho, merry Christmas!" David, backlit by the glow of the full moon, was in the cockpit listening to the message over the handheld VHF. I climbed outside.

"Must be from one of those ships," he said, smiling. "Nice, eh?"

"Except it's the twenty-fourth," I said, rubbing my eyes to focus.

"Not as of two minutes ago."

"Tell me I didn't sleep for —"

"You clearly needed it."

"Geez Louise. I'll take over. You'd better get some shut-eye, too. I want this to be the best Christmas ever."

Given the thinning freighter traffic, David conceded.

As soon as he was out, I tiptoed around the cabin, stringing garland along the ceiling handholds, hanging gold tassels on the curtain rods, placing a wreath over the wall-mounted oil lamp, suspending bows and stars from every hatch.

Early morning, he awoke to the garishness with childlike delight. "When did you ...? I can't believe you were able to ... Sue, it's really beautiful!" He did a quick check of the GPS. "I just need to point *Inia* more west so we don't run into Africa. Then let the festivities begin!"

While he went on deck, I put the kettle on to make coffee, giggling at the absurdity of running into Africa.

After altering our heading, he jumped out from behind the nav station bulkhead wearing a Santa hat of glued felt, his glasses askew, and a brightly wrapped box in hand. He began jerkily moving his shoulders and hips and singing, "Dancin' and prancin' and laughter and fun. Now the jingle bell hop's begun ..."

"Do you have any idea how you look?" I said between peals of laughter.

"Irresistibly sexy, I know," he said. Then dropping down to an Elvis voice, "And this here, my sweet li'l teddy bear, is for you."

I poured us each a cup of coffee. Then we sat on the cabin floor and began our present exchange. David watched with excitement as I carefully turned back layers of tissue paper and uncovered hand-painted ceramic plaques, four of them: an ocean beach sunrise, weathered people harvesting food along a shoreline, whitewashed dwellings with clay roofs and desert gardens, a village nestled among volcanic peaks.

"We've been to all these places. I even feel we've met these very people!" I said. "They'll be great mementos, when it's all over." I rewrapped the breakable pieces, blinking back tears.

"Thought so, too."

I lifted out a glittery gift bag from behind the port seat cushion. "Your turn. Merry Christmas, my dear."

David was elbow deep in crumpled tissue paper when we heard a bang and felt a jolt.

"It's probably Rudolph," I joked.

There was another louder bang. Then *Inia* began to shudder, decorations began to sway, and coffee began to slosh and spill.

David slipped off his hat and, amid more piercing booms and bangs, he tentatively climbed up the companionway and stepped outside. I followed close behind. We poked our heads up from the safety of the cockpit and saw that the forestay, the giant genoa, and the solid furling drum were thrashing about. The heavy-duty fitting that fastens this entire roller furling assembly to the deck had snapped off. Now its only point of attachment was at the top of the mast.

As a result, *Inia*'s hull was in obvious jeopardy, our rigging could be damaged, or lost entirely, and, without the forward stability of this forestay, we were at risk of being dismasted.

Taming this wild inorganic beast was both urgent and perilous. Winds had strengthened to 25 knots. The sea state, with cross swells, had become confused. David set the wind vane to a broad reach to minimize the flailing, loosened the jib sheets, and crawled to the bow.

"Tie yourself down and come out here," he yelled while pulling on the reefing line to haul it in.

"Who, me?"

"Now!"

Me, on the foredeck. I gasped. This was a first.

Inia jerked maniacally as I hooked myself onto a jackline, dropped to my knees, and crept to where he was.

"Okay. See that line? Bring it over. Attach it here. Then get the winch handle. Hurry." They were captain's orders: short, crisp, unequivocal.

Moving from handhold to handhold, I climbed over the cabin roof, grabbed the preventer line, climbed back across, and, reaching out over dolphins splashing in the ocean, fixed the line to the genoa drum with its snap shackle. I turned, relieved, wet with sweat. Then the winch handle fell out of my pocket. We watched it bounce and slide to the starboard gunwale. Certain that a rogue wave would send it flying, with my heart thumping in my brain, I slunk down the side and snatched it.

"Quick thinking. Way to go," David said, winching the humongous sail in.

The dolphins squawked in applause as we wrestled the sail up out of the water, over the lifeline, onto the deck. Then, while David shoved it through the forward hatch from above, I pulled it down into the V-berth from below, my eyes watering in the closeness, the heat, the concentrated odours from the head.

After the sail was stowed, he stayed out to reattach the forestay drum to the deck and raise the storm sail on the inner forestay. I remained below, vomiting strands of sour coffee until there was none left. Then I slid under our blankets and fell back asleep.

When I came to, it was again night. Seeing David's present sitting unopened where he had set it twelve hours before and him outside eating crackers from the box, I started to cry.

"Some Christmas," I said to him through the companionway. "I had all the fixings for a special turkey dinner."

"No worries, sweetie. Honestly, it'll be great whenever."

"And your present isn't even —"

"No rush for that either. C'mon out here. You gotta see this night sky. I've never seen anything like it." He slid over and I sat down. "Cracker?"

I wiped my runny nose with one sleeve of my sweatshirt and dried my eyes with the other, then took a handful of crackers.

"Look up above the moon. See that dot? That's Mars. And over there's the constellation Orion. It rises in the east and sets in the west. Supposedly it's named after a hunter in Greek mythology. Those three stars on an angle are his belt, and they point to Sirius, the brightest star in the night sky, right over there. See it?"

"I do," I said.

"Sure beats GPS, eh?"

Eventually, the constellations faded. A near-full moon illuminated the ocean and plankton flickered on its surface, like nature's own festival of lights. When the night air cooled we retreated below and picked up where we had left off, silly Santa hat and all.

David lifted the hand-thrown wine pitcher and bowl out of the gift bag and held them high.

"Look forward to testing them out."

"It's a no-return policy," I said.

We laughed.

After stowing the pieces safely in a compartment under the V-berth, David poured two glasses of Madeira and sat back down.

"To the boys," he said.

"To the boys," I responded.

"To family and to friends, old and new."

"Yes, cheers to all the wonderful people in our lives."

"To Christmas on the Atlantic."

"Dear ... if we were to die at sea —"

"Sue, it's just the forestay! We'll be —"

"Please listen. I need to say this. You need to know that if things were to go badly out here, it would have been worth it ... just sayin' ... yes, to Christmas on the Atlantic."

For the next four days, we had more of the same: lots of sunshine and wind. At the rate we were going, under storm jib only, we expected to make landfall in plenty of time to ring in the new year Cape Verdean style.

Daytime, the cross swells with sunlit spray exploding from their breaking crests looked like diamond-spewing volcanoes. The random eruptions over the wide expanse were mesmerizing to watch until, with a loud *clap*, one erupted on top of me.

"I'm laughing with you," David said, climbing up to the cockpit, howling, having witnessed the deluge from below.

"But I'm not laughing," I said, soaking wet, laughing, too, as sparkling water swirled into the cockpit scuppers.

These same seas that seemed playful in the light of day felt sinister at night. And, as it was just past the winter solstice, the nights were long. David pointed out, optimistically, that since the sun had reached its most southern declination and was moving higher and we were travelling to lower latitudes — twelve degrees lower, to be exact — daylight hours would start to increase. But as it stood, our sunrise was at 0800, sunset at 1800. If not for the moon, we would have fourteen hours of darkness on the ocean.

December 29, the wind began to slacken.

Morning of the 30th, with 160 nautical miles to go, I redid the math. Unless a dramatic change in weather occurred, which was not forecast, it was doubtful we'd make the Cape Verdes by New Year's Eve.

I struggled to conceal my disappointment, causing something in David to snap. He said if we maximized our speed and steered the most direct heading, there was still a glimmer of hope we'd get there on time. He started the engine, assumed a wide-based stance at the helm, and began to motor-sail, breaking only to pee.

Over the next ten hours, I restored order in the cabin, made food for the two of us, brought out coffees, and kept David company.

By late afternoon, a haze had developed. With no overhead shelter in the cockpit and David's face burnt, the respite from the sun was welcome.

After sunset we reduced sail, headed *Inia* slightly more west, set Bobby, and went to bed, taking turns to look about at the usual twenty-minute intervals.

At 0400 on December 31, we were both on deck, pumped for this final push. With the clouds and waning moon, it was black out. David turned on the spreader lights, high up the mast, illuminating the boat, the sails, and the water immediately around us. It was peaceful. Working together under this soft cone of light, we raised the main and poled out the storm sail.

As the sun rose, the air grew thicker with heat, humidity, and haze. David pointed *Inia* directly for the island of São Vicente and, still hopeful, he resumed steering. But by late afternoon his optimism began to leech, as did all colour from his cheeks.

"Take the helm, I need to check a few things," he said.

"What's up?"

"According to the GPS, we're less than four miles away."

"But I don't see land."

"Exactly!" he said. "With island elevations of up to seven hundred and seventy-four metres, we should!"

"You don't think we're lost, do you?"

"It's unlikely, but —"

"*Unlikely*?" I said, scanning the strangely dense air.

Minutes later he came back up and said to proceed with caution. Nick, the Polish sailor we had met in São Miguel, who had become our unofficial weather router on this leg of the journey, had emailed, none too soon, to warn us about the haze. It wasn't just low cloud cover. It was fine sand from continental Africa, being blown across the ocean by a hot wind known as a harmattan!

He wrote,

> Visibility is less than you judge. There is Sahara
> dust in the air. Beware on immediate approach.

"Keep a vigilant lookout," David said while pulling down the main. "The objective is to arrive *at* Mindelo, not on it!"

"Roger that," I said, slowing *Inia* to a crawl.

At 1730, with only two miles to go, the island of São Vicente became visible. And the doors to its immigration office became locked.

According to our Atlantic islands book, making landfall in the Cape Verdes without proper clearance could result in fines up to five million Cape Verdean escudos, the equivalent of thirty thousand pounds sterling, forty-five thousand euros, fifty-five thousand U.S. dollars — a truckload in Canadian funds. The chapter ended with "YOU HAVE BEEN WARNED!" Despite David's Herculean efforts, not only would we miss the big party, but we'd be stuck aboard *Inia* for the rest of the holiday season.

We entered the Mindelo harbour, threaded our way through decrepit commercial vessels, dropped anchor at the outer edge of the bay next to the ghostly black freighter *Jenny*, and raised the yellow quarantine flag.

Once *Inia* was secured, I reheated leftover curry and David opened a bottle of Spanish Red Reserve. We sat out in the cockpit eating dinner, sipping wine, and watching the burnt-orange setting of the sun. As the tip of the arc dipped below the horizon, fireworks exploded across the twilight sky and crowds of colourfully dressed people began to sway in song along the shoreline. Soon the sky grew darker, the lights of the harbour brighter, the music livelier.

"If only the forestay hadn't broken," I said. "And if only the wind hadn't —" Suddenly, I caught myself. Here I was, sitting on our very own boat, enjoying food and wine, in a warm Africa night breeze, alone with David. Nothing could top this. I looked over to tell him so and saw that his eyelids were heavy. He was trying gallantly, unsuccessfully, to stay awake. I urged him to go to bed, giving his hands a gentle squeeze. He recoiled with a wince. The salty knot work on the wheel had rubbed both palms raw.

"They'll be fine by morning." He stood up and kissed my cheek. "Happy new year, Sweetie," he said. Then he went below.

Still wide awake, I propped up pillows in the cockpit and continued to watch the festivities on shore. It had been only a year ago that we rang in the new year with our friends in Guelph and sold our house while we were at it. Craziness! And our life since had been, well, unbelievable! Adventure beyond my wildest dreams. Joy and love more intense than I ever before thought possible. *It's gone by so fast, too fast. Only four months until we're back home. They say experiences like these can change a person profoundly and forever. Will I have changed? Think so. Will it be for the better? Really hope so.*

The merriment built until midnight when, all at once, car horns tooted, the roar of the crowd rose to a frenzied crescendo, and a major light show erupted in celebration of the brand-new year, of the promise a fresh start holds for people the world over. And I felt every bit a part of the party after all.

TWENTY-FIVE

JANUARY 1, 0730, there was another round of fireworks, then all went quiet on shore.

I emailed family and friends.

> David and I arrived at São Vicente (16 degrees, 53 Minutes North; 24 degrees 59 Minutes West) just before sunset last night.
>
> We are at anchor in a bay off Mindelo, the capital city.
>
> Watched New Year's Eve festivities from our boat. The party was an all-nighter.
>
> Can't go to shore until we can clear customs.
>
> We'll stay here for a while.
>
> Looking forward to checking this island out. Will let you know when we head off for "the big one."

After a pancake breakfast, David and I worked aboard our floating home. I handwashed undies and T-shirts, strung a rope between the shrouds, then hung the laundry out to dry. David covered the sails; stowed the wind vane; and assembled, inflated, and launched the dinghy.

Late afternoon, while he changed the spark plug on the outboard motor and lowered the motor onto the dinghy's stern, I gathered the vacuum-packed turkey breast, pouch of mashed potatoes, box of dressing, can of peas, and envelope of gravy mix, and began to cook. With dusk descending, waves lapping against *Inia*'s hull, and the seasonal scents of sage and rich turkey gravy permeating the thick African air, we sat outside eating our yuletide feast.

"Seems different from any place we've been so far, eh?" I said, glancing at the inert landscape. The shoreline that bubbled the night before was now dull, lifeless.

"It does. They say music's big here. We need to take in some of that."

"Can't wait!"

Before going below for the night, David tested the outboard. It started on the first try. Our dinghy was ready to take us ashore as soon as we were good to go.

I took down the dried laundry. Even in the fading evening light, every article of clothing was tinged a reddish brown, as were our halyards, the sail covers, the lifelines. Sahara sand had cast a shadow over everything.

January 2, morning broke with gusting winds. I looked out the companionway to a wall of corroded steel. The freighter *Jenny* was now spitting distance away. The white caps had bounced *Inia* off the seabed shelf into deep water.

David, wearing only shorts, frantically pumped the manual windlass to raise the anchor while I, in a T-shirt and underwear, turned on the engine and began circling in search of a safer place to drop the hook.

It was midday before we felt confident *Inia* was secure and we could leave her to go to shore. David sat in the dinghy with the motor running while I stepped down into it, untied the painter from a stanchion, and shoved us off.

Our lightweight tender was inadequate in these seas. I put on my life jacket, slid low on the floorboards, and braced myself. *Lord, I know we've been blessed with common sense and I promise we'll start to use it if delivered safely to shore just this once*, I bargained, as the dinghy tossed in the waves and the outboard growled and spat and gasped to fight on.

We approached the main pier, drenched from head to toe. A tall, sombre man with piercing black eyes nodded in the direction of the dinghy dock. While I tied the painter to a cleat he stared at us from above.

"Hi there," I said with my best smile as I clambered onto the dock.

He said nothing.

"Good morning," David said when they were face to face.

"Thousand escudos" was the man's response.

I looked at David, surprised.

"Thousand escudos, one euro," he repeated impatiently, pointing to the row of inflatables crammed together, extending an open palm.

"I'm wet … *água* … lots of *água*," David said, struggling to retrieve coin from his sopping shorts pocket.

Once he'd been paid, the man slowly wrote out a receipt on a scrap of paper. This was official business. Everything was on the up and up, seemed to be his elaborate point.

With twitching grins, David and I sloshed by the marina office, past a gaggle of non-verbal men hovering around it, through the security gate held shut with clothes-hanger wire, and onto the main drag. We bee-lined it for the customs office.

The sign on the door indicated the office was still closed for the holidays. So we retraced our steps, this time noticing abandoned buildings in need of paint and dusty streets and more expressionless clusters of people.

"Downtowns can look so desolate when everything's closed up," I remarked. "And it's probably a city-wide hangover," I mused, wondering if there was more to it than that.

Once we were back in the dinghy, the man we had paid to tie up to the dock reappeared.

"I Carlos. For everytin', ask me. Unnerstan?" he said, snatching the dock line from my hands.

"Yes, of course … uh … Carlos. We completely understand. Absolutely!" I said.

He untied the line and pushed us out from between the other dinghies. I thanked him excessively as David backed us up, turned us around, and motored us off.

～～～

January 3, under hazy skies, over calmer waters, we headed back to shore where Carlos was again waiting. Without a word, he lashed the dinghy painter down and took our euro, more efficiently this time.

Walking toward the marina office with him, David broke the silence. "We're from Canada. We've never been here before…." Carlos again said nothing. David glanced at me, then persisted. "Is there a good place to eat? *Restaurante*?" he said, making silly big circles on his stomach.

Still no response.

We gladly went our separate way.

"Go Katem," Carlos yelled as we exited the gate.

Mindelo was now bustling, but no friendlier than the day before. After clearing customs and exchanging euros for escudos, we walked to the centre of town through a virtual minefield of overtly aggressive panhandlers and street vendors selling trinkets with thinly veiled hostility, all targeting us.

Spotting Katem, a snack bar, we ducked in with our newly acquired collection of beaded necklaces, painted shells, and primitive sand art. As I studied my meal of fish, maize, and runny eggs, a lanky, stooped man with disproportionately large facial features began to stare at me.

"How'd you like our island specialty?" he said in perfect English, flashing a horsy smile.

"It's good. Very, *very* good," I said, forcing a mouthful down my constricted throat.

"You two must be new to Mindelo. You seem a little lost," he said.

"You're right, we kinda are," I said.

"My name's DJ. I'd be happy to give you the grand tour if you'd like."

"We'd love that!" David and I responded in unison.

After we paid our bill, DJ took us to an open-air market where he hovered while we attempted to browse, until a grandfatherly merchant yanked David aside. After a brief chat David returned, pale-faced, and told DJ we no longer needed his services.

"The guy said every place has its gangsters. We should hide the camera and refuse offers of help. If not, we'll be sorry," David said, watching DJ scuttle off.

"But who can we trust?"

"According to him, essentially no one."

This incident put a damper on my desire to see any more of Mindelo that day. After buying some outrageously expensive oranges, onions, and carrots and sauntering up and down a few more aisles to appear unafraid, for whose benefit I wasn't quite sure, we left for home.

At the dock, without our needing or wanting his help, Mr. Omnipresent Carlos lifted our backpacks off us and tossed them into the dinghy. David clumsily tried to tip him.

"Later," Carlos said, staring.

I watched Carlos watch us motor away. *Later.* Not *thank you* or *no thanks*, but *later.* "What d'you suppose he meant by that?" I asked David.

"Don't know, but I imagine we'll soon be finding out," David replied.

While we were stowing groceries below, there was a knock on *Inia*'s hull. Neighbouring Australians — a father, mother, and adult daughter, all wearing wide-brimmed hats with chin straps — had come by to say hello on their way to shore in their homemade skiff. They said they had been anchored in the bay for a week.

"A week. Great!" I said, hoping for some sightseeing suggestions.

But they didn't have a single one. Instead, all we got were more warnings: Don't leave your vessel unattended at night. Females shouldn't wander around alone. Don't let locals onboard, ever. Be careful shopping or you'll get ripped off (too late there). And on and on.

"We're heading in to buy more diesel, then taking off for Antigua first thing in the morning," the man said.

"Can't wait to get outta here!" his daughter said.

"Be careful and good luck," his wife said.

"There's gotta be good things about this place. We just need to look for them," I said to David as the family rowed away.

January 5, we arranged a paid trip around the island for the following day through the marina manager. Then he recommended we check out Clube Náutico, a sailor's haunt down the street. So we did.

It was a large, open-roofed space beyond a pair of wide barn doors through which you could look out to sea. We chose a table with a perfect ocean view and had barely sat down when a woman ran out of the crowd toward us, yelling, "Sue! Dave! *Bonjour, mes amis!*" It was Elise.

She greeted us both with France's customary two-cheek kiss, then made it a fourer, after which she ordered a beer and pulled up a chair.

"So, where's Graham?" I said, looking around.

"Who knows and who cares?" she said. "I came 'ere on the Dutch catamaran, *mais …*"

"The crewed fifty-footer?" David asked.

"*Oui*, that one," she said.

"Must be quite the ride," he said.

"Must 'ave been," Elise clarified. She confessed she had been thrown off her third boat and went on to explain that the crew was a bunch of morons and the captain was yet another incompetent. It was their loss, not hers.

I knew it! I knew she was a prima donna the minute I laid eyes on her!

Then she smiled broadly and said, "And 'ere we three meet again. It's meant to be."

"I … I'm not sure what you're —" David began.

"See, I need a boat, you need crew, we all want to cross to the Caribbean!" Her eyes bounced back and forth excitedly between David's and mine. "*Serendipitay, n'est-ce pas?*"

I began flattening and folding my napkin, imagining how scary it'd be for her to be stuck on this inhospitable island on her own. And practically speaking, she was right: another hand aboard *Inia* would make this biggest passage easier, especially for David, since, in all honesty, he'd still be doing the lion's share. And we *could* make room for her. Then again, no boat's big enough for someone who's high maintenance, and all things considered, David had managed just fine up to now. And, selfishly, I treasured our time alone; it was the best part of the trip. But if she was truly at risk here, then taking her with us would definitely be the charitable thing, the right thing to —

"No, Elise, I'm afraid it's not," David responded without looking at me.

"*Mais ...*" she said, at a loss for words.

"But you really shouldn't stay here alone," he said.

"*Mais ...*" she repeated, looking to me for support. I folded my napkin into a swan.

"Maybe you should consider flying back to France," he suggested gently.

Elise stiffened and downed her beer. "*Et peut-être que tu devrais manger de la merde!*" she said.

"Oh! I can translate that! She said that maybe you should eat of the shit," I said as we watched her storm off.

"It's probably just 'eat shit,'" David said.

"No, see, *de* is 'of' and *la* is 'the,' and so *de la merde* is, in fact, 'of the shit.' Remember, I took French in high school. What? Quit laughing!"

January 6, as we got close to shore, I spotted our tour guide leaning against the cab of his white pickup truck parked by the marina gate. Luis was a diminutive man wearing new blue jeans; a tucked-in polo shirt with wide green, blue, and white horizontal stripes; and a baseball cap that accentuated his big ears. When he opened the passenger door, I nudged David in first, remarking that, by sitting in the middle, he could practise Portuguese to his heart's content. The truth was, it looked like communicating with Luis would be excruciating work and I wasn't up to it.

Luis climbed into the driver's side, slammed his door shut, and drove to a gas station to fill the tires with air. Then, with total disregard for pedestrians, roadside chickens, and all other living creatures, he swerved back into traffic and sped along the littered streets, through the outskirts of town, to the Cape Verdean wilderness.

The countryside was abject poverty: dirt roads, boxy concrete dwellings with no glass in the windows, no doors in the entrances, fallen clotheslines, and emaciated dogs and goats and people roaming about.

And Mount Verde was a cruel misnomer. Its severely parched terrain smelled like hot dirt. Patches of cracked and crumbling shelves carved out of the clay-coloured mountainside were evidence of failed attempts at terraced gardening in years gone by. According to Luis, islanders had long since become resigned to the fact that nothing would grow there. So fresh produce was imported, either from other islands or from the mainland, at a premium. Hence the market prices.

I began snapping pictures of this shocking scenery left, right, and centre, until I caught Luis glancing my way. The pained expression in his eyes seemed to ask, "What for?" In search of an answer, I drew an uncomfortable blank. After shamefully stowing the camera in its case, I stared out the truck window for the remainder of the trip.

Meanwhile, David did in fact seize the opportunity to practise Portuguese. It was with his usual enthusiasm to start, but, getting zero encouragement from Luis in return, for the first time ever he lost all interest in trying.

After a quick ride over the mountain and a token touch-down at the main beach, we were ready to call it quits. Luis was visibly happy to hear it. Following a silent and speedy drive back to the marina, David paid him the full day's fee for the few hours out, and Luis zoomed off without so much as a thank you.

Watching his truck fade in the cloud of dirt, I felt depressed. It seemed there was a chasm between us and these islanders that just wasn't bridgeable.

We decided to leave the Cape Verdes as soon as we could.

Brian wrote to thank us for Christmas. He had had a fantastic time with John and had reconnected with friends he hadn't seen in years. Also, the time away had enabled him to view his situation with greater clarity. He now knew the military was wrong for him.

> I have another crazy idea. There is a potential move in the near future that could be good in lots of ways, financially included. I need to figure out details first. It's just an idea for now, but another appealing one. Will keep you posted.

David wrote him back:

> Hi Bri,
> Mom and I were really pleased to get your note.
> You're very good at making things happen.
> We will be leaving the Cape Verdes soon, and will likely be a few weeks at sea.
> We're very interested in hearing about your plans. We'll try to give you a call when we land.

Over the next few days we picked up our clean laundry and bought water, diesel, more food, more trinkets.

On January 9, David picked up a fitting for the forestay from the marina manager for twelve euros. While he was attaching the steel part to the bow, Carlos blasted up in a Zodiac and, contrary to marine protocol everywhere, climbed aboard *Inia* uninvited.

"Oh, hi, Carlos," David said, unnaturally loudly to alert me.

From below I saw Carlos looking toward the jerry cans of diesel and boxes of canned food. "Look like you leavin'" he remarked.

"Not right away, but yeah, soon."

"Wit'out sayin' bye?"

"Oh, we had every intention of … uh … hey, would you like a beer?"

"Yeah, I do like."

I wedged myself into the quarter berth to be out of his sight. But as David descended the companionway to get a couple of pints from the fridge, Carlos's giant feet appeared on the rungs behind him. So I shot back out and grabbed a book to look like I had been sitting there reading all along. Soon his imposing frame blocked our exit and filled the cabin space. Although the anchorage was packed, we three were very much alone. And this was not a social visit.

We had had every intention of tipping Carlos before leaving, but he had no way of knowing that. And trust was a commodity he couldn't afford. Without a word, David emptied his wallet and handed him a fistful of money. Carlos methodically sorted and counted the mixture of bills and coin on the tabletop, nodded approvingly, and stuffed the loot in his shirt pocket.

Then, instead of leaving, as I prayed he would, he sat down and sprawled out on the main settee and began to leisurely sip his brew. David and I sat on the berth opposite and attempted to appear at ease.

As Carlos surveyed *Inia*'s interior, I did, too, as though for the first time. The cabin, which had seemed modest to me, now looked like the lap of luxury.

Fearing Carlos's misperception about our net worth, I began, "We have no other home. This is it. No mansion back in Canada. No siree. This is all we have. The sum total." And if he thought we were retirees with fat-cat pensions, well he could guess again. After this costly interlude, which, I stressed, we could ill afford in the first place, we both expected to work to our graves.

My progressively dismal financial tale came to a sudden end when Carlos blurted, "You can go. Lucky!" I studied his face and realized he hadn't heard a single word I'd said. "I twenty-five," he continued. "Five childs. No good job here. English bad. Me and my frens can no get visa. Can no leave … never, ever.…" His voice trailed off.

He was right; we were fortunate. Our sons were, too. I thought about how, in contrast to Carlos, they were free to travel, to pursue opportunity, to learn, to follow dreams, to carve out their own paths in life. They were privileged. With privilege comes responsibility. It was up to them now.

When Carlos stood up to go, David grabbed his cherished Portuguese-English dictionary off the shelf, signed the inside cover, and handed it to him. As Carlos motored off in the Zodiac, his silhouette looked slightly straighter, taller, more optimistic, I liked to tell myself.

On our last day in Mindelo, we went to the Polícia Marítima to pick up our boat registration papers. After the constable was done socializing with two women and eating the plate of chicken they had thoughtfully brought him and attending to some unfinished paperwork and digging out an annoying chunk from between his teeth with a toothpick, we were the very next. We signed the necessary forms, retrieved our documents, went back out into the muted sunshine, and walked along the waterfront to the small immigration office. After one more bout of abuse, we were free to go.

Stepping from the dock into the dinghy for the last time, I was filled with regret about our stay. I had been so impatient to get there; now I couldn't wait to leave. We had tried, but perhaps not hard enough, or for long enough. Or maybe the timing just wasn't right. By all accounts, life *was* improving in the Cape Verdes.

So, if other sailors were debating between making a stopover and passing these islands by, what would I say? What could I say? What would be fair? I hoped I wouldn't be asked — not yet anyway.

◡

January 10, we got up early to go. There was the usual closing of windows, battening of hatches, stowing, preparing, and testing. The difference this time was the absence of checkout fees to pay, bathroom keys to return, or a single soul to wave goodbye to us.

At 1150 we simply lifted anchor and motored quietly past *Jenny*, ethereally disappearing back into the haze of Sahara sand like massless, traceless spirits in the wind.

TWENTY-SIX

MARCEL LEFT THE CANARIES the same day we left the Cape Verdes. John and Freda, the retired couple who had met us and fed us on the reception dock in Portugal, wrote to say they were back out there, too. David agreed to attempt to connect with them via single-sideband radio daily at 1800 universal time. And Nick, now on the hard in Spain, volunteered to be our private weather router again.

> Me thinks I see a lovely High ride.
> Wind NE or ENE, 15-20 kts,
> Swell NW 8 ft.
> Temp 22 C

Wrong! Emerging from the dead calm of the islands' wind shadow, we were hammered with gale-force gusts from the northwest. While David manhandled *Inia* through these cresting seas like a canoeist shooting rapids, I went below and, lamenting the regrettable end to historic world weather patterns, fell asleep.

As dusk descended, David called down, "This is your captain speaking. All hands on deck. We're in the trades!"

I looked at the telltale, then out to sea. The wind had crept around. Nick was in fact bang-on after all.

We unfurled the genoa and watched it fill. Then David attached Robert, the heavy-weather wind vane, to the top of the long wooden oar and I set up camp on the cabin sole for the bouncy ride ahead.

Next morning, while David sat at the nav station logging our position and crowing about our progress, I stepped out into the glorious new day and let out a blood-curdling shriek, feeling something prickly underfoot. Lying on its belly, with its torpedo body motionless and little marble eyes staring straight ahead, was a fish — with wings.

David got up and checked it out. "Dead," he pronounced.

"Don't poke at it," I said. "What if it's faking?"

"I know dead when I see dead."

"It might be a survival technique. Innate. Nature equips animals with that ability sometimes, you know."

"Dead with a capital *D*."

"I hope you're right, that's all I can say."

After prodding the still form, he picked it up. The evidence was indisputable. Not only was the fish dead, it was hard with rigor mortis. David pulled a thin, spiky, translucent wing out. "It's a flying fish," he said. "They actually can fly."

"Hard to believe those flimsy appendages could carry it up over the gunwales," I said, looking about.

Then I spotted the tailfin of another flying fish jutting out from behind the emergency tiller's base, and a third in the folds of the mizzen sail. We both turned bow-ward to discover several more, eight in total, all without vital signs, all stiff as a board.

"It's like a grizzly crime scene," I said, illogically feeling complicit as we crawled around the deck tossing the corpses into the ocean one by one.

Not yet fully adjusted to the motion of the ocean, I went for an afternoon siesta. Cozy on the floor, I watched David tie himself to the steering pedestal to free up his hands so he could hold the sextant steady to take celestial sights. *Clever! And he's having fun. That makes me happy*, I thought as I drifted off and into the company of our boys and neighbourhood friends among the big old maple, walnut, and hickory trees in the backyard of our century cottage.

David and I were hosting a summer afternoon barbecue. He was turning skewers of beef over the hot coals. I was passing around a tray of baked brie and crackers. John was telling everyone about a bus trip he had just returned from with friends. He said that after they bought a month pass to travel east they found out Greyhound had discontinued that route. "Oh my God, that's awful," I said. "So what d'you do?" I asked. "We went west instead. No big deal. The way I see it, if I'm not somewhere, I'm somewhere else," he said. The neighbours laughed like it was the silliest thing they'd ever heard. Then Ben said, "What's so funny?" And Brian said, "It's the truth, isn't it?" And I said, "You know, I think he has a point. They all do. We can learn a lot from our kids, if we just listen. "

There was a gentle shake of my arm and I found myself on teak floorboards, entangled in blankets, tossing and turning in ocean waves, with David looking down at me. It took time to clear my head, to sort out fact from fiction; my dream was so believable, my reality so damned farfetched.

It was an hour until the scheduled radio calls. Anticipating I was ready for food, David had a pot of rice with tomatoes, onions, canned chicken, and Cape Verdean hot sauce simmering on the camping stove. I was famished. It hit the spot.

At 1745 we sat together on the nav station seat. Radio waves need to bounce or skip off ionospheric layers in the sky to travel long distances. The weather, the season, and the amount of light all affect their ability to move. Sunspot cycles also alter the transmission of radio signals from one year to the next. The general consensus among hams was that propagation had been poor of late. So we knew better than to get our hopes up.

David turned on the radio and adjusted the dial to the agreed-upon bandwidth. Then we waited and listened to rumbling and static and snippets of conversations, too distorted for us to make out what was being said until, cutting through all the audio clutter, Marcel boomed, "*Inia, Inia, Inia.* This is *Cygnus, Cygnus, Cygnus.* Over."

David responded, "*Cygnus,* you're coming through loud and clear. Over."

"Hey, Dave, what d'you know? Six hundred miles apart and I can hear you, too, five by four I'd say. Over."

David and Marcel were mindful to keep it brief. After reporting longitudes and latitudes, wind and waves, breakages and repairs, it was over and out.

As soon as David hung the microphone on its hook, John and Freda called. They were clear as a bell too. Freda had just gotten over seasickness, so they had decided to head straight for Barbados rather than stopping.

After the calls, we checked for emails. Nick wrote that, on this relentless downwind course, there were two tactical approaches to choose between:

> to sail low (south of west) to midway, then gybe,
> or
> to sail high as far as reasonable, then gybe.

We chose to veer north of west.

And so began our evening ritual on our classic trade-winds passage home.

Yawing to the left, then to the right. Turning. Swerving. Climbing the swells. Cresting. Pitching. Dropping and thrusting forward with the power and spirit of a jaguar in the wild.

Splash. Clap. WHOOSH. Lurch and lunge ahead.

The wind vane works full out. The whisker pole holds firm. We eat sparingly, maybe one hot meal a day. We ration power; water, too. We hardly wash. Salt's on our clothes, in our noses, our mouths, our pores. We brace to sit, grasp to move. There's motion around the clock. It just never lets up.

Splash. Clap. WHOOSH. Lurch and lunge ahead.

Mornings are fresh. Night skies are brilliant. There are no dramatic wind shifts, no calms, no storms, no problems, no worries.

Splash. Clap. WHOOSH. Lurch and lunge ahead.

I surrender to the motion, the open sea, time. One day melds into the next.

I read a lot. Steinbeck, Anne Frank, Hemingway, Atwood, Irving. True and invented tales of pain and love and adversity and triumph, of what it is to be human.

There is abundance in the vast emptiness. Dolphins cut through the water to visit us, driven by the desire for company. Seabirds soar above in migration to distant feeding grounds off continental shelves, guiding many a sailor to land. But I know where we are by the sky. The North Star's altitude signals our latitude. By observing its position in the night sky, I know our progress south. And I know we're on course by watching the sun make its daily path: rising behind *Inia*'s port stern, crossing due south midday, setting beyond her starboard bow. I can determine how long we've been at sea by noting the moon relative to the setting sun. A new moon sets with the sun. A full moon rises in the east just as the sun kisses the western horizon. To every thing there is a purpose under heaven.

Insight wells from the silences. Love fills my heart, inspiration my soul, clarity of purpose my mind. I pledge that, when I am back home, I will live simply, honestly, creatively, with gratitude. I will invest in the people I love, in the things I do. I will face my life journey with a new spirit of adventure and courage. I will take time for reflection. And I will always, always remember the night sky.

Splash. Clap. WHOOSH. Lurch and lunge ahead.

Day nineteen, strange and fickle winds arrived. The whisker pole was taken off. We reefed the jib and raised the main. We lowered the main. And let out the mizzen. Unfurled the genoa. The whisker pole was back on. Raised the main. Tacked. Tightened. Reefed. Lowered. Raised. Progress was slowed. We were made to work for every inch.

Nick assured us landfall was imminent; moreover, it would be an exciting ride.

> Grab the opportunity to fuel up, charge the batteries, eat up, sleep up, and make sure all your way points are in the GPS and all your charts are on the table. For there'll be some spray flying high.

We heeded his advice. If he said so, we knew it would be true.

January 30, 0400, I was awakened by difference: different feels, different sounds. David was on deck already. The winds had indeed clocked around and built. We had a northwest blow with gusts to 30 knots. I made a Thermos of coffee and joined him outside. We furled the genoa, double reefed the main, aimed straight for the British Virgin Islands, and away we went!

Inia screamed along close-hauled. Soon, lights flickered in the distance. Islands rose in the mist. The dawn shimmered gloriously. Dolphins and birds gathered to escort us on this final run.

Thoughts crept in of a hot shower, stretching and walking, fresh food, John's visit, anchoring, snorkelling, and rum punch.

Approaching land, David started the engine. We dropped the sails and my heart rate spiked. The sudden tranquility in the Sir Francis Drake Channel marked a safe end to our second transatlantic crossing and the longest passage of our trip. I was relieved, proud, ecstatic.

Inia purred along, centre channel. As charter boats flitted every which way, I was gripped with nostalgia. This was the very spot we had spent two magnificent weeks with our sons eight years earlier, our last holiday as a family.

"Looks the same, doesn't it?" I said to David, choking back tears.

"Exactly the same. It's like we were here just yesterday."

"But with all that's happened since, *I'm* not the same, none of us are."

As he looked about, David's eyes glistened. "That's an understatement," he said.

TWENTY-SEVEN

WE STOOD IN the long customs line on the island of Tortola as two overfed men in undersized uniforms shuffled forms and berated customers, all of whom, invariably, thanked them in return.

We reboarded *Inia*, numb with exhaustion. When David lifted off the companionway doors, the stench of dirty laundry, sprouting potatoes, and lime toilet-bowl crystals rose up from the cabin as an instant reminder we had been three weeks at sea. We opened all the hatches and portholes to let fresh air in, then pulled out the main berth and slept for the afternoon.

Early evening, we went by dinghy over the pink-tinged waves to shore, determined to pull out all the stops in celebration of this momentous occasion. After an extravagantly long, hot shower in the marina washroom, I put on a sundress, jewellery, lipstick, even perfume, and headed out onto the boardwalk where David, dressed in taupe shorts and a royal-blue cotton shirt, was waiting for me.

In an upscale restaurant, at a table overlooking the harbour, he ordered a bottle of their best Cab Sav. Wine had never tasted better. We ordered charbroiled steaks medium rare, with baked potatoes and sour cream and large country salads on the side. We ate at a leisurely pace and, short of licking our plates clean, savoured every morsel.

It was night when, satiated and a little giddy, we walked out into the onshore breeze. I slid into the dinghy, wobbled, and sat with a thud. David followed me down, turned on the engine, and pushed us off the dock.

"They all look alike!" I said, looking at the bay full of boats, black on black.

"Not to worry. We're to the left, near the other side," David said. We wove through that entire area. No *Inia*.

"I distinctly remember mooring beside a ketch," I said. We couldn't see any ketches. When it became obvious we were lost, the outboard sputtered to a stop. I knelt at the bow, calling out random directions, while he rowed in circles, in zigzags, and in reverse.

A half hour later, when *Inia* appeared, I was sober, clammy, and more than ready for bed.

But David wasn't. I felt his hands on my butt cheeks while I clambered aboard and knew that little hiccup hadn't dampened his spirits in the slightest. Once he was on deck, he lit candles around the cockpit, then went below, passed up two pillows and resurfaced with a plate of dark chocolate in one hand, two plastic wine glasses in the other, a blanket draped over his shoulder, and the bottle of Madeira tucked under his armpit, confirming sleep was the furthest thing from his mind.

I watched him pour us each a nightcap and thought about how he put his heart and soul into everything he did, how his care and attention to the details of life not only kept us safe on the ocean, but also sane in ordinary times; how he had this unique ability to make the mundane exciting, lean times enriching, dark days a little lighter and, yes, even cool, damp nights sparkle with romance.

Our little corner of the world was now dreamily aglow. David looked tanned, fit, rested, and more handsome than ever.

I lifted my glass of Madeira. "This is to you, my dear, the best blue-water skipper there is."

"We make a great team," he said.

I melted into his warm embrace and felt him fiddle to undo the clasp at the back of my dress, then unzip the zipper.

"Here?" I asked.

No reply. None really wanted.

In the flickering candle light, in the fresh salt air, under the moonless night sky, intimately, passionately, well into the night, we celebrated.

February 1, dawn was announced by a chorus of roosters, loud enough to wake the dead. We motored to the marina in Road Town to spend a few days cleaning *Inia*, doing laundry, and stocking up on food, after which we planned to anchor among the islands for two weeks while waiting for John.

Brian wrote that he was following through with his latest idea; he was moving to Lethbridge, Alberta. The flight was only ninety-nine dollars.

> Apparently, Lethbridge has more days of sun than any other Canadian city. And it has the Chinooks, so it's one of Canada's mildest inland cities. There are three BMX tracks that I'm aware of and it isn't far from the mountains for downhill biking.
>
> Being as the economy is booming, I'm sure I will get a job quickly.
>
> Everything should go fairly smoothly (unless I find out that light at the end of the tunnel was just painted on the side of that cliff

by some wassquawy wabbit! ha ha). Just a few
loose ends to tie up and I'm off.

He informed us he still didn't have a phone and had decided
to leave his computer behind, so he wouldn't have internet for
a little while either. Patrick, a buddy from Whistler, had moved
back to Lethbridge and was living with his mom. Until he got
settled, Brian could stay with them.

After plugging *Inia* into shore power, we walked over to
phone booths on the main pier and called other family. John said
he was as prepared as he could be for his final recital, Brahms,
four days away. He assured us he knew we'd be there in spirit.
And he confirmed that his flight to the U.S. Virgin Islands was
February 16. My mom said she'd arrange to meet us in Nassau
mid-March, since she'd be off on a golf trip in April.

February 3 was Super Bowl Sunday: New York Giants versus
New England Patriots. David's interest in football had waned
over the years, but this was billed as an exceptionally exciting
match-up. The Giants were seeking to become the first wildcard
team to win a Super Bowl, but the Patriots were the first in over
thirty years to enter the game after completing a perfect season.

We sat below and listened to the game over the ham radio,
hearing the rise and fall of cheers and jeers from neighbouring boats
with every play. Fourth quarter, with the Giants down 14–10 and
just over two minutes left in the game, New York got the ball and
marched it eighty-three yards down the field for the winning drive.
"It's the finest Super Bowl, and possibly one of the biggest upsets
in the history of sport," the announcer blared over the radio. And
we could hear a rumble of hysteria throughout the whole marina.

"Wow!" I looked over. David's mind was elsewhere. "What's up?"

"Got thinking about when Ben played football," he said.

"To this day, it amazes me *that* he did."

"I wanted to, too, when I was his age, but my mom was dead set against it."

"I can see why. If I had been a single mom, I'd have been the same. God! I remember taking him to that first practice. Most of the guys were twice his size and they acted like they ate nails for breakfast. I was certain he'd get crushed out there."

"But he never did. Too bad you missed that Brantford game. You had the flu or something," he said. "Anyway, I had volunteered to hold one of the yard markers on on the sidelines." David continued. "Ben was defensive end. Fourth quarter, a minute left in the game, a Brantford receiver caught the ball, broke away from the crowd, and was galloping toward the goal line. Ben charged up from behind, leapt into the air, and caught him by his heels. It was a classic shoestring tackle, less than a yard from the end zone. I tried to contain myself, managing the sticks and all, but damn near burst with pride. He couldn't wait to get home to tell you. Neither of us could."

"I remember the two of you flying in through the door, talking over each other. Ben was so happy. And you were so happy."

"What he lacked in girth he made up for in guts. *That* was the best game in the history of sport."

∿

February 4, we stopped at a school bus that had been converted into a take-out food joint by two young guys. Over the reggae blaring from their radio, we ordered two tubs of their "bang good" barbecued chicken with sides of potatoes and a cabbage salad. With laundry done and groceries bought, we took off for Peter Island to anchor.

"Seems like everyone's rushing to relax," I said, watching the charter boats from competing companies race throughout the channel. That had been us. That was the lifestyle we had left behind, the rat race I had all but forgotten and didn't miss, and feared being part of again.

We got an early start, but the cove off Peter Island was already packed when we arrived. As the newcomer in the anchorage, it was our daunting responsibility to calculate enough swinging room to prevent collisions with the other vessels that were there first; moreover, we had to respect the personal space of their crews. Following our third attempt, certain we had managed to disrupt the peace and tranquility of the entire bay, I cowered behind the dodger. One look at me and David knew there would be no prospect of relaxation if he didn't get us the hell out of there.

Soon we were secured to a mooring ball in Norman Island's Bight, a bay we had visited as a family. We wrote the boys:

> Hi guys,
> We feel the need to drop you a line to let you know we are tied to a mooring ball in Norman's Bight … about a hundred yards from the first mooring of our Sunsail charter. And there, at that mooring, lies an identical 34-foot charter boat, with a Canadian flag! This has brought back such warm feelings and wonderful memories of the trip that we had with you, so many years ago now.
>
> We hope you're doing well and we love you always.

February 8 was overcast, breezy, warm. At my cajoling, we went by dinghy to the beach.

"There aren't sharks here," I said, standing in the white sand. "C'mon. Baby steps. They call it systematic desensitization, and it works." I carried our bag of snorkelling gear to the water's edge. "Either you come with me or I go alone."

"That's stupid and you know it. I won't let you —"

"Here I go ... I'm going ..." I teased, wading into the rolling waves.

"If you meet up with a great white, don't blame me," he yelled.

"Maybe never to return ..." I continued.

Predictably, he ran in after me.

We sat side by side, waist deep, wearing masks with snorkels dangling from the sides, wrestling our feet into our flippers.

"You can be a royal pain at times, d'you know that?" he said, looking out to the undulating grey-green.

I bit on my snorkel mouthpiece and dove below. He followed. We nodded to each other and gave A-okay signals like expert frogmen. Then we kicked our flippered feet and swam off.

Floating lazily along the surface above the reef, I watched the miniature marine world: crabs scuttling between fanning plants; sapphire, black-and-yellow striped, and glowing orange fish darting in and out of crevices; minuscule shells propelling themselves on filament-like legs along velvety, antler-shaped pink coral.

I pointed them out to David with delight. He looked over and began to dog paddle like a child. I giggled at his silly antics. Then he flailed and splashed and bobbed up to the surface, and I realized he wasn't joking. His mask had filled with salt water, stinging his eyes, blocking his nose. He yanked the goggles up and gasped for air, swallowing more of the sea. Then he swam to shore, coughing and spitting, and I followed close behind. We stood in the sand and quietly dried ourselves off.

"I panicked," he said.

"I won't ask again," I said.

It began to drizzle and I shivered as we motored back to *Inia*.

∿

February 9, David woke up determined to anchor again. Between here and home there were a lot of anchorages. We couldn't afford marinas or mooring balls all the time.

"Look, we've anchored during storms, in tides, over rocks, by derelict freighters," he said.

"It's a well-known fact that the challenge of anchoring increases exponentially with the size of the audience," I said.

"Nonsense," David said.

"While the joy's inversely proportional."

"If anchoring's doable in these crowded harbours, then, damn it, we're gonna learn to do it! No gawker sipping a whatnot on the back of his Barbie boat'll scare us off again."

We headed back to Road Town. As David circled in the busy basin, he stressed that timing, especially among so many vessels, was of the essence. I agreed. And that valuable seconds were lost between his communication of instructions to me from the bow and my reactions at the helm.

"Come to think of it, you're right," I said.

And he said that it wasn't even necessary. I knew what to do. So, starting now, *he* would take instructions from *me*!

Weak-kneed, I took the wheel. He went to the bow and waited. I spotted an opening and headed into the 20-knot wind, past a large sailing school, by a ferry, between anchored boats, to the anchoring area. Following a final glance about, I put the engine in neutral and, once forward momentum had ceased, signalled to David to drop the anchor. With a scope of seven to one, ninety-four feet of chain scrambled out of the anchor well and off the deck, after which *Inia* lurched sideways, drifted back … and back … and back toward a Hunter 54, then stopped.

"I did it!" I yelled as she began to swing.

"Of course," David said with a grin. He locked the companionway.

Stoked by my anchoring triumph, I drove the dinghy when we went to shore. As we passed the Hunter, its highball-drinking skipper stood in his cockpit and gave me a big thumbs-up.

I waved back, thrilled he was there.

February 11, Brian used Patrick's computer to write us to say he didn't have a job yet, but he had an interview the following day. We could call him on the home phone after.

February 12, we walked back to the phone booth on the pier and David called at the pre-arranged time. "Hi, Brian. It's me, Dad. Finally! We've been thinking about you, your move, your job search and everything. It's been frustrating not being able to connect. So, how'd the interview — what's so funny? You thought what? Stop laughing, I can't understand a thing you're — did you say something about a cat? Damn it, Brian, not everything's a joke! You've had five jobs in the last — is that right? Really? Sorry to hear that. We had no idea. Well … so … good luck with the other interviews. Keep us posted."

David hung up, white as a ghost.

"What on earth happened?" I said.

David explained that Brian thought he had applied to a company that builds custom timber homes. Midway through the interview, he learned there were two companies in town with the same name. He was at the other one; it makes kitty litter. He thought that was hilarious.

David continued, telling me that Brian went on to assure him he didn't think everything was a joke. For instance, it was no joke when all the guys at the fibreglass plant ate lunch in the cabs of their trucks and he had no truck to go to. He didn't think it was humorous when he went to a staff barbecue and got pummelled in a boxing ring by an assembly-line colleague-slash-psycho-slash-local welterweight champ. He didn't laugh when he discovered the cost of living in Victoria is one of the highest in the country; when, after paying for rent and food, he couldn't afford a bus pass; or when he was fined for reckless operation of a bicycle on his 23-mile commute to work. And he wasn't one bit amused when the superintendent of his apartment building kept his damage deposit without reason and he was forced to leave with only the airfare in his pocket and the shirt on his back.

I stared at David and absorbed every last heart-wrenching detail. And I thought back over the year and Brian's communications with us: the absence of any mention of fun since the Sonny Rollins concert six months earlier, his curious "Canon in D" and *Sleuth* emails, his sudden and uncharacteristic interest in the military, his "bit of a problemo" remark about money. He had been treading water to stay afloat the entire time he was in Victoria, but he was slowly going under. He didn't want to worry us. Still, I should have known.

"I feel just sick!" I said.

"Me, too," David said.

David emailed Brian to say we were sending him money to tide him over until he got on his feet, and that he was so, so sorry; obviously the kitty-litter interview was funny.

Brian replied,

> I've been proud not to ask for your help in these last few years. But thanks. Got a little stressed there for a bit.

Over the next week, we took daily strolls on shore among the tamarind trees and hibiscus shrubs and chickens, stopping for local music and the occasional roti. And aboard *Inia* — when we weren't entertained by newcomers attempting to anchor — we read, watched brash and quirky pelicans by the hour, and read some more.

February 15, after an even lazier, gum-smacking customs woman stamped us out of the BVI, we moseyed on over to the U.S. Virgins next door.

TWENTY-EIGHT

FEBRUARY 16, we headed to the island of St. Thomas. The entrance to the town of Red Hook, where we were to meet John, was filled with wrecks — all manner of wrecks: motorboats, speedboats, sailboats, houseboats, in varying depths of water and stages of rot.

"It's like a boat graveyard," I said, circling back to set anchor as far away from the skeletal cadavers as possible. "What on earth ...?"

"I think I know!" David said. "I think this is from Hurricane Marilyn. 1995. If so, *Dove's* one of them."

"Not *the Dove!*"

His eyes went misty.

Dove was the twenty-four-foot sloop belonging to Robin Lee Graham, who, at sixteen years old, set off to sail around the world alone. His five-year odyssey, chronicled in *National Geographic*, had fuelled David's dream. And here he was — here we were — over four decades later.

At 1500, with *Inia* secured, we went by dinghy along the shoreline of mangrove shrubs to the dinghy dock, where a cat-sized iguana watched us tie up with a disapproving glare before retreating into the greenery.

At the waterfront café, Molly Molones, we sat at a table in the shade, sipped fresh pineapple smoothies, and waited impatiently for John. Right on schedule, he emerged through a crowd off the airport bus, tired from the rigours of travel and burning up in his February-in-Canada clothes.

The instant we boarded *Inia*, he took his duffel bag below. Minutes later, he resurfaced in shorts, stepped over the lifelines, and threw his pasty-white self into the bay, yelling "Cannonball!" and creating a massive explosion of spray on impact. When he popped back up and saw we, too, were now wet, he apologized through fits of laughter and gulps of water. It was with all the remorse of a gnat, I mused. Classic John. He was now in his early twenties, but apparently some things never changed. And thank God for that. I've always loved his impishness, even when I was the brunt of it. It was great to have him there!

Following a good night's sleep and a light breakfast on deck, we lifted anchor and left for St. John. The island, donated by the Rockefellers to the United States with the proviso that its rich biodiversity be protected, was spectacularly unspoiled and uncluttered. We explored Caneel Bay, Watermelon Cay, Leinster Bay, Cruz Bay, and Christmas Cove. The reefs were phenomenal: mountainous coral; flowerlike coral; tubular, ribbon, lobed, knobby, and pillar coral; coral resembling elk horns; and coral grooved like the human brain. Giant purple sea fans and small fluorescent green ones swayed in the ocean current. Parrotfish, angelfish, and shimmering schools of jacks swam by. Spiny lobsters and tiny crabs ambled about. Closer to shore, solitary starfish gracefully embellished the clean basin floor. John and I snorkelled every day, sometimes twice a day, and as the week progressed, David joined us.

We hiked up hilly trails through native palms and wild orchids, lizards and mongooses darting across our paths.

And, pleasantly tired, we spent evenings aboard, eating fashionably late dinners, listening to music, watching crimson and gold setting suns, and talking. John had six weeks left of university. He and a few of his classmates were discussing the possibility of collaborating on various music projects. His future, post-school, was vague but exciting, uncertain but full of promise.

Before we knew it, the week was over. After a final misty morning swim, we stowed items below and left for the capital city, Charlotte Amalie. John played harmonica throughout our three-hour sail across. The blues felt apt.

We pulled into our assigned slip — next to a commuter ferry terminal, by the Tickles Dockside Pub, across from people conducting mini-tours of a docked submarine, near a shipyard, minutes from the airport — and back into the din of urban life.

Brian called with good news. He had a job. It was making fountains, concrete fountains. Like the Trevi in Rome, only smaller, for residential use. He was beautifying the country, one backyard at a time, he said with a laugh. His job was to pour concrete into the frog and angel and lion moulds. And he had secured an apartment for half of what he had paid in rent in Victoria and was back to having a phone. So, essentially things were falling into place in Lethbridge. He thought we'd be happy to know it.

"We are," I said, unsure.

On John's last day, we walked to the heart of the city in search of souvenirs. Charlotte Amalie was an unabashed mecca for tourists, but only tourists with money and a penchant for diamonds, rubies, and fine crystal. Even window-shopping felt out of our league.

"Look! Two for the price of one," David said, pointing to a pub sign promoting what they called a "Bushwhacker Bonanza." It sounded appealing and affordable. In we went.

When the waitress came by, David and John ordered the advertised special, but after reading that it was Kahlúa, rum, Baileys Irish Cream, and amaretto in coconut milk, I opted for wine. Soon she returned carrying two tall creamy drinks and my glass of red. After tentative sips, David and John, in near-perfect unison, declared, "They're like coffee-flavoured milkshakes!"

Watching the Bushwhackers disappear with the ease and speed of milkshakes, my alarm bell sounded. Then David grandly gestured for another round for himself and his fine son, who had come here all the way from Toronto, Canada. I discreetly voiced concern, but he assured me I had nothing to worry my pretty little nogoogian about.

John agreed. "Mom, relax! They're ninety-nine percent cream!"

After downing his second Bushwhacker, faster than the first, the normally responsible, shopping-phobic husband and father jumped to his feet and said, "Bottoms up, John, my boy. We've got some serious bargain-hunting to do."

"Let's get at 'er," John exclaimed with uncharacteristic zeal.

Back in the shopping district, David decided to stop communicating in English.

"From now on, I only speak Portuguese," he announced.

"Don't be silly," I said.

"*Tu não entende. Eu falo só português,*" he said, leading us into the first store on a strip.

The two of them bounced into one shop after another and rolled back out onto the street in stitches, David certain he was pulling off the best caper ever, John thoroughly entertained by the father he never knew he had. When their shopping spree wound down, John, now wearing a T-shirt displaying a possessed lizard, was toting a forty-ouncer of rum and a box of cigars. And David emerged in a new bright-blue polyester shirt plastered with neon sunrises, orange blossoms, and windswept lime-green trees, for which he had haggled ruthlessly, allegedly entirely in Portuguese.

Eager to savour what was left of the visit, we went for a stretched-out dinner of authentic Caribbean fare: curries with sides of plantain, rice, beans, sweet potato, and green bananas, and johnnycakes all around for dessert. Once we got back at the boat, even karaoke night at Tickles couldn't keep us awake any longer.

~

Departure morning inevitably came. Watching John pack up was bittersweet. We'd had so much fun. It had gone by way too fast. But I knew he had to leave. He had to get back to his own life. It was right. It was time.

"This is for you," I said, handing him a card with money in it. "We want you to splurge on something special for your graduation. You've certainly earned it."

"Awesome. Thanks," John said.

"We'll celebrate when we're home," David said.

"Sounds good," he replied.

The three of us stood on the side of the road, watching the airport cab approach.

"Well, Johnny baby, as they say, all good things have to come to an end," I said, trying not to cry.

John gave us each a hug. Then he piled into the car with his duffel bag and shut the door.

"You might want to steer clear of those Bushwhackers," he said through the open window.

"Hey, I'm the dad here," David said.

They both laughed.

"Love you, John."

"Love you, too. Thanks a lot for everything," he replied. Looking rested, content, and nicely brown, he waved goodbye as the cab pulled away.

David put his arm around my shoulders and we watched the cab drive off. Then he gave me a gentle squeeze. "It's time to get ourselves home, too."

"That's for sure," I replied.

On the walk back to the marina, I thought about how our life back home wasn't all bad. How I enjoyed my job, had great friends, loved my family. Who knew when we'd see Brian next, if we'd ever hear from Ben? I thought about how, right then, I missed them more than anything.

I reboarded *Inia*, ready to go.

TWENTY-NINE

THE DAY AFTER John left, we left, too. Destination: Grand
Turk Island, 400 nautical miles to our northwest.

On Thursday, February 28, David updated family:

> We are two days at sea. Day One we logged 130
> NM, and we should be close to that again today.
> Our current position is 20 degrees 22 minutes
> north, 068 degrees 31 minutes west.
>
> We are heading for the Turks and Caicos and
> should arrive there late Friday or early Saturday
> at this rate.
>
> We'll likely send our next update after our
> landfall.

There was an incoming email. My mom had written with
flight information. She'd arrive in Nassau March 12 at 1:00 p.m.
on USAir, with more books. *Yay!* Our mail. *Uggh!* And an income
tax form. *Shit!*

Predawn February 29, David woke me. We were nearing shoals. Coming about was a two-person job with the main up and the whisker pole out. No sooner were we done than the wind shifted. So we changed tacks from running with the wind to a broad reach and took down the whisker pole entirely. Once we were past the hazards, David reset the wind vane and the alarm, and we both went to bed.

When I awoke, it was three whole hours later. I apologized. "Seems I died. Honestly, I didn't even hear the alarm!" I said.

By the terror in David's eyes, it was clear he hadn't heard it either. While we slept, *Inia* had chosen to head back through the shoal-ridden waters toward Europe.

We brought her back on course in silence.

But that unplanned detour was costly. We approached Grand Turk Island past evening twilight, too late to go in.

So we carried on, hoping to hit the Caicos Banks at dawn.

Our arrival at the edge of the Caicos Banks, 240 miles of turquoise sea, was right on schedule.

As striking as the area is, because it's shallow and riddled with coral heads, it's also potentially hazardous. Neither GPS nor charts alone can determine a safe route across. Visual navigation, for which one needs a clear day, sun from behind or overhead, relatively calm waters, and a lookout on bow, is essential. Change in water colour is key. Lightness indicates a shallow. Cloud-like patches are coral heads, treacherously close to the water's surface.

We had ideal weather. With David at the helm and me on bow, we threaded around sand bars and between coral heads. It soon became a fun game, like spotting licence plates on a road trip, only in utopia.

Approaching noon, two thirds of the way across, I suggested we stop, since anchoring on the banks is doable in good weather, and it was gorgeous out, and the forecast was for more of the same. "How 'bout it?" I said.

David looked around at the turquoise water, in every direction as far as the eye could see, and said, "How could we not?"

We left our course and found a clearing. He dropped the hook in twelve feet of crystal-clear water.

"Pretty amazing!" I said, watching the anchor nestle into the white sand bottom.

He continued to mete out chain.

"No land, no obstacles, not a single other boat in sight," I continued.

And more chain.

"This is definitely my kind of anchoring!"

He let out all one hundred feet of chain, followed by an additional thirty feet of rope, after which he set the anchor alarm.

"Dear, just wondering, have you lost your mind?" I said.

In the absence of a proper anchor snubber, the elasticity of rope would be more forgiving than chain, he explained. As for setting the anchor alarm, it's force of habit, he added with a shrug. Besides, better to be safe than sorry, he blurted out as a mildly defensive afterthought.

"Very, very valid points — for an incorrigible paranoid whose glass's three quarters empty," I teased.

Although I felt it was overkill, it was indisputable that we were as safe as we could be, and we could both relax.

As I looked out from the bow, blue-green ocean and azure sky was spectacularly all there was to see. I decided to swim. Noticing there was a current, David tied a rope around my waist so I wouldn't be carried off. He watched me from the deck and took pictures and joked about sharks and barracudas and woman-eating turtles. And I splashed him ruthlessly in return.

Then we sat on the bow, the gentle breeze like silk on our skin.

And we ate lightly: salad, cheeses, bread, and fruit.

And we watched the pink setting of the sun.

And we had sex.

And we drifted off into extravagantly deep sleeps below.

At 0400 I heard a shrill siren and saw that David did, too.

"Shit! It's the anchor alarm!" he exclaimed, suddenly wide awake.

"Can't be!"

"It is."

"You must've set the perimeters too close together."

"Nope." According to the GPS, *Inia* was moving, in a straight line and fast.

We went topside and raced to the bow. David held up a few splayed ends of rope in the dull glow of the waning crescent moon. The anchor rode had bounced out of its track and chaffed on an adjacent steel edge. The chain and the rope and the anchor, all that ground tackle, was now resting on the floor of the banks.

And *Inia* was adrift, among coral heads, in the dark, at sea!

"No need to panic. We've got a backup!" David turned on the engine and ordered me to get *Inia* back to where we had anchored, as it was the only place we knew for certain coral heads weren't. While I steered to the GPS waypoint, he dug out the old fisherman's anchor from the lazarette, hustled to assemble it, and attached what spare anchor rode we had.

"We're here!" I announced as soon as I hit the spot.

"Great!" he said, hurling the entire kit and caboodle overboard.

After resetting the alarm, this time with my tacit approval, we sat out in the darkness.

"Lucky or what!" I said.

We both laughed nervously at how disaster had once more been averted, until the alarm sounded again.

David looked down through the companionway at the GPS screen.

"Please tell me we're not —"

"I wish I could," he said.

After restarting the engine, I took the wheel while he went back to the bow to investigate. This time the anchor rode was still intact, but there was nothing at the far end of it. In his haste to put the anchor together, he had missed the final step of inserting a tiny cotter pin. As a result, we lost our second, and only other, anchor.

And *Inia* was adrift, among coral heads, in the dark, at sea, for the second damn time.

Without daylight, it was impossible to tell where danger lay. We couldn't move on, but now neither could we stop. So we did figure eights around the anchor waypoint for three and a half hours, until dawn.

When the sun had risen sufficiently, we left the banks for deeper waters and shot for the closest place that had a marina that we could get into and that might sell anchors. It was Long Island in the Bahamas, another three days away.

THIRTY

ON MARCH 4 at 1310, we arrived at Flying Fish Marina in Clarence Town, on the southeast coast of Long Island. It was small, accommodating sixteen boats, and quaint, its clapboard building painted buttercup yellow. But there was nothing small or quaint about its clientele.

We were surrounded by large men on large boats, catching large fish, telling humungous fish stories. These were men's men. Hemingway types.

"Whatever you do, don't tell them about the anchors," I said. "It'd be social suicide."

David agreed. We barely nodded to send out the right kind of signal as we walked down the dock to the marina office.

As we approached the building, a couple jumped out of a car and flagged us down. They both needed to pee. I pointed to the marina washrooms, and we went into the office to register. On our way out, we ran into them again and began to chat. It turned out they, Linda and Ralph, were sailors, too. Their boat was at a mooring at the very north end of the island. And it just so happened they had three anchors and were willing to part with one.

"Are you sure?" David said.

"You'll have to come up and get it, but yeah, absolutely," Ralph said. "Around here, sailors take care of other sailors."

We said we had already booked the marina's rental car for the following morning to drive to the customs office.

"Perfect. Meet you at the government dock at Burnt Ground! Radio when you're close," Ralph said.

Long Island is, as the name suggests, long — seventy-five miles from tip to tip, but only four miles wide at its widest.

March 5, in the humid, pungent predawn stillness, we hopped into the compact car and headed up the island's thin, winding road of cracked asphalt, through a sleeping village with a prominent white stucco church, past miles of dormant farmland, to our first stop.

The customs building, an aluminum portable, was hidden behind trucks parked on a gravel lot in field of tall grass. We waited in the reception area while the transport drivers had their bills of lading signed and gossiped with their uniformed buddy behind the desk in the other room. When they had all cleared out, we went in.

After the usual stamping of this and initialling of that, we were handed an invoice for three hundred dollars. David asked what it was for.

"It's for the privilege of being on the Bahamian part of the Atlantic Ocean," the agent answered.

"But we're just passing through," David clarified.

"Doesn't matter," he clarified back, adding that they only accepted cash. After a side trip to find a bank, we paid up and carried on.

Continuing north, we passed more farmland, Deadman's Cay, dried salt ponds, cliffs, beaches of pink sand, Lower Deadman's

Cay, and, at the island's narrowest points, aquamarine water off both shoulders of the road.

Early afternoon, we arrived at the wharf just as Ralph pulled up in his dinghy. After he tied his painter to a dock cleat, he pulled the anchor out from under his seat. It was a small rusty plow anchor with thirty-six feet of chain, insufficient for a boat in rough weather, inadequate for our boat in any weather, but it was better than nothing.

"Okay, so how much do I owe you?" David said.

"Five hundred," Ralph said, without blinking an eye.

That was more than it was worth new. David paid up and threw the corroded steel in the car trunk.

And we drove back to the south end of the island, another eight hundred dollars poorer.

March 6, after attaching the anchor, we decided to go.

Winds were high. There was no room to manoeuvre between our dock and the breakwater of enormous boulders. Going astern with *Inia* was always unpredictable. As we stood on the dock discussing our departure strategy, an alpha male sauntered over to give us a hand. Then two others joined him.

David expressed guarded appreciation for their help. "These full-keel boats are a bugger to back up," he said to them.

"Hop aboard, cap'n," the first one said, and he started to undo a dock line.

"I tell ya, she's got a mind of her own," David said.

"What woman doesn't?" the man said. They all chuckled.

Realizing David's warnings about *Inia's* idiosyncrasies were falling on deaf ears, we climbed into the cockpit and watched the men in silent resignation. After they undid each and every line, all ten tons of her began to buck and bounce off the dock and pilings, dragging them and their egos along until, one by one, they released their grips in humiliating defeat.

Without time to think, I hauled the lines onboard and held *Inia* off the posts midships while David gunned the engine in reverse. Then he backed her up, turned her on a dime, and headed her out to the open seas.

Once past the breakwater, he exclaimed, "Holy shit!"

"To tell you the truth, I'm surprised we got outta there in one piece."

"Me too! *Inia* co-operated like never before. This might sound crazy, but I'd swear she took over."

That notion would've indeed seemed off the wall to me years ago. But not anymore.

"That's my girl!" I said, lovingly stroking her teak port rail.

THIRTY-ONE

NASSAU IS 130 NAUTICAL MILES from Long Island as the crow flies. We hoped to get there by March 9 so we'd be rested and ready for my mom's arrival on the 12th.

Back-to-back fronts were forecast. Twenty-four hours out, sailing north in the deep waters of the Exuma Sound, David suggested we leave the sound, spend the night in the lee of the Exuma island chain on the shallower Bahama Banks, then scoot over to Nassau in the morning. I was game.

We headed for the Dotham Cut, where *Inia* was chewed up in the perilous turbulence between walls of jagged rock, then spat out onto the other side. As we travelled north along the west side of the cays looking for a place to put in, the winds began to shift.

"It's not as calm as I thought it'd be," I eventually said.

"Yeah, I'm surprised too," David said. "But I see an anchorage." He pointed to a bay full of masts and turned *Inia* toward it.

I watched the masts swaying in the chop as we got closer and closer.

Almost there, I blurted, "Dear, let's not."

He looked at me. "Let's not what?"

"Anchor. Let's not anchor. It's shallow. We've got pathetic ground tackle. They're packed in there like sardines. Sea room's what we need right now. Let's go back out and heave to. Pretty please. We'd be much safer!"

David's eyes went wide and he smiled. "Only an ocean sailor thinks like that. And you're absolutely right!" He circled *Inia* around.

We ploughed back through the hurly-burly between islands into deeper water, then sailed close-hauled 20 nautical miles off-shore. We hove to upwind of Highborne Cut.

March 8, after a fitful night of watches, we were pleased to find ourselves ten miles closer to the cut. David checked the GRIB files. The stronger front was coming.

Once we were through the gap, high cirrus clouds formed, a sign the front was closing in. The crossing would be a commitment and, God forbid, we didn't want to be in the middle of these coral-ridden shallows when the front hit. But we didn't want to be stuck in the Exumas either. With a safe haven beckoning behind us, the yellow banks looming ahead, we took off for New Providence Island.

After seven hours of a stiffening breeze and diminishing visibility, we pulled into our slip in the Nassau marina. Men jumped off neighbouring vessels to tie our lines on the dock, which was six feet above us in low tide. Then the sky went purple, a deafening clatter of halyards erupted, and a raging deluge fell.

Once again, we were damn lucky.

March 9 was overcast with the passing of the front. We opened up *Inia*'s hatches and let fresh air flow through.

The Nassau marina was basic, with rundown docks, rotten pilings, tired boats, and washrooms with overflowing toilets.

"It's one thing for us, another for my mom," I said.

"I'll loan her my boots."

"Very funny. Seriously, I want her to have a great time. It's probably been a tough year for her with us away."

"Dear, she must realize that the very reason we're hanging around here is for her."

"Still, it's important to me that she —"

"We'll make sure she has fun. We always do. You always do."

We cleaned up *Inia* and ourselves and headed off to check out the sights.

East Bay, the main street, was dirty and grey, lined with shops with duct-taped windows. In glaring contrast, a short walk across the bridge, was Paradise Island, home to the rich and famous like Nicolas Cage and Michael Jackson, and Atlantis, the epitome of opulence with its Vegas-style casino, beach bars, mega-yacht marina, live theatre, open-air marine reserve, man-made water-falls, and Mayan Temple waterslides.

March 12, we took a cab to the airport and waited for my mom. After everyone else had walked through the arrival doors and taken off, she appeared, dragging her red suitcase on wheels behind her.

"Welcome to Nassau," I said, giving her petite frame a big hug.

"They lost my damn luggage," she responded.

"Well, good that they found it. All's well that ends well," David said. He grabbed her suitcase and hailed a cab. "It's great that you're here, Marty!"

Aboard *Inia*, we made a light dinner of conch salad and rolls.

"This is popular here. It's essentially conch meat from those giant snail-like shells, some chopped cilantro, onions, and garlic, drizzled with a little lime," David said. "We were introduced to it at a neat place called Potter's Cay. There's a string of local food vendors under a bridge. We'll have to take you there."

"I'm not very hungry," she said, pushing her plate away.

"Hard to believe, eh, Ma? Us meeting in Nassau?" I said. "David and I getting here by —"

"It's been the worst damn winter in years, snow up to the rafters, and —"

"We heard," I said. "It sounded just —"

"And medical appointments coming out my yingyang."

"Medical appointments? For what?"

"A lump, on my back. It was biopsied around Christmas."

"Oh no! Why didn't you —"

"You said you didn't want to be told."

"I never said that!"

"In any event, your brothers were great. They called all the time. Tony was a sweetheart, too. And of course I couldn't have a better friend than Ron. He helped write my obituary."

"God! No!" I shrieked.

"Fortunately, the lump was benign."

I looked at David, upset by being upset by this second false alarm.

"That must've been scary," David said. "Thankfully you're —"

"You have no idea. I'm still reeling."

"Well, Nassau'll be the perfect tonic," he continued. "There's lots to do here. So you name your pleasure."

"Well, there's nothing that a few hands of blackjack can't cure."

It was decided. We'd hit the casino first thing in the morning.

After dropping my mother off at a blackjack table, David and I wandered around. Atlantis was a gambler's smorgasbord with penny slot machines for the nibblers, ten-thousand-dollar baccarat tables for those with an appetite for high stakes, and a dizzying array of risk options in between. Even at this early hour, the place was bustling with dealers dealing, roulette wheels whirring, and players making signs of the cross.

We stopped to watch people at the one-armed bandits and saw a guy sitting, staring at his machine. "Can't stay, but can't go home either," he said to no one in particular.

"What the hell are we doing here?" I said to David.

"You said you wanted your mother to have fun."

"I guess I was thinking *with* us, for her to have fun with us."

Over breakfast the following morning, I asked my mom if she wanted to try snorkelling.

"It is just so amaz—"

"Don't waste your breath, Sue," she said. "I have no interest in being shark bait."

"I'm with you there, Marty," David said, smiling at me.

Then, suddenly realizing it was David's birthday, I suggested we check out the Straw Market, an outdoor venue where Bahamian crafters make and sell their stuff. I thought I'd maybe find a small gift for him, and it'd be an ideal place for my mom to pick up a few souvenirs.

While David and I attempted to browse, she lagged two paces behind.

"Ma, is something wrong?" I finally said, slowing down to wait for her for the umpteenth time.

"The last thing people my age need is another piece of junk," she said.

David had stopped up ahead to watch a carver turn a stump of wood into a pelican.

"He makes it look easy," he said when we caught up with him.

"I want to buy it for your birthday," I said.

"Buy me a pelican?"

"Oh, that's right. Happy birthday, Dave," my mom said. "It's Ron's birthday, too. He's in Arizona right now. I must remember to email him. And I really should've let Ruth know I'd be away."

"Maybe we should head back then," David said.

"Wait," I said. Fighting back tears, I paid for the wooden pelican, and then we headed out.

That night Brian called with birthday wishes, and to report he had made another job change because, with composites taking over the world, there was no future in concrete fountains. He was now conducting seminars on deck construction at a building-supply store, even though he knew diddly-squat about decks, he told David. *Yet!* he added with a restrained laugh. And John wrote that he hoped David had a great day and that the end of his final semester was mere weeks away.

～

March 14, with four days left of my mom's visit, David poured each of us a coffee and laid out brochures of other Nassau tourist attractions on the table.

"How we spend the rest of the week's your call," David said.

She looked them over and responded that she couldn't tolerate being out in the heat, certainly didn't feel like more shopping, wasn't a fan of steel drums, could learn about the history of Nassau from a book, had already told us snorkelling was out of the question. And, needless to say, Mayan waterslides weren't her thing.

So we returned to Atlantis that day. March 15, too. March 16, we bused it to the casino in Cable Beach. March 17, we went back to Atlantis for the fourth and final time.

The last night, my mom treated us to dinner out at Arawak Cay. Throughout the meal she talked non-stop. Did we know she'd had an operation? An operation! It was elective surgery, cosmetic, to fix a toe, but still, it was really yucky, she said. She had lots of support, thank goodness. Great, just as David expected, I was worried for nothing, I said. And she had had a fantastic time with Brian and John at Christmas. She had no idea how happy I was to know that, I said. And as soon as she got back from Nassau she'd be dusting off her golf clubs, and Easter weekend would be super-busy with —

"So, Marty, what do you think of your daughter crossing the Atlantic?" David interrupted. "Not once, but twice, in one year." I kicked him under the table, but at the same time, I wanted to know, too. I needed to know.

"Big whoop-dee-ding," she replied.

March 18, my mom packed up her things and arranged a taxi for first thing in the morning, for her afternoon flight.

I was despondent watching her go.

"Well, that was a terrible, terrible visit," I finally said, as David and I turned to walk back to *Inia*. "And I can't believe she'd actually say —"

"Sue, I don't believe she meant it for a minute," David said. "I bet she's driving everyone at home crazy with stories about our trip. She was in a rare mood the whole time. And I'm beginning to wonder if perhaps it's got to do with how she's feeling about herself, her own life."

"But she's got a perfectly good life. She's pretty and stylish and smart and funny and good at absolutely everything she does and she's had all kinds of interesting —"

"According to you."

"According to everyone!"

"Are you sure she thinks so? The reality is, she has far more days behind her than ahead. Our trip might have been complicated for her in ways we'll never know, is all I'm trying to say."

THIRTY-TWO

AFTER MY MOM LEFT, we waited for favourable weather so we could cross the notorious Gulf Stream. The body of water between the Bahamas and Florida has a strong north-setting current. When contrary winds blow over it, treacherous conditions referred to as *square seas* — high waves with short wavelengths — develop.

Local boaters warned us that a safe passage can only be made on the Gulf Stream's terms. And we were told, over and over again, that we should never, ever set out when there was an *N* in the forecast, and we should only set out after the last nor'easter. We'd have to be fools to ignore the advice. I just hoped we could tell which nor'easter was the last!

Every day we followed the same ritual: checking weather sites, listening to radio forecasts, walking down the docks to compare notes with the other sailors heading to Florida, and emailing family and friends to say, "Still here, the wait continues, Happy Vernal Equinox, haven't left yet, will keep you posted."

Finally, on March 25 it was evident that, in a day or two, we'd have the break in the weather we needed to be on our way. Both of us were suddenly struck by the significance of it.

David updated family about our impending departure and said,

Once the Gulf Stream's behind us, it'll be the end
of ocean passages.
  Both Sue and I are feeling some sadness that
our open water days are nearing an end.

March 27, 0730, we uncleated the dock lines and backed *Inia* out
of her slip. I knew we wouldn't be leaving alone, but I didn't expect
the size of the crowd, nor the frenzy. Nassau Harbour was con-
gested with vessels, all speeding, vying for position, competing to
get out ahead of the pack with the intensity of the Daytona 500. It
was an irrational race to the open seas.

  Past land, the normal fanning out didn't happen. Most of the
boats were crossing with chart plotters and electronic autohelms,
and obviously all were using the exact same waypoints. Before
long, we unwittingly found ourselves in the middle of a peculiar
motor-sailing conga line that extended to the horizons ahead and
behind us, with no boats on either side.

  And there was radio chatter — incessant, inane, social chatter, entirely over the VHF.

  There was no more need for our single-sideband radio. Come
to think of it, we no longer needed our self-steering wind vane, or
our wind generator, or solar panels, or even our sails, for the most
part.

  And there was no more sense of adventure, self-reliance, or
daring to tug at a sailor's heartstrings; no more silences, or solitude, or awesomeness of space, or sublimeness of time, that nour-
ishes one's soul.

  This last crossing was not blue-water sailing. I was so disappointed.

March 28, 1430, a sunny afternoon, we entered Fort Worth Inlet, Florida.

If the end of our ocean adventure was significant to me, it had to be monumental to David. Yet he accepted it with such grace. As we slowly made our way down the channel, passing buff bodies in Speedos and bikinis partying on cigar boats, I tried my best not to cry, but I was unsuccessful.

"It's a little-known fact that Floridian women have evolved with built-in floatation due to their proximity to the ocean. They're bad swimmers — it's a safety feature," David said in a goofy attempt to make me laugh. I cried some more.

Fat tears plopped on the nav station as I wrote family and friends.

> Now that we are heading for the Intracoastal Waterway, which will be mainly motoring home, I'm feeling our trip is coming to a close, and I must say I'm pretty emotional at the thought. It has been such an amazing adventure despite, maybe even partly because of, the challenges we've faced along the way. I wouldn't trade this experience for the world. It has truly been a trip of a lifetime. I can't tell you how lucky and grateful I feel to have had this year away.

My mom wrote back.

> The weather at this end is sloppy rain and cold, and that makes me even more thankful for your treat of my visit to Nassau.
> Somehow I ended up with the marina key. Please send me their address and I'll mail it back. Sorry about it.

There are no words to adequately express how impressed I am with your accomplishments, your voyage. I hope this next leg will be just enjoying the scenery.
Love and thanks,
Ma

"What'd I tell ya," David said. And I began to sob. Then I saw another email. It was from Ben! He wrote,

I am proud of you. I hope you had an amazing time. You did your dream.
Call me when your trip is finished.
Ben

Now David cried, too.

THIRTY-THREE

IT WAS UNSEASONABLY COLD for May. With flurries in the forecast, David and I reluctantly dug out and put on our musty snowsuits, toques, and mitts, and headed out. There was hoarfrost on the riggings and icy mist hovering above the water's surface. A class of underdressed eight-year-olds shivered along the rail at the top of Lock 10 on the Erie Canal.

"A boat! Look!" a teacher shouted on our approach, relieved their field trip wouldn't be a total flop.

The students waved and cheered maniacally as we drew nearer.

"Shit!" David said.

"Just great," I concurred, waving back, fanning the excitement flames.

We were close to home, but with over thirty locks to contend with between here and Lake Ontario, we were still not home free. Securing *Inia* to the lock wall was, in itself, a daunting task. But with our dismantled masts sticking out horizontally beyond her rails, she was more difficult to manoeuvre. And with our disengaged wind generator and radar and whisker pole and mast stays and solar panels and jerry cans cluttering her deck, she was hazardous to move about on. Our focus was required. An audience was the very last thing we needed.

There was a collective groan from above when we entered the bottom of the lock and went temporarily out of their line of sight.

"Thank the Lord," I said, grateful for the privacy at the most critical stage.

I glanced at the thick slimy ropes dangling down the mossy wall. Eager to surface like the experienced sailor I had become, I grabbed the very next one. As *Inia* kept moving, I tripped over the radar, my arm did a one-eighty, and a piercing jolt flashed down my left side.

I yelped, but the kids' hooting and hollering drowned me out.

"Christ, Sue! You okay?" David yelled, while reaching precariously beyond the gunwales with a boat hook to snatch the last rope.

"No, I'm seriously not." I hustled to get up, tears streaming down my cheeks.

The pain was searing. But we had to hold *Inia* in the lock, and like it or not, there was a boisterous class of eight-year-olds waiting to be entertained at the top.

Once I was seated on a small clearing on the bow, with the rope in my right hand and my throbbing left arm propped on my lap, the water level began to rise.

"I see their heads," a youngster squealed.

"Me, too! Me, too!" others chimed in.

"It's like we're a pair of chimps in a zoo," I said.

"On with the show. This is it!" David sighed.

The children watched in awe as we slowly rose up from the depths until we were face to face with them, staring back, still clinging to our vines.

A scrawny boy with turned-in shoulders and big coal eyes blurted, "Ma'am is that a cannon on your boat?"

He was referring to the main mast. His classmates snickered. He cringed. And I was transported back to the ugly side of grade three. This situation was no longer about my pain, but about his.

"Very good question," I said, making deliberate eye contact with him. "It does look like a cannon, but it's a mast. This is a sail-boat. It happens to have two masts. Normally they're upright, but we had to take them down to clear the canal bridges. They hold sails so we can move with the power of wind alone. Pretty neat, eh?"

He nodded, his mouth agape, and his classmates fell silent. Suddenly, I had thirty impressionable little beings — little Bens and Brians and Johns, grade-three Davids, eight-year-old me — all staring my way.

"Do you sometimes dream?" I asked him.

He nodded again.

"I thought so. I bet you all do. Well, you'll never guess what we just did. We sailed across the Atlantic Ocean to Europe and back. And all because of a dream. So keep dreaming, boys and girls. Dare to dream big. And never, ever give up."

With that, the lock gate opened and we slipped away, as did the analgesic effects of wide-eyed wonderment. I couldn't move my arm at all. Even the tiniest change of position sent shock waves through my entire body.

"Shiiit! Owwwww!" I wailed as David attempted to pull my coat sleeve down.

He rushed below deck and came back up with first-aid supplies.

"I think it's dislocated," I said, eagerly swallowing the pills he gave me. "Seriously, it felt like it was yanked right out of the socket." I watched him calmly rip a pillowcase. "What if only skin's holding it on? Oh God. Duck! I think I'm gonna puke," I said as he carefully wrapped my arm in the makeshift sling.

In a matter of minutes he had my arm immobilized and my body pumped full of codeine, which quickly began to take effect.

"Sue, that was amazing, what you said to those kids," he said, wiping my sweaty forehead with a cool damp cloth. "Absolutely amazing!"

I couldn't reach over water beyond the bow gunwale to grab ropes and cables because of the pain. I was certain I'd fall overboard and sink like a stone if I tried. At Lock 11, I yelled up to the lockmaster and requested that he swing the rope to me. He did, but with such a scowl I didn't dare ask again. In Lock 12, David brought *Inia* to a halt, then scrambled forward and aft over the clutter to grab both lines. That was too dangerous to repeat.

We stopped in Fonda, New York, to pause and figure out what to do. First things first, did I need medical attention? If so, as much as we both hated the idea of stopping, this would be the place, and we still had travel insurance.

I winced spasmodically as David slowly peeled back the layers of clothing to have a look. My left side, from the chest wall, across the shoulder, and down the arm to my elbow, was swollen, angry, black and blue. But, as far as he could tell, my shoulder joint was back together and no bones were broken.

I emailed my friend Donna, a physiotherapist, with the details and asked for some long-distance advice. She wrote back:

> Oh dear — sounds like maybe a rotator cuff tear/ injury? — If so, ICE!!!! — pendular excercises only — i.e. bend over from the waist and let the arm dangle — try to let gravity gently move it away from your body — avoid provocative movements as much as possible — for now, passive only.
>
> Initially pain killers were probably necessary, but an anti-inflammatory might be better at this point.
>
> Looking forward to hearing you are home — stay safe — you are soooooooooooo close!!!

Perfect! I had no desire to move provocatively right then, and everything she suggested I do was entirely doable on the move. Just what I wanted to hear; we could carry on.

The next question was how exactly would we carry on? Locking-through requires teamwork, and there were still many of these feats of engineering ingenuity ahead.

David's face lit up. He had the perfect solution. Why hadn't he thought of it sooner? *I'd* helm and *he'd* reach at the bow. Sensing my horror, he reminded me of the anchoring successes.

"Anchoring's different," I said.

"And what about Poughkeepsie? Docking in that blinding rain in a three-knot current?"

"But that's 'cause *Inia* was drifting away with me alone on her," I said. "And besides, I had two fully functional arms."

"Well, you're now a single-handed sailor," he joked. "Seriously, you're capable of bringing her through the rest of the locks."

"Okay," I squeaked, in the absence of a viable alternative.

Considering the matter settled, David propped me up with pillows and pills, then pulled a blanket over himself and dozed off. I sat up, fully dressed, the long moonlit night through, nursing my arm, regretting my stupidity, worrying if we'd make it back all right, dreading the morning.

The next morning, we approached Lock 13. I took over the helm and figured out that, with my right hand, I could manage the throttle on the same side of the console, cross over to reach the gear shift on its left, and steer the wheel in the middle. To hold it steady, I'd use my belly. David stood at the bow and waited for the gate to open, counting on my help, believing in me, trusting I would keep him safe. Holy crow. What if he was wrong?

As the lock light turned green, arm belly arm, I entered at a crawl, sidled up to the wall, shifted into neutral, gave a little reverse, stopped, and grabbed the rope by the cockpit, adjusting my grip as water levels changed. I then waited for the go light, after which I set the line free and exited the lock, slow and steady. Once we were successfully on the other side, David bolted back into the cockpit and planted a big kiss on my cheek.

"One lock at a time," he said.

The canal system, our last new frontier, was a charming marriage of technology and nature, then and now, with railway trestles, foot-bridges, towpaths from which mules had pulled barges along in days gone by, and birds chirping melodies over the hum of highway traffic and the rhythmic beat of each passing train.

As we moved along, midday temperatures crept up, burning off the early morning chills. Treetops were turning lime green and mustard yellow, pussy willows were budding, patches of crocuses and daffodils were fragrantly in bloom, cyclists and joggers were hitting the towpaths in droves, and quaint villages were coming out of hibernation to prepare for the seasonal influx of boating business. Everything and everyone along the canal was coming to life.

It was spring, the season of renewal and new beginnings. And we were heading home.

In a twenty-four-mile stretch of the Oswego Canal we dropped from 363 to 245 feet above sea level.

May 24, beyond the final two locks straight ahead was the shimmering expanse of Lake Ontario, welcoming us back.

May 25, 0500, in light, cold winds we motored across to the Canadian side. David plotted and charted every last nautical mile, whether he needed to or not. I sat out the entire time, a blanket on my lap, wondering how I'd feel being home; how I'd *be*; what, if anything, I'd take away from this adventure in the long run; if I'd remember to look at the moon.

In the wee hours of May 26, exactly a year to the day after we'd left Whitby, *Inia* crossed her wake, and another wave of emotion hit. Even though we weren't home yet, we had come full circle. At 0230, she was secured to the gas dock in the Whitby marina, essentially marking the end to our journey.

THIRTY-FOUR

BY 0830 DAVID AND I were standing outside the Whitby marina office, waiting for it to open.

"Well, hello there!" I said, seeing the young desk clerk we had dealt with before we left on our trip.

"Mornin'" he said, unlocking the door, yawning like the Grand Canyon.

Once inside, David told him we needed a transient slip for two nights and wanted to arrange help to raise our masts.

"Oh, and we need to *clear customs* too!" I said, hoping to jog his memory.

But no. He pointed to the wall-mounted phones and handed David the magnetic washroom key.

May 27, I got off the boat to be out of the way while our masts were being stepped. Looking around, I saw that everything was the same. The marina grounds were no different. Same boats were in the water. Same boaters were strolling the docks. And the same dockhands, who had helped launch *Inia* the year before, were giving David a hand, wearing the same jackets, complaining about the exact same weather.

Oh God! Could it be …?

I jumped back onboard and made a mad dash below to the drawer under the quarter berth. There, in a sealed plastic bag, were the courtesy flags of the countries we had visited, all worn and neatly folded. Then I noticed the butane camping stove we had clamped to the counter in Portugal and, back outside, the crusty salt on *Inia*'s riggings from the Atlantic and the brown moustache on her hull from the waters of the Intracoastal Waterway. And I felt my arm throb. Yes, of course our journey had been real!

May 28, before our departure for home, David strung a line within my limited reach between the mizzen and main, on which I painstakingly tied each flag in order. The Azores: nothing could compare to the glorious feeling of that first landfall after twenty-three days at sea, good friends waiting to catch our lines, sitting among blue-water sailors from around the globe. Portugal: what a magnificent sight Cabo de São Vicente had been after that harrowing eleven-day crossing. Admittedly, once we got there, living on the hard in southern Portugal for two and a half months while *Inia* was restored to her seaworthy self had been anything but hard. I wondered how Chris was doing. Karine and Alex, too. God, we had such a fantastic afternoon at their place. I hoped they would get back to Brazil, get back to their kids, build that house. I wondered if Carl and Kate were still out there somewhere. No one had been more astonished than me at my readiness, even eagerness, to cast off again. The Madeiran Islands: majestically rising up out of the ocean, so beautiful in starkly different ways. This was where we got to know Manuel, who embraced life's simple pleasures, and the four lone sailors, the four unique ships in motion: James, Raimo, Graham, and Keith. *They call them weather cloths on this side of the pond, Graham!* Then the Canary Islands, where Spanish is spoken and clothing's optional. Marcel was back in Nova Scotia already. *Do you have any idea how far I have to walk to make coffee in the morning now?* he had written from home. That was so funny! And the dry, dusty Cape Verdes: Carlos's unanticipated visit, Elise's unanticipated request. Did she ever find boat number four? Then our classic trade-winds passage with Nick expertly guiding us the whole way over, right into the British Virgin Islands. Nick, of Nick and Dagmara. *I think I understand their seventy-two-day passage now.* After the BVI, the big push north through the Bahamas, island jewels in a turquoise sea. Then, finally, through the States via the Intracoastal Waterway and the New York State Canal System, where we negotiated New York Harbor among tugs and ferries and tour boats and hung a right at the Statue of Liberty — that was right up there on the scale of awesome.

What an incredible adventure!

I couldn't possibly forget it, could I?

THIRTY-FIVE

WITH BANNERS FLYING high, *Inia* headed into our Hamilton Harbour slip, where a small crowd was waiting to welcome us home.

After a champagne celebration on the dock, the well-wishers dispersed and David and I went below. I packed up the few perishable fridge items — after all, wasting food was unthinkable. And I loaded our knapsacks with toiletries and clothes. And David reflexively emptied the bilge, checked the battery charge, covered up the GPS, and made sure the radio was off. Then we climbed back up the companionway. With an air of finality, David locked *Inia* up and checked her dock lines one last time. And, as a matter of course, we both glanced over our shoulders as we walked away. There was *Inia's* bright-red boot stripe smiling back at us, assuring us we could go; she'd be all right.

Good news: Leiah still loved us. If she wagged that tail of hers any faster, I feared it'd fall right off. She bounded into the back seat of the car, clearly no worse for wear.

Ben, already in Toronto for a bike courier event, swung by Guelph for an overnight visit. He told us that he was growing his own vegetables now and that he hoped to one day live entirely off the grid. The earth's a beautiful planet and we have to take care of it, he said. I couldn't agree more.

"And I'm sorry I didn't write, but somehow I ... it's hard to explain, but I felt I had to —"

"Just glad you're here, Ben," I said.

Brian announced he had yet another move in mind. "My next-door neighbour was at one of my seminars. So gotta get outta Dodge before his friggin' deck collapses," he said, laughing. "But, seriously, I've got another idea, a very, very —"

"For heaven's sake, Brian, you just barely —"

"I'd really like to move home, Mom."

"To move home? You mean, *home* as in *here?*"

"To go back to school. I'd qualify as a mature student. And I'd get a job, and I'd pay room and board, and —"

"That's an excellent, excellent idea," I said. It takes courage to cast off, but, sometimes, so too does it take courage to return home.

John told us that to celebrate the end of school, he had bought himself a clarinet mic and an ice-cream cone and walked around Toronto in brilliant sunshine. It couldn't have been more perfect. And he had started a new band, The Boxcar Boys, which played gypsy jazz klezmer folk blues.

"I feel pretty solid about my life now," he said. "Still, until my career really takes off, I'm gonna need to supplement my income."

"So, you thinking of teaching?" I asked.

"No, postering."

"That's ideal. You're so great at art, too," I said.

"Oh, I'm not *designing* posters, I'm just hanging them up. You know, with a stapler?"

"And stapling."

"Just got me a deal on roller blades."

"Music, art, *and* stapling," I said.

In the summer, David was hired, on a contract-to-contract basis, to teach business courses at the local community college. The pay was a fraction of what he had earned before our trip; there was no pension and no job security whatsoever; and, faced with large classes, confused students, and hours and hours of lesson planning, he was every bit as busy as he had been in industry. But it was a different kind of busy. He felt that if he could help these kids, or rather, these young adults, get on with their lives in some small way, it would all be worthwhile. It soon became obvious that teaching wasn't just his new job; it was his calling.

Here we were: home safe and sound; reunited with our family, our friends, our loyal pet; moved into the cutest little house on earth; both of us engaged in meaningful work. This after having an adventure of a lifetime.

So how come I felt so miserable? The phone installers irritated me. I was a basket case in traffic. And conversations over the fence seemed exceedingly banal. When I burst out crying watching the movie *Captain Ron*, I knew I was in rough shape. But why?

Re-entry shock was Charna's diagnosis. She explained it as a common phenomenon of feeling like an alien when returning home after a life-altering experience. She had been afflicted herself. And she assured me the condition was highly curable if I took three simple steps: One, preserve memories of the trip in whatever way I could. Two, embrace what was good about the life I'd returned to. Three, create new dreams for the future.

Well, in terms of preserving memories, we sorted and archived all our pictures; we found special spots for the pottery, the plaques, and the pelican; and, having stumbled on a Portuguese district in Hamilton, we agreed we'd visit whenever we had a hankering for *pastéis de nata* or David had an uncontrollable urge to annoy the hell out of unsuspecting merchants.

With respect to step number two, I happily resumed chatting with my mom on the phone every morning, walking Leiah every afternoon, showering more often, swearing less, and, when outdoors, almost always keeping my clothes on.

And as for the need for a new dream, I took care of that, too. Over a Saturday morning breakfast of bacon and eggs at the Apollo with David, I said, "Dear, what do you say we truck *Inia* to Alaska, sail her down the B.C. coast, and head off into the Pacific?"

Expecting to discuss which home reno to tackle first, the leaky roof or the crumbling plaster walls, David stared at me for a second. Then he laughed so hard coffee ran out his nose, which I interpreted as meaning anything was possible.

Now that a fresh seed has been planted, I know I'll be all right going forward. Whether or not it germinates, who can say for sure?

But that's not the point.

EPILOGUE

STACKS OF FILE FOLDERS covered the kitchen table. A fresh pot of Kenyan dark roast brewed. I needed to get my new caseload under control. Working at home was the only hope.

But mere minutes into it, my cellphone rang. Then it jingled, telling me I had a message. Then it rang again. It was a case manager, and it seemed important. I had to pick up.

"Hey, Sue. Welcome back. Clearly you survived the high seas. How was it?"

"Oh, hi, Joan. Truth be told, we had lots of wild times out there. But it was amazing, life altering really."

"I'd love to hear all about it."

"At least I'd like to think it was life altering. But sometimes I find myself wondering," I said, signing a report and moving the client's chart onto the "completed" pile. "Days like today it feels like I never even —"

"Well, I can definitely confirm you were away. And sorely missed by us all, I might add. Which brings me to my reason for calling. Just got an urgent referral from Nancy, the hospital discharge planner. It's an unusual case. We need an experienced occupational therapist. Please say you can take it."

"What's the situation?"

"A woman. Eighty. Had both legs amputated midthigh last winter because of gangrene. Her stint in rehab's just about done."

"And?"

"She's insisting on going back home."

"Go on."

"She lives in an apartment, a basement apartment."

"With an elevator?"

"Nope."

"Does she have family?"

"Wanda, her twelve-year-old cat."

"Let me get this straight; she has no legs, she can't get out of her place, and she's elderly and on her own."

"Yup. And did I mention she smokes?"

"You've gotta be kidding."

"I wish I were. But she's adamant. So, Nancy needs a functional assessment of this woman in her home environment, ASAP."

"Fax the paperwork over," I sighed. "Elsewhere, Joan, I'd love to tell you about our adventures, or should I say misadventures. Over lunch. My treat."

"Sounds like a plan. When things slow down. Looking forward to your report on this woman."

"Should be pretty straightforward."

On the day of the home visit, I walked up to the ambulance by the dumpsters in the parking lot behind Esther's building.

"Hi there," I said to the paramedics as they got out of the cab. "I take it you'll be bringing this woman back to the hospital when we're done."

"Yes, ma'am. In three hours or so, right?" the driver said.

"That's usually right. But don't venture too far off. I seriously doubt we'll be that long."

When they opened the back doors of the ambulance, Esther's head poked up from the top of her legless torso, which was strapped flat on the gurney. She was toothless, wrinkled like cracked porcelain, with a thin white ponytail sprouting up from her crown. But there was something in her steel-grey eyes that belied any notion of frail vulnerability. And I thought better of attempting to expedite the assessment.

While she was being lifted out, I introduced myself with a professionally friendly "Hi. I'm Sue Williams, the occupational therapist," to which she reacted with a glare that could kill.

The men carried Esther down the eight stairs and through the newspaper-strewn hall to her dark, dank apartment, which reeked of cat and cigarettes. After transferring her into her cracked vinyl wheelchair, they left.

I sat at her card table beneath the basement casement window. As I took the Home Safety Assessment Tool from my file and a pen from my pocket, Esther began to propel about, stopping at a dresser to root through its rickety drawers, then yanking back a sheet nailed to the ceiling to inspect the shelves behind it.

"I understand it's been quite a while. Hope everything's as you left it," I said.

She rolled past me and into the kitchenette, shoving the kitty-litter bag out of her way.

"I gather you have a cat. We do, too. Wasn't a 'cat person' before," I said, making quotation marks in the air. "But, have to admit, she's won me over. I've joined the club."

"Bread, bologna, Coke," she muttered while looking into her almost-empty fridge. "Jam too. Fuckin' marmalade's grown fur," she added, tossing the jar into a bin under the sink.

"Esther, this is for you. It's our brochure," I said, a bit louder, firmer, holding the piece of paper at the end of my outstretched arm.

She carried on, frenetically opening this, moving that, like I wasn't there.

"It tells you about our services. My contact information's on it." I placed the pamphlet on the corner of the table. "It's here so you can read it ... whenever."

Esther glanced over at it. I took this flicker of attention as my cue to proceed and launched into my well-practised spiel about the purpose of this meeting, closing with "to determine if you can return home," upon which her flurry of activity came to an abrupt halt.

Esther slowly wheeled over to the table, and applied the left wheelchair brake, followed by the right. She then took out a pack of tobacco, a thin paper rectangle, and a lighter from the purse on her lap and rolled herself a cigarette. Holding it up near her cheek between her index and middle fingers, she studied me with an ice-cold gaze. "To determine if I can return home, you say?"

"Yes. If you'll be all right here."

She took a deep, long drag to light it. "So, *you* are going to determine that about *me*?"

"I'm an occupational therapist," I said. She exhaled a series of smoke rings and my eyes began to sting. "We're trained to do this sort of thing." I coughed and sputtered.

She took a few more slow puffs.

"Ooooh! Trained, eh?"

"Mmm-hmm," I said.

She took excessive time to stub the butt out in the souvenir ashtray from Niagara Falls, then she said, "Kee-rist! You so-called experts are all alike. You wiggle-waggle about like you know every-thing. Like you know me. Like you know what I can and can't do, and what's best for me. Well, if you think I'm gonna move outta here, then you don't know a goddamn thing. It's like this: I've lived in this place for fifteen years, my friends want me back here, my cat needs me here, I like it here, and it's damn well where I'm gonna stay 'til they carry me out in a pine box. I've got just one life to live and no one — and that includes you, Madame Occupational Therapist — is gonna tell me how to live it. So unless you're here to help me, get the hell out, 'cause you're wasting my time and yours."

I welled up, but not from the smoke. Esther was right. I didn't have a bloody clue about her. I was guilty as charged.

But as she continued to tear this strip out of me, I received a crash course in what I needed to know. I learned that, even though most people in her condition would opt for an easier environment, Esther wasn't most people; that she understood the risks and was prepared to face them; and that she had grit, the power and magic of which, I'd come to believe, knows no bounds.

By the time Esther was through, even if I could have convinced her to move, I was no longer at all inclined to try. Imagining her sitting by a nursing station in some sterile facility on my say-so felt wrong, even tragic. Maybe she'd be safer elsewhere, but at what cost?

Living according to someone else's script wears down a spirit and assails the unique essence of a life. Fundamental to occupational therapy is the realization that there are lots of ways to live a life, and autonomy and self-determination is what makes us whole.

I now truly believe that as a mother, too. Given the freedom to make their own choices, our sons are growing into the unique men they were each meant to be.

And we ocean sailors know that quality of life is not dependent on how much we have or how easy we have it. It's being able to sail our own ships. It's choosing our own destinations. It's developing our own heavy-weather tactics. It's self-discovery through passage-making and riding out the storms. It's appreciating when the sun re-emerges, as it always does. And it's the incomparable thrill of landfall that can be experienced only if one first takes the risk to cast off.

The notion of relinquishing control was a greater personal threat to Esther than any physical barrier she was up against. She, too, needed to be in charge.

In weighing potential routes for this last stretch of her journey, she chose to stay the course. My gut feel was that she had spent much of her life helming over turbulent waters, through which she'd developed skills and competence in her own right. If anyone could handle this rough passage, she could. Maybe she'd ultimately have to change tacks; then again, maybe she wouldn't. But that would be her call as skipper. No questions asked.

As I collected my thoughts and refocused, I saw that Esther was still staring my way.

"I hear you," I said.

And her eyes changed to a softer, warmer grey.

Sue Williams, off the eastern seaboard and approaching
New York Harbor.

ACKNOWLEDGEMENTS

Thank you to my friend, Charna Galper, a life force who influenced me and my family profoundly and forever.

I am grateful to Susan Scadding, the first person, other than David, who told me I can write, and who provided invaluable feedback as I made my way through the very initial draft of the story. And to other first draft readers: Donna Lychwa, Rob Simpson, and Al Metzger. Their early and ongoing enthusiasm was pivotal.

Thank you to the writing community. To Barbara Kyle, whose expert lectures on the art and craft of storytelling armed me with the tools I needed to transform a rough manuscript into a memoir that attracted literary agents and publishers. To Adam Lindsay Honsinger. When I write, my notes of his insightful musings about the fundamentals of a good story are by my side at all times. And to Miriam Toews, for her mind-blowing course in creative writing at the University of Toronto, and for her generous support of my memoir and her personal encouragement of me since.

Thank you to the team of professionals at Dundurn Press. To acquisitions editor Scott Fraser, for loving the sound of my story, for championing it internally, and for welcoming me into the fold. To developmental editor Allison Hirst, for her wisdom, respect, and humour in handling *Ready to Come About.* To artistic director Laura Boyle, for the fantastic cover design. To project editor Jenny McWha, for skillfully overseeing the final stages of publication. And to copy editor Susan Fitzgerald. I am in awe of her eye for detail and ear for nuance.

Thank you to my sons, Ben, Brian, and John, for being the most inspiring life coaches a mom could ever have, for supporting my desire to share some of our family's story, and, together with my daughters-in-law, Allison Williams and Emilyn Stam, for cheering me on along the daunting road to getting published. Also, special thanks to Brian for the book title *Ready to Come About.* It is just so perfect!

Thank you to my husband, David. Of course, if not for his cockamamie dream, there wouldn't be this story to tell. But I am also grateful for his steadfast belief in my ability to tell it, for encouraging me to quit my job to complete the manuscript, for reading passages to family and friends whether they wanted to hear them or not, for never once complaining when he discovered he had been carrying on a conversation with himself (which happened more often than I care to admit), for reviewing whole drafts more times than I can count, for listening to me practise my elevator pitch at 3:00 a.m. in a hotel room, and for insisting I was a writer, well before I believed it myself. Without him this memoir simply would not exist.

And thank you, *Inia*, for taking us far and keeping us safe. Godspeed, my sweetheart!